BUSINESS/SCIENCE/TECHNOLOGY DIVISION
CHICAGO PUBLIC LIBRARY
400 SOUTH STATE STREET
CHICAGO, ILLINOIS 60605

HD
30.
.B8
199

HWB

ironmen

Business and the Natural Environment

Chicago Public Library

REFERENCE

Form 178 rev. 1-94

BUSINESS/SCIENCE/TECHNOLOGY DIVISION
CHICAGO PUBLIC LIBRARY
400 SOUTH STATE STREET
CHICAGO, ILLINOIS 60605

DISCARD

R0127442591

BUSINESS/SCIENCE/TECHNOLOGY DIVISION
CHICAGO PUBLIC LIBRARY
400 SOUTH STATE STREET
CHICAGO, ILLINOIS 60605

Business and the Natural Environment

Edited by
Pratima Bansal

and

Elizabeth Howard

Butterworth-Heinemann
Linacre House, Jordan Hill, Oxford OX2 8DP
A division of Reed Educational and Professional Publishing Ltd

ℝ A member of the Reed Elsevier plc group

OXFORD   BOSTON   JOHANNESBURG
MELBOURNE   NEW DELHI   SINGAPORE

First published 1997

© Elizabeth Howard and Pratima Bansal 1997

All rights reserved. No part of this publication may be reproduced
in any material form (including photocopying or sorting in any medium by
electronic means and whether or not transiently or incidentally to some
other use of this publication) without the written permission of
the copyright holder except in accordance with the provisions of the Copyright,
Designs and Patents Act 1988 or under the terms of a licence issued by the
Copyright Licensing Agency Ltd, 90 Tottenham Court Road, London,
England W1P 9HE. Applications for the copyright holder's written
permission to reproduce any part of this publication should be addressed to the publishers

British Library Cataloguing in Publication Data

Business and the natural environment
   1. Industrial management – Europe – Environmental aspects
   2. Environmental responsibility
   I. Bansal, Pratima   II. Howard, Elizabeth B. (Elizabeth
   Barbara), 1949–
   658.4'08

ISBN 0 7506 2051 X

Typeset by Acorn Bookwork, Salisbury, Wilts.
Printed and bound in Great Britain by Biddles Ltd, Guildford and King's Lynn

Contents

Contributors

Pratima Bansal is an Assistant Professor in the Department of Management at Georgia State University in Atlanta, Georgia. She received her doctorate in Management Studies from the University of Oxford. Her research interests lie in the application of business strategy and organizational theory to corporate environmental management, in strategic decision-making in an international context, and in paradigm commensurability.

James Cameron is a practising barrister and Director of the Foundation for International Environmental Law and Development (FIELD) at the School of Oriental and African Studies (SOAS), University of London. He is Visiting Professor at the College of Europe in Bruges, and Life Member of Clare Hall, Cambridge University, Fellow of the Royal Society for the Arts Manufacturing and Commerce (FRSA) and Fellow of the Royal Geographical Society (FRGS). His specific research interests lie in the area of trade and the environment, and the precautionary principle, and he has authored and edited five books in the field.

Thomas N. Gladwin received his PhD in international business and natural resource policy from the University of Michigan. He is a Professor of International Business and Management and Director of the Global Environment Program at the Leonard N. Stern School of Business, New York University. His research focuses on environmental management, global sustainability and corporate social responsibility.

Keith Grint is a Fellow in Organizational Behaviour and Lecturer in Management Studies at Templeton College, Oxford University. A sociologist by training, his current research interests concern theories of technology, the sociology of knowledge, the practical significance of organizational theory, and the role of leadership. He has authored and edited six books including *Fuzzy Management* (Oxford University Press, 1997) *The Machine at Work: Technology Work and Society* (Polity Press, 1997) and *The Sociology of Work: An Introduction* (Polity Press, 1997).

Elizabeth Howard is a Fellow of Templeton College and lecturer in Management Studies at the University of Oxford. Her degrees are in geography and town and regional planning. She formerly worked in local government as a town planner. Her research focuses on retailing, environmental issues and especially the impact of retail development. She undertook to edit this book as part of her work to encourage the examination of business by students of environmental issues and of the environment by business students.

James J. Kennelly received his PhD in international business and management from the Leonard N. Stern School of Business, New York University. He is currently Assistant Professor of Business at Skidmore College. His research focuses upon the environmental and social performance of multinational corporations, social sustainability, and the relationships between multinational corporations and local communities.

Ruth Mackenzie is a staff lawyer at the Foundation for International Environmental Law and Development, and Visiting Lecturer at the School of Oriental and African Studies, University of London. Her main areas of interest are the law of international institutions, natural resources law, and international and European Union environmental law, particularly in the field of biological diversity.

Kay Milton is a Senior Lecturer in Social Anthropology at Queen's University, Belfast. She obtained her PhD in Social Anthropology from Queen's University in 1981. Her research focuses on environmental issues and their interpretation through anthropological approaches. Her recent publications in this field include *Environmentalism and Cultural Theory* (Routledge, 1996) and an edited volume, *Environmentalism – the View from Anthropology* (Routledge, 1993).

Mike Monaghan obtained a PhD in Chemical Engineering from Sheffield University, England in 1963 following which he worked for approximately ten years in the international oil and gas industry in the UK and overseas. He joined the P&O transport, shipping and construction group in 1974, and was a director of international transport companies before taking the position as Group Director for Environment in 1991. He is responsible for policy, auditing and development of environmental matters worldwide.

David Pearce is Professor of Environmental Economics at University College London and Associate Director of the Centre for Social and

Economic Research on the Global Environment (CSERGE). He is the author or editor of nearly fifty books, including the seminal *Blueprint for a Green Economy* (Earthscan, 1989) which he co-authored with A. Markyanda and E. B. Barbier, holds the United Nations '*Global 500*' award for services to the world environment. His degree is from Oxford University and his research interests cover the whole field of environmental and resource economics, cost benefit analysis and the ethical foundations of environmental policy.

Ken Peattie is a Senior Lecturer in Strategic Management at Cardiff Business School, UK. His educational training has been in management and geography. He became a lecturer in marketing after working in information systems and marketing for paper multi-national Kimberly-Clark and as a strategic planner for AB Electronics. His research interests centre on the impact of environmental concern on corporate and marketing strategies, and he is the author of two books on the subject, *Green Marketing* (1992) and *Environmental Marketing Management: Meeting the Green Challenge* (1996), both published by Pitman.

Nigel Roome is the Erivan K. Haub Chair in Business and the Environment in the School of Business at York University, Canada. He also holds the Chair in Environmental Management in the Faculty of Economics at Tilburg University, The Netherlands. His doctorate is from Cambridge University's Department of Land Economy. He was the architect of business and environment concentration as part of the York MBA and has been active in establishing environmental research and education programmes in North America and Europe. He has taught environmental management in schools of environmental science as well as business.

Allerd Stikker is the Chairman of the Ecological Management Foundation in Amsterdam. His early training was in chemical engineering which was later complemented with an MA in theology and religious studies. In over forty years of employment, he has held senior executive positions at the Dutch Engineering and Shipbuilding Group RSV, AKZO, Royal Netherlands Salt Industries, and SIKKENS Group. In addition, he has held non-executive directorships in nine different companies including Heineken, Rothmans, and Cargill. He has also written several articles in journals and two books titled *The Transformation Factor* (Element, 1992) and *The Price of a Miracle* (BRES, 1988).

Richard H. Williams is an Associate Director of the Centre for Research in European Urban Environments and Director of the

Masters Programme in the Department of Town and Country Planning, University of Newcastle upon Tyne, UK. His training is in geography and town and regional planning. His main research interest is supranational planning policy and the spatial (environmental, regional, urban, infrastructure) policies of the European Union.

Introduction

Pratima Bansal and Elizabeth Howard

The Toyota Corporation group of companies has said that it sees the environment as the single most important societal and business issue confronting it.[1] It is not alone. Other major companies and business leaders have recently said similar things. Twenty years ago there would have been little discussion about the environment in business; today few dare say it is unimportant. Yet businesses deal with environmental issues in varied ways. Even some of the very largest companies, when closely examined, have done little to develop new practices or attitudes. Among the mass of smaller companies, the environment is often not really on the agenda at all. There are many statements of good intentions, but there is much uncertainty about what, if anything, should be done.

Previous books on the subject of business and environment tend to the normative and prescriptive – espousing what managers should do rather than providing them with the analytical tools to derive a solution which is most appropriate to their circumstances. Our own research has shown us that in practice companies have difficulty in knowing what to do, in defining the priorities and indeed in identifying why new approaches are necessary – especially after the initial 'easy wins' have been obtained. This book is about understanding the relationships between business and the environment, recognizing that there are multiple perspectives – from philosophy, anthropology, sociology, economics, law, ethics, and management systems. The perspective taken in analysing the issue will define the context, the framework for analysis, and the underlying assumptions. Because environmental issues cut across the boundaries of business functions, companies and states, and because of their value-laden nature, we believe our understanding of the business–environment relationship will be helped by explicitly applying different lenses. The chapters of this book are written from different points of view. From the contrasts, we can start to understand the conflicts and ambiguity businesses confront, and we can use these contrasts to inform business management.

The relationships between business and the environment have been redefined over the last decade. New science, new ideas about responsibilities for environmental change, and new management concepts within business have all helped to define what we see as a new era for business–environment relationships. However, this new era is characterized by dispute within business: why particular businesses should change their approach to environmental questions; what they should be concerned with, how they should proceed, and what sort of benefits, and for whom, may arise. These arguments are not surprising. Environmental questions in business are full of scientific uncertainty, alternative prescriptions are heavily value laden, and the issues are mostly complex and cross the boundaries of management functions, organizations and academic disciplines. We have attempted to provide a set of analyses so that the sources of the arguments may be better understood and the complexity recognized. *Business and the Natural Environment* is a series of views of the context within which businesses are managed and the ways that the relationships of businesses and the natural environment may be seen.

We do suggest that a new era in business–environment relationships has arrived. In science, relatively recent concerns about change in the environment have been added to long-standing problems of human impact on natural systems. Debates about climate change, biodiversity and congestion are absorbing the attention of the scientific and business communities in addition to worries about land, water and air pollution. Environmental responsibilities have been reframed. In particular, the notion of sustainable development has emerged. Little consensus exists on the meaning of sustainable development, yet its rhetoric has increasingly permeated organizations since the late 1980s. In business management, ideas about what the environment is, and which environmental matters should concern managers, have begun to change. Management books mainly describe social and economic systems, disregarding the biological and chemical systems on which we depend, and which the ecologists and other scientists emphasize. New environmental management systems are however now appearing for businesses to apply, and fierce debates are taking place about their worth.

In the last decade environmental matters have come to be defined as the concern of all businesses, not just the traditional heavy polluters or natural resource extractors. Even so, it is not clear what aspects of business behaviour have altered – or ought to be altered.

Public and business awareness of environmental concerns has certainly risen, if inconsistently, over recent years, as scientific knowledge has advanced and as, indeed, environmental problems have been seen to increase. There are long-standing environmental concerns about pollution, desertification and resource depletion, whose significance is interpreted and reinterpreted by each generation. It is difficult to disentangle human effects within the complex processes of ecological change. Systems are inter-related. For example, whether river flooding in particular places is caused more by building than increases in rainfall, and what might be the significance of altered vegetation (itself partly, but only partly, related to human activity) can be uncertain. But it seems clear that there are trends in human impact on the environment (Goudie, 1990). The ways we affect the environment are increasing; new pesticides, new nuclear reactors have appeared. Some environmental issues have become more widespread; pollutants exist far beyond their place of origin for example. The complexity and intensity of the impact of activity is increasing as technology and construction projects grow. Population growth and the increase in per capita consumption compound any effects which exist. Readers who wish to explore these matters will find assistance particularly from Goudie (1990) and O'Riordan (1995).

If it is possible to mark the beginning of the new era, we would assign it to 1972. In that year, we saw the first United Nations (UN) world conference on the environment. At that time articles in newspapers attempted to explain the word 'environment' for their readers. Since then, 'environment' has become a word frequently used as a matter of course in places from primary school to the councils of government. In the most general sense, interest in the commercial environment has affected language and concerns. The metaphors of business have been stretched to include competition as ecology. In practice, the 1970s and early 1980s saw major efforts by large corporations in heavy industry to reduce or control air, water and land pollution. The rhetoric of 'pollution prevention pays' (3M's slogan) spread, highlighting the potential to enhance not only corporate reputation but also profits through active environmental measures. Highly publicized environmental disasters (Bhopal, *Exxon Valdez*, Brent Spar) increased the attention given to the idea that the licence to operate conferred by public opinion on a business might be infringed by the environmental impact of corporate activities.

Another key era-defining event was the 1987 World Commission on Environment and Development and the publication of the Brundtland Report (WCED, 1987). It epitomized the idea that sustainable development is necessary for social, economic and environmental ends, and that business is not the problem, but the agent of change to be harnessed. Development is necessary, environmental care is necessary, and both should be equitable between countries and generations, if human welfare is to be maintained or increased – and all of these things are needed together.

Whether or not we accept the argument that environmental concern is a luxury good in western economies – and that concerns lessen in tougher times – interest in protecting the environment has continued into the 1990s. The demand for greater environmental responsibility by business has been ratcheted up and formal environmental management has become relevant to many businesses. Economic models of business activity now compete with ecoefficiency and sustainable development models.

There may be a new era, but there is little consensus about what environmental matters should concern business in practice and how they should be dealt with. We suggest three reasons: environmental issues are ultimately global in concern, they cross disciplinary boundaries, and they are laden with value.

First, environmental issues know few borders. The concerns are becoming increasingly global, and transboundary. They extend beyond the usual context of business and of business textbooks. Questions of climate change, ozone depletion, and water and air pollution cross regional and national borders. Any one business may impact the environment in ways which affect many individuals, households and organizations. The issues extend beyond markets or legal jurisdictions. Consequences may be far removed in time or space from actions. Where cause and effect are obscure, action is difficult to organize and, indeed, the need for action may be difficult to see. Furthermore, businesses struggle with the level of the response they should make to calls for environmental action to deal with matters of possible and debatable global and social urgency, yet where their actions may have small effect. There seems to be major incongruence between social responsibility and individual responsibility.

Second, the reach of environmental issues extends not just across geography, but also across disciplinary domains. How do we know how to analyse the issue when there are repercussions across all disciplinary boundaries and, therefore, the matter can be viewed from multiple perspectives? Environmental management is grounded in science. Without good science, the identification and discussion of environmental issues lacks a rudder. Science rarely offers a prescription however. It may in itself be incomplete or uncertain. Its significance for business is mediated through economic, political and social systems.

It was the scientists who suggested that the depletion of atmospheric ozone caused by the catalytic action of certain chemicals, whose human production is being increased, has produced 'ozone holes' over the poles. Once the scientific community was able to capture an image of this hole, public concern rose rapidly. Industrial actions to change production processes, products and marketing activities however depended on businesses' interpretations of the meaning of the science, and of the implications of public understanding of the science, of political and legal changes in controls over certain chemicals, themselves related to social pressures. The economic structures are important: environmental damage has not been a cost for producers of ozone depleting chemicals; legal controls over certain chemicals and the demands of customers mean that the costs of research into new products and processes have now become more acceptable. Costing changes to processes involving substances which are not prohibited but may be implicated in ozone depletion is an interesting matter involving among other things an assessment of risk – future regulatory change, future change in public perceptions and so on. The ozone problem is often cited to show the importance of environmental matters in business, with widespread changes to reduce the use of chlorofluorocarbons (CFC) and other chemicals yet it is not clear what businesses should do in response to the problem. Many substances are involved in atmospheric changes however, and it may be that significant damage is being done and will continue to be done by those which are not controlled by the Montreal Protocol. Economics sets certain parameters for business, social and legal systems set others. How should businesses determine how to act? Should they test what they can or should they do what is environmentally significant as well as what is economic and legal? How will regulatory and economic systems take account of changing environmental concerns?

This leads us to the question of values. The relationship between business and environment is laden with value. If we are to commit resources to environmental solutions, we must be able to choose between alternative environmental issues on which to focus attention and then be able to value costs and benefits of action. Much business activity is tested against its financial implications, whereas the issue of environment pertains to ethics, values, responsibilities, which are only sometimes translated into economics. The effects of the depletion of the ozone layer on solar radiation at ground level are not absolutely certain, nor the link with human health, nor indeed are we certain of the effects of eliminating the designated chemicals. The decisions which are taken or not taken involve the values we ascribe to human health, to present and future resources and situations, to self and others. Entirely different value systems, eco-centred or human centred, may be applied. The task is complicated by the fact that different constituents will value resources differently. So, what starts in the realm of science, moves into the domain of economics, ethics and politics.

Management fashions come and go but there does not even seem to be a fashion in environmental management. For many businesses, there is little that seems to be necessary. There is too much ambiguity, too much conflict, too little focus. It is because environmental questions are so wide and touch so many aspects of what we do in business, because the issues are so bound up with competing value systems, and because there is so much uncertainty in interpreting human impact on the environment, that the business of environmental management is so difficult. The result is that we are locked into inaction as organizational stakeholders vie for the loudest and most powerful voice.

When assembling this book, we chose contributors who were leaders in their disciplines. We asked them to set the directions, to explore what they saw as important and to suggest how we should think about the business–environment relationships. We are very pleased with the results. There is a range of issues covered, the underlying assumptions and the writing styles permitting the reader to easily detect some of the key differences in perspective. Furthermore, many of the authors provide insights which have not been discussed elsewhere. In the remaining part of this introduction, we summarize each chapter. In the conclusion, we follow up by identifying some of the obvious ways in which the chapters differ: how they reach different answers to the same question. Finally, we summarize by outlining some of the messages which are common to all of the chapters.

The first chapter by Gladwin and Kennelly studies the issue of business–environment from a *philosophical* position by considering the question of sustainable development. They set out for us some of the complexities of sustainable development and more importantly they show why and how it calls into question so much of the technocentric worldview which pervades business thinking. They cannot prove that a sustainable development paradigm is better or more valid than another – that, they point out is impossible because we must use values in the choice. The fundamental lack of communication between 'Greens' and people of different world views seems to us to lie behind some of the bitterest disputes about what environmental management is or should be. Gladwin and Kennelly help us to understand this mutual incomprehension.

Roome, in Chapter 2, explores an area which offers rich insights into the business–environment relationship, that of *corporate social responsibility and applied ethics*. Roome covers a wide scope of management literature to assemble a map of the field and the way in which business interacts with environment. He highlights the importance of considering all aspects of business operations and performance if we are to consider the relevance of environment in business and vice versa. Furthermore, he shows the importance of individual values in assessing the importance of environment to business.

Three chapters then deal with the contrasting approaches of three key disciplines: anthropology, sociology and economics. Milton takes the position of an *anthropologist* in exploring the business–environment relationship. She begins by mapping out the key issues relevant to anthropologists and then applies them to the discussion of business and environment. The key issue to anthropologists is the one of culture; how it is defined and how it informs human actions. She applies the model of cultural diversity to show that the way in which we define the environment is influenced by the way in which we engage it. This mode of engagement influences not only definitions and understandings but also shapes the symbols and discourse which are applied.

Grint's chapter develops an approach to the business of the environment rooted in *sociological* analysis, approaching the material from three angles. The structural and action approaches have long traditions and imply that phenomena can be explained either as a consequence of external structures which tend to determine individuals' actions, or as a consequence of the interpretative action of individuals. A third approach, constructivism, is then explored. This asserts that the critical issue is epistemological – how we know things to be as they are claimed to be. It is rooted in a scepticism of truth claims but has significant practical consequences. The debate hinges on modernist notions of science and technology and offers an alternative route into the complex issues that confront all those engaged in the environmental debate.

Pearce explores the business-environment relationship from the perspective of *economics*, placing environmental investment decisions into a benefit–cost framework but without assuming that profit maximization is the only goal of the firm. He addresses the question of why firms would engage in environmentally responsible activities beyond the point where the marginal cost exceeds the marginal benefit. If the dominant forces in business are the imperatives of economics, Pearce's chapter is especially useful in that he identifies how economics defines certain business–environment relationships and, second, how developments in environmental economics might change those relationships.

The two chapters in Part Three deal with regulatory frameworks. Williams considers the *government environmental policies* which influence the business–environment relationship. He argues that businesses must understand the logic of these, particularly if they want to operate across borders. Williams outlines the treaties and powers which influence the development of environmental policy. By better understanding the structures and principles which bind the policy-making bodies, businesses will be better able to respond to them in such a way so as to not jeopardize their operations. In particular, Williams identifies the main international, European Union (EU) and United Kingdom specific treaties and agencies relevant to good business management.

Cameron and Mackenzie consider similar subject matter to Williams but incorporate the specifics of *law* to policy and governing structures. Cameron and Mackenzie too suggest that the interlocking systems of international, EU and UK law impose operational constraints on organizations. They identify the specific statutes which are relevant to business respecting the environment and the significance for business of changes in them and in legal concepts related to the natural environment. Of particular interest is the discussion of trends which are appearing in law-making. They outline cases which illuminate the implications.

In Part Four we begin to look specifically at the degree to which management studies informs our understanding of the business–environment relationship. We start with the concerns of strategic management and marketing, and then look at the specific ways in which businesses apply environmental management systems.

Bansal explores the relevance of the business–environment relationship to *strategic management*. She argues that the environment can be perceived as an opportunity or threat. When changes in the natural environment or concepts of it are perceived as an opportunity, the firm can enhance its competitiveness, and when perceived as a threat, the firm can strengthen its legitimacy by showing sensitivity to concerns about the environment. Her stance is not predicated on ethics or managerial values, but on principles of improving competitive performance and more confidently securing organizational survival.

Peattie discusses the role of *marketing*. He takes on the difficult task of defining key marketing terms in the context of the environment and then demonstrating how they fit with traditional discussions of marketing, and how they supplement those discussions. He makes suggestions about ways in which marketing can enhance our understanding of business and environment. Most importantly, he argues that marketing does not suggest more consumption but, rather, wise consumption so that the needs of society, past and present are adequately met.

Stikker moves the discussion to the question of how *organizations* are able to implement environmental strategies. He outlines six steps. First organizations must build awareness of the issue, then they must develop specific goals. Firms must be able to measure their performance, and benchmark against competitors. Finally, they must engage in environmental cost accounting, and then communicate their activities. Stikker supplies managers with a specific approach to ensure that environmentally sensitive change is focused and achieves results in a systematic manner.

Monaghan's chapter considers the nature of *environmental management systems*. He distinguishes five elements: carrying out an environmental review; developing an environmental policy, establishing a management organization for environment, establishing objectives; and engaging in an environmental audit. He provides managers with specific sound advice, based on his experiences and those borrowed from numerous others of the efficacy of the results if the environmental management system is applied intelligently.

Monaghan and Stikker provide us the perspectives of managers. They write with the authority of experience and get to the heart of the questions confronting managers. More striking than the differences between these two chapters are their similarities. They move us from defining the problems to trying to solve them.

In our concluding remarks at the end of the book we will summarize some of the key questions and answers in the eleven perspectives presented here.

Note

1 *Environment Briefing*, Issue 17 December 1996, P & O SN Co.

References

World Commission on Environment and Development (1987). *Our Common Future*. Oxford University Press.
Goudie, A. (1990). *The Human Impact on the Natural Environment*. (3rd edn) Basil Blackwell.
O'Riordan, T. (ed.) (1995) *Environmental Science for Environmental Management*. Longman.

Part One

Philosophical and Ethical Questions

1 Sustainable development: a new paradigm for management theory and practice[1]

Thomas N. Gladwin and James J. Kennelly

'Nothing in this world is so powerful as an idea whose time has come.' (Victor Hugo, 1802–85)

This chapter surveys the meaning and principal requisites of sustainable development, the paradigms or worldviews that tend to support or oppose it, and the implications of this paradigmatic battle for the nature of the business–environment relationship. More fundamentally, the chapter asks managers to ponder the question of 'how do we wish to live and what is the role of business organizations in such living?' Ultimately, it asks managers to confront perhaps the most important question of our time: what is the impact of business organizations on the full human community, the natural environment and a sustainable future?

There has been, and remains, a profound *dissociation* between business education and practice, and the natural environment. Much of business education proceeds as if organizations lack biophysical foundations. Organic and biotic limits in the natural world are excluded from the realm of organizational science, ignoring the myriad ecosystem service transactions that keep organizations alive. Quite simply, how many organizations could exist in the absence of oxygen production, fresh water supply or fertile soil?

Such constricted sense-making on the part of managers may be dysfunctional at best, or pathological at worst, with profound consequences for both the natural environment and human life on earth. This chapter provides managers with an opportunity for self-reflection, as the meaning and requisites of sustainable development are explored. It appraises the conventional paradigm of *techno-centrism* and its generated opposite of *ecocentrism*, and finds both deficient according to the requirements of sustainable development. A new integrative paradigm of *sustaincentrism* is then proposed as more fruitful in yielding sustainability when put into practice. The chapter concludes with a broad set of implications for informing the role of managers in support of sustainable development.

Toward a meaning of sustainable development

There is no lack of definitions of sustainable development. It has been considered an expression of a vision (Lee, 1993), a change of values (Clark, 1989), a stage of moral development (Rolston, 1994), a social reorganization (Gore, 1992) and a transformational process (Viederman, 1994). The core idea was defined most influentially by the World Commission on Environment and Development (i.e. the Brundtland Commission) as 'development which meets the needs of the present without compromising the ability of future generations to meet their own needs' (WCED, 1987: 8). In its broadest sense, this normative abstraction has been widely endorsed by thousands of governmental, corporate and other organizations worldwide.

Definitions of sustainable development

Since the time of the Brundtland Commission's report, scores of alternative definitions of sustainable development have been proposed. The boxed text presents a gallery of some of the leading conceptions of sustainable development.

Representative conceptions of sustainable development

To maximize simultaneously the biological system goals (genetic diversity, resilience, biological productivity), economic system goals (satisfaction of basic needs, enhancement of equity, increasing useful goods and services), and social system goals (cultural diversity, institutional sustainability, social justice, participation) (Barbier, 1987: 103).

Improving the quality of human life while living within the carrying capacity of supporting ecosystems (WCU, UNEP, WWF, 1991: 10).

Sustainability is a relationship between dynamic human economic systems and larger dynamic, but normally slower-changing ecological systems, in which 1) human life can continue indefinitely, 2) human individuals can flourish, and 3) human cultures can develop; but in which effects of human activities remain within bounds, so as not to destroy the diversity, complexity, and function of the ecological life support system (Costanza, Daly and Bartholomew, 1991: 8).

A sustainable society is one that can persist over generations, one that is far-seeing enough, flexible enough, and wise enough not to undermine either its physical or its social

---

systems of support (Meadows, Meadows and Randers, 1992: 209).

Sustainability is an economic state where the demands placed upon the environment by people and commerce can be met without reducing the capacity of the environment to provide for future generations. It can also be expressed ... leave the world better than you found it, take no more than you need, try not to harm life or the environment, make amends if you do (Hawken, 1993: 139).

Our vision is of a life-sustaining earth. We are committed to the achievement of a dignified, peaceful, and equitable existence. We believe a sustainable United States will have an economy that equitably provides opportunities for satisfying livelihoods and a safe, healthy, high quality of life for current and future generations. Our nation will protect its environment, its natural resource base, and the functions and viability of natural systems on which all life depends (USPCSD, 1994: 1).

Sustainability is a participatory process that creates and pursues a vision of community that respects and makes prudent use of all its resources – natural, human, human-created, social, cultural, scientific, etc. Sustainability seeks to ensure, to the degree possible, that present generations attain a high degree of economic security and can realize democracy and popular participation in control of their communities, while maintaining the integrity of the ecological systems upon which all life and all production depends, while assuming responsibility to future generations to provide them with the where-with-all for their vision, hoping that they have the wisdom and intelligence to use what is provided in an appropriate manner (Viederman, 1994: 5).

A perusal of the boxed text shows a construct infused with multiple objectives and complex interdependencies. As a consequence, some forecast that the concept of sustainable development will remain fuzzy, elusive and controversial for some time to come (Beckerman, 1994; Dowie, 1995; Levin, 1993).

Components of sustainable development

For now, we are forced to deal with the topic of sustainable development at a rather high level of abstraction. It is, however, possible to deduce principal components of the idea that are generally accepted (and common to most of the definitions in the boxed text). These suggest that sustainable development is a process of achieving *human development* (widening or enlarging the range of people's choices; UNDP, 1994) in an inclusive, connected, equitable, prudent, and secure manner. *Inclusiveness* implies human development over time and space. *Connectivity* embraces ecological, social and economic interdependence. *Equity* suggests fairness, within and across generations and species. *Prudence* connotes duties of care and prevention, technologically, scientifically and politically. *Security* demands safety from chronic threats and protection from harmful disruption.

We accept that debate over the meaning of sustainable development will go on, and *should* go on, for a long time, and that our chosen abstract conception is but one of many. The formula is very simple, in that human development is subjected to five constraints. In this view, development is unsustainable when an enlargement of human choice excludes, disconnects, promotes inequity, reflects imprudence or raises insecurity. We recognize that all of these terms are challenging to define, with notions such as security or prudence more easily identified by their absence than their presence. Yet if the reader contemplates the representative definitions in the boxed text, we believe that these constraints on the range of human choice represent a reasonable basis upon which to move the debate forward. Each of the five components is further amplified below.

Inclusiveness

The definitions of sustainable development presented in the previous section suggest that sustainability embraces both present and future environmental *and* human systems. An understanding of the human dimensions of sustainability must encompass the forces of global environmental change: population growth, economic growth, technological change, political and economic institutions, and attitudes and beliefs (Stern, Young and Druckman, 1992). Sustainability thus goes beyond a sole concern with the natural environment, to also encompass social and economic dimensions.

Connectivity

Sustainability demands an understanding of the world's problems as systemically interconnected and interdependent. Social equity and biospheric respect are required for enhanced welfare anywhere on the planet: improved human welfare and social equity are necessary to motivate biospheric respect; and enhanced welfare and biospheric respect are needed to facilitate social equity (Gladwin, Krause and Kennelly, 1995). Efforts aimed only towards ecological health and integrity, in the absence of efforts to alleviate poverty, stabilize population and redistribute economic opportunity, may produce trivial results at best. Any gains may be counteracted by global ecosystem degradation and sociopolitical instability induced by the poverty–population nexus (Dasgupta, 1995).

Equity

Fair distribution of resources, both within and between generations, is a central dimension of nearly all conceptions of sustainable development. Some place special emphasis on providing for the needs of the least advantaged in society. Few address human obligations regarding the non-human world. While acknowledging the intensity of the debate regarding fairness, equity and justice, the definitions supplied previously in this chapter imply that sustainability, at a minimum, means that human activities should not shift costs on to, or appropriate the property or resource rights of, other human interests, today or tomorrow, without proper compensation.

Prudence

Most definitions of sustainable development argue for the maintenance of resilient life supporting ecosystems and inter-related socioeconomic systems, the avoidance of actions that may be irreversible, and the containment of the scale and impact of human activities within regenerative and carrying capacities. Most analysts call for prudence and humility in the pursuit of sustainable development, given the massive uncertainty, unknown thresholds and complex dynamics of ecological and social systems (Costanza, Wainger, Folke and Mäler, 1993). This constraint demands precaution, pre-emptive safeguards, reversible actions, safety margins, and preparation for perpetual surprise (Ludwig, Hilborn and Walters, 1993).

Security

Sustainable development is a human-centred construct, aimed at ensuring 'a safe, healthy, high quality of life for current and future generations' (USPCSD, 1994: 1). There are a number of overlapping conditions that must be fulfilled in support of this goal. At a minimum, sustainability mandates *no net loss* of:

1   *ecosystem and social system health*, i.e. capacities of natural and
social systems to provide life-support services to humanity
(Costanza, Norton and Haskell, 1992);
2   *critical natural capital*, i.e. stocks of irreplaceable natural assets
such as biological diversity, the ozone layer, and biogeochemical
cycles (Daly, 1994);
3   *self-organization*, i.e. capacities of living systems to carry out self-
renewal, self-maintenance and self-transformation;
4   *carrying capacity*, i.e. long-run capacities of biophysical and
social systems to support human enterprise (Daily and Ehrlich,
1992);
5   *human freedom*, i.e. civil society, with democracy and full realization of human rights in day-to-day living dependent on participation, accountability, reciprocity and transparency (Veiderman,
1994), including the fulfilment of basic human needs.

Appraising paradigms versus sustainable development

'Men and women become civilized, not in proportion to their
willingness to believe, but in proportion to their readiness to
doubt.'
(Henry Louis Mencken, 1880–1956)

In this section, we dialectically examine three paradigms or worldviews: the conventional *technocentric* worldview (thesis) versus its
generated opposite, the *ecocentric* worldview (antithesis), versus an
emergent integrated *sustaincentric* worldview (synthesis).

Worldviews refer to 'the constellations of beliefs, values and
concepts that give shape and meaning to the world a person experiences and acts within' (Norton, 1991: 75). They rarely take the form
of highly developed philosophies, but rather are sets of background
assumptions that *tend* to organize language, thoughts, perceptions
and actions (Morgan, 1980). Such assumptions about how the world
works are usually fragmented, and often not even recognized by their
holders. Despite this, they are highly resistant to change.

This typology constructs alternate worldviews based on sets of
shared fundamental assumptions. The three worldviews are not
closed, but merely represent broad camps in which many schools of
thought flourish. Given that worldviews in practice are taken for
granted, it is reasonable to expect that no one person or institution
would strictly hold to all of the assumptions within any one
worldview. Human and organizational mindsets may very well mix
assumptions from the different camps in a variety of complex,
conflicting, and ill-defined ways.

Nor is this a matter of correctness; no given worldview is either right or wrong. We cannot proclaim that either technocentrism, ecocentrism or sustaincentrism are true or false, good or evil, beautiful or ugly. We can, however, posit a criterion of relative fitness for sustainable development. In other words, which set of assumptions is most consistent with our prescriptions for inclusiveness, connectivity, equity, prudence and security? The following is an elaboration of the three paradigms.

The technocentric paradigm

The origins of the technocentric paradigm can be traced back to the Scientific Revolution and the bias toward human dominion over nature some see embedded in western religion (Capra, 1982; Daly and Cobb, 1994; Merchant, 1992; Orr, 1992). The technocentric worldview is dominant today in mainstream elements of business. Its apparent fundamental assumptions are summarized in Table 1.1.

Technocentric ontology and ethics

The earth is inert, passive and legitimately exploitable. Nature is composed of infinitely divisible objects, moved by external rather than internal forces. The dominant metaphor is mechanical, with the whole nothing more than the sum of its parts. Understanding is achieved by reductionist and positivistic modes of reasoning. System structure is hierarchical.

Humankind is *separate from* and *superior to* nature. Humans are the only locus of intrinsic value. They have a right to master natural creation for human benefit. The natural world has only instrumental and typically monetarily quantifiable value as a commodity. Ethics are human-centred and utilitarian, for human beings matter most. Sacrifices on behalf of future generations, non-human nature or even less fortunate but geographically distant current generations are generally unwarranted, unless market signals dictate otherwise. Assuming continued economic growth and technological innovation, today's generation need only pass on to the next an aggregate capital stock no less than the one enjoyed currently. Reasoning is egoistic, linear, instrumental and rational.

Technocentric science and technology

Nature is resilient in the face of disturbance, with damage generally reversible. Nature changes gradually, fast enough to be detected yet slow enough to be controlled. The earth's physical resources are

Table 1.1 Alternative environmental paradigms

Key assumptions	Technocentrism	Sustaincentrism	Ecocentrism
Ontological and Ethical			
1. Metaphor of earth	Vast machine	Life support system	Mother/web of life
2. Perception of earth	Dead/passive	Home/managed	Alive/sensitive
3. System composition	Atomistic/parts	Parts and wholes	Organic/wholes
4. System structure	Hierarchical	Holistic	Egalitarian
5. Humans and nature	Dissociation	Interdependence	Association
6. Human role	Domination	Stewardship	Plain member
7. Value of nature	Anthropocentric	Inherent	Intrinsic
8. Ethical grounding	Narrow homocentric	Broad homocentric	Whole earth
9. Time/space scales	Short/near	Multiscale	Indefinite
10. Logic/reason	Egoist-rational	Vision/network	Holism/spiritualism
Scientific and Technological			
1. Resilience of nature	Tough/robust	Varied/fragile	Highly vulnerable
2. Carrying capacity limits	No limits	Approaching	Already exceed
3. Population size	No problem	Stabilize soon	Freeze/reduce
4. Growth pattern	Exponential	Logistic	Hyperbolic
5. Severity of problems	Trivial	Consequential	Catastrophic
6. Urgency of solutions	Little/wait	Great/decades	Extraordinary/now
7. Risk orientation	Risk-taking	Precaution	Risk aversion
8. Faith in technology	Optimism	Scepticism	Pessimism
9. Technological pathways	Big/centralized	Benign/decoupled	Small/decentralized
10. Human vs. natural capital	Full substitutes	Partial substitutes	Complements

Economic and psychological

1. Primary objective	Efficient allocation	Quality of life	Ecological integrity
2. The good life	Materialism	Postmaterialism	Anti-materialism
3. Human nature	Homo economicus	Homo sapient	Homo animalist
4. Economic structure	Free market	Green economy	Steady state
5. Role of growth	Good/necessary	Mixed/modify	Bad/eliminate
6. Poverty alleviation	Growth trickle	Equal opportunity	Redistribution
7. Natural capital	Exploit/convert	Conserve/maintain	Enhance/expand
8. Discount rate	High/normal	Low/complement	Zero/inappropriate
9. Trade orientation	Global	National	Bioregional
10. Political structure	Centralized	Devolved	Decentralized

virtually inexhaustible because of infinite human ingenuity in exploiting them. Population growth is a positive force for improvement; it sparks creativity and ingenuity within societies (Simon 1981).

There is no cause for drastic action, since environmental dangers are greatly exaggerated (Easterbrook, 1995). There is plenty of time to improve scientific understanding. Humans can manage any technology (e.g. nuclear energy, genetic engineering) safely and without corruption.

Technocentric economics and psychology

The economy is a closed linear system, isolated from nature, where exchange value circulates between industries and households. The primary economic objective is to efficiently allocate resources. Human wants are central and unlimited, and individuals behave in a self-interested and consistent manner to maximize their utility. The optimal economic structure for satisfying wants and allocating resources most efficiently is *laissez-faire* capitalism. Goods and services are allocated to the most valued ends based upon the willingness to pay. Externalities arising from market failures should be internalized if cost effective (i.e. if gains in social welfare from correcting the externality outweigh the costs of doing so).

The world is largely empty. Growth is good and more growth is better; growth enables governments to tax and raise resources for environmental protection and leads to less polluting industries and adoption of cleaner technologies. Global growth and its trickle-down benefits are the key to bettering the lives of the poor without sacrifices by the rich. Free or unregulated trade increases economic efficiency through comparative advantage. Global economic integration and free mobility of capital across national borders maximizes welfare. With nearly infinite substitution possibilities, scarcity is relative rather than absolute. The future can thus be discounted at conventional rates because people universally exhibit short-term time preference and rates of productivity of natural and human-made capital are likely to increase through time.

Appraising technocentrism versus sustainability

We proposed earlier that for a worldview to be congruent with sustainable development it must manifest inclusiveness, connectivity, equity, prudence and security. The technocentric worldview, in our opinion, performs poorly on all five tests.

1 *Inclusiveness*. Technocentrism dissociates the human economy from non-human nature. It disregards a broad range of scientific understandings regarding limits on resource availability, irreversibilities associated with losses of critical natural capital, biophysical interdependence between human capital and natural capital, and the finite, materially closed character of the global ecosystem (Jannson, Hammer, Folke and Costanza, 1994). Its overarching economic efficiency calculus represses attention to matters of appropriate ecological scale and fair distribution of resources and property rights. Its exclusive reliance on markets subordinates concern with community, nature, the poor, marginalized elements of society, and the interests of future generations.

2 *Connectivity*. Technocentrism may be a fractured worldview that 'drastically separates mind and body, subject and object, culture and nature, thoughts and things, values and facts, spirit and matter, human and nonhuman' (Wilber, 1995: 4). Such gross reductionism severs the connections and complex interlinkages at the crux of the sustainability challenge.

3 *Equity*. Technocentrism is viewed as 'arrogantly' human-centred (Ehrenfeld, 1981). Many argue that technocentrism's logic of growth via market mechanisms perpetuates poverty and under-development, deepens economic and social disparities, privileges a wealthy minority at the expense of the human majority, and serves to exhaust a one-time inheritance of natural capital. (Daly and Cobb, 1994; Ehrlich, 1994; Korten, 1990).

4 *Prudence*. The core economic and technological assumptions of technocentrism are all rather dangerous, we believe, given great uncertainty and complexity. Technocentrism's heavy discounting of the future, by which distant catastrophic consequences become virtually irrelevant in the short-term present, also biases policies toward inaction. Continuing with technocentrism as usual may, quite simply, represent a huge gamble with survival.

5 *Security*. While it is unfair to trace all world problems to technocentrism's doorstep, it is clearly correlated with a world 'in agony' (Council for a Parliament of the World's Religions, 1994: 67). Evidence of declining renewable resources, persistent pollution, and a threatened biological base are well documented (Ayres, 1993; Vitousek, 1994; World Resources Institute, 1994). Even within developed countries, most important environmental indicators remain negative, and trends are not improving (Scharf and Williamson, 1994). In the social realm, data clearly suggest persistent deprivation for the human majority, widening disparities within and between nations, and gathering forces of social decomposition and divisiveness posing

threats to human security (Gladwin, Krause and Kennelly, 1995; UNDP, 1994).

In summary, technocentrism fails, in our view, the litmus tests of sustainability. It pathologically dissociates or represses many critical components bearing upon life support systems. It fractures or severs the connections that sustainability requires. It fails to deal adequately with intergenerational, intragenerational and inter-species equity. It places an extremely large and risky wager on the future. Finally, while producing material wealth and power for a privileged minority, it gives rise to risks which threaten the future of the entire human community. If society does indeed adopt sustainable development as a fundamental organizing principle (Gore, 1992), then the dominant paradigm of technocentrism will clearly become a paradigm in crisis.

The ecocentric paradigm

Supporters of the ecocentric worldview draw philosophical inspiration from: Eastern philosophies calling for conformance with the critical order of nature, indigenous reverence for life-giving earth, transcendental and preservationist movements, the 'land ethic' of conservationist Aldo Leopold (1949), the deep ecology movement which rejects human domination over nature (Devall and Sessions, 1985; Sessions, 1995); and New Age systems thinking (Capra, 1982; Jantsch, 1980). Its core assumptions (see Table 1.1) follow.

Ecocentric ontology and ethics

The earth is the nurturing mother of life, a great interlocking order, and a web of life in which humans are but one strand. The earth is alive, active and sensitive to human action, and sacred. The governing metaphor is organic, with wholeness representing the basic principle of ecocentrism. Everything is connected to every-thing else, and internal relations and process take primacy over parts.

Ecocentrism rejects the premise that humans occupy a privileged place in nature. Non-human nature has intrinsic value, indepen-dent of human values and consciousness. It should be used by humans only to satisfy vital needs of sustenance. Non-interference in naturally evolving systems is a primary moral duty. Ethical priority is given to wholes over parts: 'a thing is right when it tends to preserve the integrity, stability and beauty of the biotic community. It is wrong when it tends otherwise' (Leopold, 1949: 224–225).

Ecocentric science and technology

Nature is fragile, easily stressed and vulnerable. Damage to human interests is essentially irreversible in cases of biodiversity and topsoil loss, groundwater depletion, and interference with biogeochemical cycles. The current human population size and its material demands already exceed the long-term biophysical carrying capacity of the planet; the optimum human population is in the vicinity of 1.5 to 2 thousand million people (Daily, Ehrlich and Ehrlich, 1994). The flourishing of non-human life requires a substantial *decrease* in the human population.

Humanity and the natural world are on a collision course which will result in global decay and chaos in the absence of urgent and radical reform (Kaplan, 1994). This view of fundamental instability correlates with a high degree of pessimism regarding human capacities to generate and use technology wisely. Technology is viewed as a Faustian bargain, trading current gain against future survival. Persistence is only feasible via small, simple, resilient and decentralized systems and technologies that make minimal demands on nature. Such pathways are necessary because man-made capital and natural capital are fundamentally complements, rather than substitutes. Virtually all production and welfare are totally dependent on ecological health, integrity and abundance. Technological substitutes are not plausible for most critical non-renewable natural resources and life support functions.

Ecocentric economics and psychology

Human well-being is secondary to the well-being of the earth. Ideal human nature calls for full immersion into the biosphere (Naess, 1995). With the world already full, material growth increases environmental and social costs faster than benefits of production and consumption. Ultimately, this makes humanity and the rest of nature poorer, not richer. Economic order implies more ecological disorder. Given that the scale of material and energy throughput must be drastically reduced, a minimalist development strategy is needed. The good life resides in voluntary simplicity.

The achievement of human security, dignity, and satisfaction can be reached through steady state economics (Daly, 1992). Poverty can be dealt with via redistribution. Natural capital must be preserved and enhanced. This necessitates drastically reduced rates of energy and matter throughput across ecosystem–economy boundaries. With ecologically optimal scale as the overarching objective, collective decisions over-ride the free play of market forces. Since uncontrolled capital mobility reduces economic security and ecological integrity, capital must be rooted in community, and trade restricted to the exchange of true ecological surpluses. Finally, the tyranny of discounting against the future fosters exhaustion of natural capital and must be overcome.

Appraising ecocentrism versus sustainability

In reacting to technocentrism, ecocentrists offer a worldview that is decidely more holistic. However, it also fails the litmus tests of sustainable development.

1 *Inclusiveness*. Ecocentrism emphasizes harmony in nature and downplays its harshness. Yet, as a species in a biotic community, some mix of human subduing and caring is essential; as Nash states 'some degree of domination of nature by humans is necessary to prevent the domination of humans by nature (1991: 106). Ecocentrism, on the other hand, clearly subordinates humans to the biosphere. It dispenses with human distinctiveness in a hierarchically evolving universe (Weinberg, 1994). Ultimately, it removes the 'wisdom' from the term 'homosapien', and fails to embrace the capacity of human intellect and thus the whole of reality.
2 *Connectivity*. A renowned proponent of deep ecology recently opined that pursuit of ecological sustainability would be accep-table regardless of the state of affairs in the domains of peace and justice (Naess, 1995). This view falls considerably short of the argument that ecological sustainability is a necessary, but not sufficient, condition for sustainable development. Ecological sustainability is simply unachievable under conditions of social or economic unsustainability. Ecocentrism offers little guidance concerning the horrors of expanding poverty, human rights abuse and massive displacement that currently beset much of the developing world. It fails adequately to address issues of unemployment, income inequality and other social pathologies that grip the industrial world. Ecocentrism does not ensure sustainable livelihoods.
3 *Equity*. Ecocentrism privileges the biosphere, levels distinctions within it and, by emphasizing the whole, depreciates the impor-tance of the suffering of individual parts (human or non-human). In the absence of principles for adjudicating conflicts of interest between human and non-human nature, ecocentrism offers little policy guidance beyond that of taking all legitimate human and non-human interests into account in decision-making (Norton, 1989). This may paralyse pragmatic action of any sort.

4 *Prudence.* Ecocentrism eulogizes a primal state when matter, life and mind were undifferentiated and whole (Goldsmith, 1993; Roszak, 1992). It is a vision of return to a pristine communion with nature in a new Golden Age. The reality today, however, is that humans may already have brought about 'the end of nature' as a force independent of humanity (McKibben, 1989). Human alteration of natural cycles and land use/land cover is already so vast that 'any clear dichotomy between pristine ecosystems and human-altered areas that may have existed in the past has vanished' (Vitousek, 1994: 1861). There is no longer a primal relationship to which to return. Projections suggest that the human population will double in the next century (World Resources Institute, 1994). Ecocentrism suggests a substantial decrease of the human population from current levels is required. How this is to be achieved in the absence of profound social re-engineering is difficult to imagine.

5 *Security.* The United Nations Development Programme has emphasized that 'it will not be possible for the community of nations to achieve any of its goals – not peace, not environmental protection, not human rights or democratization, not fertility reduction, not social integration – except in the context of sustainable development that leads to human security' (1994: 1). In our view, ecocentrism as articulated so far offers little guidance as to how the achievement of ecological sustainability is possible, under current social conditions, without a gross diminishment of universal pluralism, altruism and freedom (Taylor, 1989).

In summary, eocentrism diminishes human distinctiveness, ignores fundamental relationships bearing upon human security and therefore ecological integrity, and rests on philosophical grounds that cannot currently be accepted as practical guides to human conduct. Despite its perhaps attractive ideology and admirable intent, ecocentrism, like technocentrism, is beset by internal contradictions and fails to truly integrate culture and nature. It is to this integrative perspective that we now turn.

The sustaincentric paradigm

We have argued above that neither technocentrism nor ecocentrism offers a basis upon which to achieve sustainable development. Both paradigms, by setting in motion self-defeating counterforces, fail to promote development or to conserve nature. As competing paradigms, they appear locked in a state of mutual negation (Myers and Simon, 1994). The idea of a paradigm centred on sustainable development can be understood as a dialectical outgrowth of this colossal struggle.

The sustaincentric paradigm represents an emergent synthesis, an attempt at higher and deeper integration. While technocentrism and ecocentrism have long histories, the paradigm of sustainability is embryonic. While many are working to 'green' technocentrism, a complete reconciliation of the two opposing paradigms remains elusive. The task is extraordinary and perhaps even impossible. The articulation of a sustaincentric worldview below must necessarily be seen as but a tentative step in the search for reconciliation.

Sustaincentrism draws its inspiration from claims of the universalism of life, the stewardship admonitions common to the major religions, the field of ecological economics (Costanza, 1991), traditions of conservationism and scientific resource management (Norton, 1991), and emerging scientific theories based on nature's dynamic complexity and inherent self-organizing properties (Botkin, 1990; Prigogine and Stengers, 1984; Wheatley, 1992). Efforts to sort out its emergent dimensions and principles can be found in many recent works (Brown, 1994; Daly and Cobb, 1994; Gladwin, 1992; Gladwin and Krause, forthcoming; Gore, 1992; Jannson, Hammer, Folke and Costanza, 1994; Korten, 1990; Porritt, 1991; Stead and Stead, 1992). The core assumptions tending to unite such work follow (see Table 1.2).

Sustaincentric ontology and ethics

The earth is humanity's home, to be kept clean, healthy and properly managed for the sake of human survival and welfare. There are no wholes and no parts anywhere in the universe; there are only holons (i.e. whole/parts). Economic and human activities are inextricably linked with natural systems. Because dynamism and cyclicality are fundamental, synthetic, non-linear and intuitive modes of understanding are required.

Humans are neither totally disengaged from, nor totally immersed in, the rest of nature. Although part of the biosphere in organic and ecological terms, they are above the biosphere in intellectual terms. The biosphere is more fundamental for existence than humans, yet humans are more significant than the biosphere because they embrace a much deeper and greater wholeness (Wilber, 1995). The crucial consequence is that humans 'have become, by the power of a glorious evolutionary accident called intelligence, the stewards of life's continuity on earth. We did not ask for this role, but we cannot abjure it. We may not be suited for it, but here we are' (Gould, in Calvin, 1994: 107).

Sustaincentrism favours moral pluralism. Ethics are broadly

grounded in the good of both human and non-human nature. Sustaincentric ethics actively embrace the full conceptualization of political, civil, social, economic and cultural human rights. Human consciousness is the repository of all value in human nature, but some of this value is not dependent on instrumental human values (Norton, 1991). Just as a parent might value a child, not only instrumentally but also inherently, the same can and should apply between humans and other species. Inter-generationally, a chain of moral obligation stretches across time (Howarth, 1992), and current generations are obligated not to reduce the liberties, opportunities or welfare-generating potentials available to future generations (Weiss, 1989). Intragenerationally, current generations are obligated to ensure equitable opportunities for all of humanity, most especially the satisfaction of vital basic needs of the marginalized, poor and most vulnerable segments of society.

Sustaincentric science and technology

The extent to which natural systems can absorb human-caused disruptions in their autonomous processes varies widely (Norton, 1991). The global ecosystem is finite and closed, vulnerable to human interference, and limited in its regenerative and assimilative capacities. Some natural limits are being approached, particularly in regard to the maximum amount of food that the earth can produce (Brown and Kane, 1994). The scale of material and energy throughput must be limited to levels below which deterioration of natural systems may not occur.

Such concerns lead to the generation of crude axioms such as waste emissions should not exceed natural assimilative capacity, harvest rates for renewable resources should not exceed natural regeneration rates, and human activities should result in no net loss of genetic, species or ecosystem diversity (Costanza and Daly, 1992; Daly, 1990; Gladwin, 1992; Hawken, 1993; Robèrt, 1994). A set of operational principles and associated techniques of biophy-sically sustainable behaviour is presented in Table 1.2.

Sustaincentrism holds that population must be stabilized soon. Consumption in developed countries must be scaled down. The challenge is one of logistic growth, managing a difficult socio-economic and environmental transition to a sustainable plateau (Holling, 1994). Problems are grave and urgent, with the Union of Concerned Scientists (1992: 1) warning that 'no more than one or a few decades remain before the chance to avert the threats we now confront will be lost and the prospects for humanity immea-surably diminished'.

Table **1.2** Operational principles and techniques of biophysically sustainable behaviour

Sustainability principles	Operational principles	Sample techniques
Assimilation	Waste emissions £ Natural assimilative capacity	Pollution prevention Natural products Detoxification Biodegradability Low input agriculture Synthetic reduction
Regeneration	Renewable harvest rate £ Natural regeneration rate	Sustained yield management Safe minimum standards Harvest certification Access restriction Exclusive harvest zones Resource right systems
Diversification	Biodiversity loss £ Biodiversity preservation	Biosphere reserves Extractive reserves Buffer zones Polyculture farming Ecotourism Debt for nature swaps
Restoration	Ecosystem damage £ Ecosystem rehabilitation	Reforestation Mine reclamation Site decontamination Bioremediation Species reintroduction Habitat restoration
Conservation	Energy–matter throughput per unit of output (time 2) £ Energy–matter throughput per unit of output (time 1)	Fuel efficiency Mass transit Cogeneration Computer controls Demand side management Smart buildings
Dissipation	Energy–matter throughput (time 2) £ Energy–matter throughput (time 1)	Depackaging Durable design Repair/reconditioning Telecommuting Bioregional sourcing Dematerialization

Table 1.2 Continued

Sustainability principles	Operational principles	Sample techniques
Perpetuation	Nonrenewable resource depletion £ Renewable resource substitution	Solar energy Wind power Hydrogen fuel Bioenergy Hydropower Geothermal energy
Circulation	Virgin, recycled material use (time 2) £ Virgin, Recycled material use (time 1)	Closed loop manufacturing Industrial ecosystems Internal recycling Waste recovery Design for disassembly Water recirculation

In the face of threats of serious or irreversible damage, requirements for scientific certainty cannot be used as a reason to postpone measures to prevent environmental degradation. Precautionary principles (O'Riordan, 1995) and safe-minimum standards (Ciriacy-Wantrup, 1963) are needed to minimize irreversible losses of renewable resources, provide ecological 'slack,' and shift the burden of proof from the victims to the nature-alterers. Sustaincentrism is not anti-technology, but also does not accept it uncritically. Technologies should be developed and employed in appropriate, just and humane ways. Stringent ecological, social and economic impact assessments should be made of new technologies before introduction in order to minimize adverse side effects.

Sustaincentric economics and psychology

The economic system which provides humanity with its material goods is underpinned by ecological systems; changes in one affect the other. Humans are capable of learning and appreciating the full range of aesthetic, economic and other values residing in nature. Humans can learn to satisfy non-material needs in non-material ways, and to reduce preoccupation with material rather than intellectual or spiritual concerns.

A prosperous economy depends on a healthy ecology, and vice versa. A green and equitable economy is possible in which ecological and social externalities are internalized. Markets are required to efficiently allocate resources, but other policy instruments and economic incentives are required to constrain natural resource use. Taxation and other public policies are shifted to favour labour intensity over capital intensity, as well as to promote income and saving versus energy/matter throughput. Poverty reduction in sustaincentrism depends on

> two equally important elements. The first element is to promote the productive use of the poor's most abundant asset – labor (sic). It calls for policies that harness market incentives, social and political institutions, infrastructure, and technology to that end. The second is to provide basic social services to the poor. Primary health care, family planning, nutrition, and primary education are especially important. The two elements are mutually reinforcing; one without the other is not sufficient. (World Bank, 1990: 3)

The sustaincentric paradigm accepts that material and energy growth are bounded by ecological limits; growth cannot go on forever in a closed system. It asserts that the benefits of past growth have not been distributed equally; the richest 20 per cent of the population on the earth possess 83 per cent of its financial wealth and consume an estimated 80 per cent of the world's resources (UNDP, 1994). Resource consumption in developed countries must be reduced, but least developed nations need transitional opportunities for material growth in order to help alleviate poverty and stabilize population. There is a recognition that trade may spatially separate the costs from the benefits of environmental and labour exploitation. Uncontrolled capital mobility may work to lower worker remuneration and environmental health and safety standards. Sustaincentrism calls for the removal of any ecological, economic and social inequities associated with international commerce.

Portions of the natural capital stock are deemed non-substitutable by man-made alternatives, for example, irreplaceable genetic or species biodiversity and the ozone layer. Sustaincentrism calls for such critical natural capital to remain intact or preserved via preemptive constraints. Other less critical natural capital, however, can be converted into man-made capital possessing equivalent welfare-generating capacity.

Appraising sustaincentrism versus sustainability

Sustaincentrism offers a vision of development which is both people centred (concentrating on improvement in the human condition) and conservation based (maintaining the variety and integrity of non-human nature). As with ecocentrism, it is a paradigm not yet manifest in reality. Some might claim that as an expression of ecological humanism, it is fundamentally a contradiction in terms. We believe, however, that sustaincentrism represents the perspective that is most congruent with the requirements of sustainable development.

1 *Inclusiveness.* The sustaincentric paradigm allows the interests of today and tomorrow, of rich and poor, of North and South to acquire fuller and deeper attention. Whereas ecocentrism is biased toward ecology and rights of nature, and technocentrism is biased toward the economy and market-based rights, sustaincentrism transcends these with a more pluralist embrace of the world. However, this comprehensiveness adds a bewildering amount of complexity with which human institutions may be unable to cope.
2 *Connectivity.* Sustaincentrism also adds dynamic complexity, focusing on inter-relationships of causality, such as among poverty, population, gender bias, overconsumption, and ecosystem degradation. It shifts awareness to human actors and their organizations and the feedback processes that impact upon sustainability (Senge, 1990). However, one can question whether humans and their institutions are capable of such systemic thinking.
3 *Justice.* Sustaincentrism recognizes that all human values depend on a healthy ecological, social and economic context. It seeks a hierarchically organized and integrated system of values (Norton, 1991) to guide practical action by differentiating grades of both instrumental and intrinsic value, while proposing that all living things have value independent of their usefulness to human purposes (Birch and Cobb, 1981). Ecocentric critics claim that moral pluralism inevitably implies moral chaos (see Callicott, 1989). Others wonder whether principled positions can be worked out in relation to the non-instrumental dimensions of sustainability, given difficult questions about the limits of moral obligation, boundaries of moral considerability, and inevitable tradeoffs (Owens, 1994).
4 *Prudence.* Sustaincentrism embodies the precautionary principle and urges humility in the face of uncertainty and complexity in ecological and human systems. It assumes the ability of human knowledge and institutions to reveal limits and thresholds, determine carrying capacities, and pinpoint stress and collapse, such that human activities can be kept within such bounds. Although some question whether we possess the wisdom and

the will to 'manage the planet' in such a fashion (Worster, 1995), the same could be asked of the other paradigms.

5   *Security.* We contend that sustaincentrism is more likely to keep ecosystems resilient to change than technocentrism; it is also more likely to keep socioeconomic systems resilient to change than ecocentrism, given current historical realities (e.g. poverty, population growth, unemployment).

In summary, sustaincentrism is seen as too radical, naïve and Utopian by conventional technocentrists. It is not radical, humble and transformative enough to deal with our global ecological crisis in the eyes of ecocentrists. We would reject charges, however, that it merely travels the easy road of political compromise or sells out, in the end, to pragmatism. We believe it transcends or supersedes, at once both negating what is dysfunctional and preserving what is beneficial, in the alienated poles of technocentrism and ecocentrism.

Implications for management practice

'Life has no meaning except in terms of responsibility.'
(Reinhold Niebuhr, 1892–1971)

Since the Enlightenment, we have progressively differentiated humanity from the rest of nature, and separated objective truth from subjective morality. The greatest challenge of post-modernity may reside in their reintegration (Habermas, 1990; Taylor, 1989). A similar challenge may exist for managers and the organizations they lead.

This challenge is particularly problematic since the operationalization and measurement of sustainability (along the lines of the principles offered in Table 1.2) are only in their infancy. Practical decision support tools are needed to systematically include sustainability criteria in evaluating the design and selection of products, processes and projects. Further development of tools such as design for environment, life cycle analysis, full cost pricing, and industrial ecology models may be useful in this quest (Allenby and Richards, 1994). These tools of 'greening', however, which focus on instrumental or process objectives such as pollution reduction or continuous improvement, will need to be transformed into tools of 'sustaining' that focus on ultimate or outcome objectives such as assuring ecosystem and sociosystem health and integrity. Tools of greening, in other words, move organizations in the right direction, but fail to inform them about the distance from or variance with the ultimate destination of sustainability. We must shift from the prevailing metaphor of greening (Walley and Whitehead, 1994) which merely 'reduces the bads,' to that of sustaining or 'realizing the goods.'

According to the World Bank, 'the achievement of sustained and equitable development remains the greatest challenge facing the human race' (1992: 1). Transforming business practice so it positively contributes to sustainable development is, in our view, the greatest challenge facing managers today. Indeed, it is difficult to imagine the impact business enterprise could have if it genuinely accepted, and acted upon, 'The earth pledge' of the June 1992 United Nations Conference on Environment and Development: 'Recognizing that people's actions toward nature and each other are the source of growing damage to the environment and resources needed to meet human needs and ensure survival and development, I PLEDGE to act to the best of my ability to help make the Earth a secure and hospitable home for present and future generations.'

Note

1 The authors express their appreciation to AT&T, The Energy Foundation (a joint initiative of The John D. and Catherine T. MacArthur Foundation, The Pew Charitable Trusts and The Rockefeller Foundation), The Management Institute for Environment and Business, The Merck Family Fund and the Winslow Foundation for their support of The Global Environment Program at New York University, which partially financed preparation of this article. We also thank Richard N. L. Andrews, Gloria Asuncion, Robert U. Ayres, Max Bazerman, Allan Bird, Elena Cabada, Herman E. Daly, William R. Dill, E. Andres Garcia, Ann Gladwin, Carl Henn, Andrew King, Bryan G. Norton, David W. Orr, Stephen Viederman and anonymous reviewers for the *Academy of Management Review* for their helpful comments and assistance. This chapter reflects a shortened version of an article previously published in the *Academy of Management Review*. The viewpoints herein should be attributed only to the authors.

References

Allenby, B. R. and Richards, D. J. (eds) (1994). *The Greening of Industrial Ecosystems.* National Academy Press.

Ayres, R. U. (1993). Cowboys, cornucopians and long run sustainability. *Ecological Economics*, **8**, 189–207.

Barbier, E. (1987). The concept of sustainable economic development. *Environmental Conservation*, **14**(2), 101–10.

Beckerman, W. (1994). 'Sustainable development': Is it a useful concept? *Environmental Values*, 3(3), 191–209.

Birch, C. and Cobb, J. B. (1981). *The Liberation of Life*. Cambridge University Press.

Botkin, D. B. (1990). *Discordant Harmonies: A New Ecology for the Twenty-First Century*. Oxford University Press.

Brown, L. R. and Kane, H. (1994). *Full House: Reassessing the Earth's Population Carrying Capacity*. W. W. Norton.

Brown, L. R. (1994). *State of the World: 1994*. W. W. Norton.

Callicott, J. B. (1989). *In Defense of the Land Ethic*. State University of New York Press.

Calvin, W. H. (1994). The emergence of intelligence. *Scientific American*, 271(4), 101–7.

Capra, F. (1982). *The Turning Point: Science, Society and the Rising Culture*. Bantam Books.

Ciriacy-Wantrup, S. V. (1963). *Resource Conservation: Economics and Policies*. University of California Press.

Clark, W. C. (1989). Managing planet Earth. *Scientific American*, 261(3), 47–54.

Costanza, R. (ed.) (1991). *Ecological Economics: The Science and Management of Sustainability*. Columbia University Press.

Costanza, R. and Daly, H. E. (1992). Natural capital and sustainable development. *Conservation Biology*, 6, 37–46.

Costanza, R., Daly, H. E. and Bartholomew, J. A. (1991). Goals, agenda and policy recommendations for ecological economics. In *Ecological Economics: The Science and Management of Sustainability* (R. Costanza, ed.) pp. 1–20, Columbia University Press.

Costanza, R., Norton, B. G. and Haskell, B. D. (eds) (1992). *Ecosystem Health: New Goals for Environmental Management*. Island Press.

Costanza, R., Wainger, L., Folke, C. and Mäler, K. G. (1993). Modeling complex ecological-economic systems. *Bioscience*, 43(8), 545–55.

Council for a Parliament of the World's Religions (1994). Toward a global ethic. *World Business Academy Perspectives*, 8(1), 67–76.

Daily, G. C. and Ehrlich, P. R. (1992). Population, sustainability, and Earth's carrying capacity. *Bioscience*, 42, 761–71.

Daily, G. C., Ehrlich, A. H. and Ehrlich, P. R. (1994). Optimum human population size. *Population and Environment*, 15, 469–75.

Daly, H. E. (1990). Toward some operational principles of sustainable development. *Ecological Economics*, 2(1), 1–6.

Daly, H. E. (1992). *Steady-state Economics*. Earthscan.

Daly, H. E. (1994). Operationalizing sustainable development by investing in natural capital. In *Investing in Natural Capital: The Ecological Economics Approach to Sustainability* (A. Jansson, M. Hammer, C. Folke and R. Costanza, eds) pp. 22–37, Island Press.

Daly, H. E. and Cobb, J. B. (1994). *For the Common Good: Redirecting the Economy Toward Community, the Environment, and a Sustainable Future*. Beacon Press.

Dasgupta, P. S. (1995). Population, poverty and the local environment. *Scientific American*, 272(2), 40–5.

Devall, B. and Sessions, G. (1985). *Deep Ecology*. Gibbs Smith.

Dowie, M. (1995). *Losing Ground: American Environmentalism at the Close of the Twentieth Century*. MIT Press.

Easterbrook, G. (1995). *A Moment on the Earth: The Coming Age of Environmental Optimism*. Viking.

Ehrenfeld, D. (1981). *The Arrogance of Humanism*. Oxford University Press.

Ehrlich, P. (1994). Ecological economics and the carrying capacity of Earth. In *Investing in Natural Capital: The Ecological Economics Approach to Sustainability* (A. Jansson, M. Hammer, C. Folke and R. Costanza, eds) pp. 38–56, Island Press.

Gladwin, T. N. (1992). *Building the Sustainable Corporation: Creating Environmental Sustainability and Competitive Advantage*. National Wildlife Federation.

Gladwin, T. N. and Krause, T. (forthcoming). *Business, Nature and Society: Toward Sustainable Enterprise*. Richard D. Irwin.

Gladwin, T. N., Krause, T. and Kennelly, J. J. (1995) Beyond eco-efficiency: towards socially sustainable business. *Sustainable Development*, John Wiley & Sons Ltd.

Goldsmith, E. (1993) *The Way: An Ecological World View*. Shambhala.

Gore, A. (1992). *Earth in Balance: Ecology and the Human Spirit*. Houghton Mifflin.

Habermas, J. (1990). *The Philosophical Discourse of Modernity* (F. Lawrence, trans), MIT Press.

Hawken, P. (1993). *The Ecology of Commerce: A Declaration of Sustainability*. HarperBusiness.

Holling, C. S. (1994). New science and new investments for a sustainable biosphere. In *Investing in Natural Capital: The Ecological Economics Approach to Sustainability*. (A. Jansson, M. Hammer, C. Folke and R. Costanza, eds), pp. 57–73, Island Press.

Howarth, R. B. (1992). Intergenerational justice and the chain of obligation. *Environmental Values*, **1**, 133–40.

Jansson, A., Hammer, M., Folke, C. and Costanza, R. (eds) (1994). *Investing in Natural Capital: The Ecological Economics Approach to Sustainability*. Island Press.

Jantsch, E. (1980). *The Self-Organizing Universe*. Pergamon Press.

Kaplan, R. D. (1994). The coming anarchy. *Atlantic Monthly*, **273**(2), 43–76.

Korten, D.C. (1990). *Getting to the 21st Century: Voluntary Action and the Global Agenda*. Kumarian Press.

Lee, K. N. (1993). Greed, scale mismatch and learning. *Ecological Applications*, **3**(4), 560–4.

Leopold, A. (1949). *A Sand County Almanac*. Oxford University Press.

Levin, S. A. (1993). Science and sustainability. *Ecological Applications*, **3**(4), 1–2.

Ludwig, D., Hilbron, R. and Walters, C. (1993). Uncertainty, resource exploitation, and conservation: lessons from history. *Science*, **260**, 2 April, pp. 17, 36.

McKibben, B. (1989). *The End of Nature*. Anchor Books/Doubleday.

Meadows, D. H., Meadows, D. L. and Randers, J. (1992). *Beyond the*

Limits: Confronting Global Collapse – Envisioning a Sustainable Future.
Chelsea Green.

Merchant, C. (1992). *Radical Ecology: The Search for a Livable World.*
Routledge.

Morgan, G. (1980). Paradigms, metaphors, and puzzle solving in organization theory. *Administrative Science Quarterly*, **25**, 605–22.

Myers, N. and Simon, J. L. (1994). *Scarcity or Abundance: A Debate on the Environment.* W. W. Norton.

Naess, A. (1995). Politics and the ecological crisis: an introductory note. In *Deep Ecology for the 21st Century* (G. Sessions, ed.) pp. 445–53, Shambhala.

Nash, J. A. (1991). *Loving Nature: Ecological Integrity and Christian Responsibility.* Abingdon Press.

Norton, B. G. (1989). Intergenerational equity and environmental decisions: a model using Rawls' veil of ignorance. *Ecological Economics*, 1(2), 137–59.

Norton, B. G. (1991). *Toward Unity Among Environmentalists.* Oxford University Press.

O'Riordan, T. (1995). *Environmental Science for Environmental Management.* Longman Group.

Orr, D. W. (1992). *Ecological Literacy: Education and the Transition to a Postmodern World.* SUNY Press.

Owens, S. (1994). Sustainability and environmental policy: five fundamental questions. In *Reinventing the Left* (D. Milbrand, ed.) pp. 207–15, Polity Press.

Porritt, J. (1991). *Save the Earth.* Turner Publishing.

Prigogine, I. and Stengers, I. (1984). *Order Out of Chaos.* Bantam Books.

Robèrt, K. H. (1994). *Den Naturliga Utmaningen.* (The Natural Challenge) Ekerlids Förlag. (English version in press.)

Rolston, H. (1994). *Conserving Natural Value.* Columbia University Press.

Roszak, T. (1992). *The Voice of the Earth.* Simon and Schuster.

Scharf, A. and Williamson, T. (1994). *Index of Environmental Trends: An Assessment of 21 Key Environmental Indicators in 9 Industrialized Countries.* National Center for Economic Alternatives.

Senge, P. M. (1990). *The Fifth Discipline: The Art and Practice of the Learning Organization.* Doubleday.

Sessions, G. (ed.) (1995). *Deep Ecology for the 21st Century.* Shambhala.

Simon, J. G. (1981). *The Ultimate Resource.* Princeton University Press.

Stead, W. E. and Stead, J. G. (1992). *Management for a Small Planet: Strategic Decision Making and the Environment.* Sage.

Stern, P. C., Young, O. R. and Druckman, D. (eds) (1992). *Global Environmental Change: Understanding the Human Dimensions.* National Academy Press.

Taylor, C. (1989). *Sources of the Self: The Making of the Modern Identity.* Harvard University Press.

Union of Concerned Scientists (1992). *World Scientists' Warning to Humanity.* Union of Concerned Scientists.

United Nations Development Programme (UNDP) (1994). *Human Development Report 1994.* UNDP.

US President's Council on Sustainable Development (USPCSD) (1994). *A Vision for a Sustainable U.S. and Principles of Sustainable Development.* President's Council on Sustainable Development, July.

Viederman, S. (1994). The economics of sustainability challenges, Paper presented at the workshop The Economics of Sustainability, Fundacao Joaquim Nabuco, Recife, Brazil.

Vitousek, P. M. (1994). Beyond global warming: ecology and global change. *Ecology,* **75**, 1861–76.

Walley, N. and Whitehead, B. (1994). It's not easy being green. *Harvard Business Review,* **72**(3), 46–53.

Weinberg, S. (1994). Life in the universe. *Scientific American,* **271**(4), 44–9.

Weiss, E. B. (1989). *In Fairness to Future Generations: International Law, Common Patrimony, and Intergenerational Equity.* The United Nations University and Transnational Publishers.

Wheatley, M. J. (1992). *Leadership and the New Science: Learning About Organizations from an Orderly Universe.* Berrett-Koehler.

Wilber, K. (1995). *Sex, Ecology, Spirituality: The Spirit of Evolution.* Shambhala.

World Bank (1990). *World Development Report 1990: Poverty.* Oxford University Press.

World Bank (1992) *World Development Report 1992: Development and the Environment.* Oxford University Press.

World Commission on Environment and Development (1987). *Our Common Future.* Oxford University Press.

World Conservation Union, United Nations Environment Programme and Worldwide Fund for Nature (WCU, UNEP, WWF) (1991). *Caring for the Earth: A Strategy for Sustainable Living.* IUCN, UNEP and WWF.

World Resources Institute (1994). *World Resources 1994–95: A Guide to the Global Environment.* Oxford University Press.

Worster, D. (1995). The shaky ground of sustainability. In *Deep Ecology for the 21st Century* (G. Sessions, ed.) pp. 417–27, Shambhala.

2 Corporate environmental responsibility

Nigel Roome

Introduction

Concern about the impact of human activity on the earth's systems and resources has generated a rich debate about the balance between economic development and environmental protection. The richness of the debate stems from its focus on issues that are so fundamental to human and non-human existence, which operate at each and every level and form of social organization – individual, household, community, business, state and global – while drawing on thinking from across the social, physical and natural sciences and humanities. The debate is also strongly veined with normative ideas and demands to reappraise past theory and understanding.

A key issue is the suggestion that previous relationships between human society and the environment are no longer adequate in meeting the demands of environmental change. This parallels Kuhn's (1970) description of paradigmatic change in scientific understanding and leads to the view that we might be in a period of potentially revolutionary change in thinking from which a new paradigm will emerge to explain inadequacies in existing orthodoxies. For this reason the issues dealt with in this chapter are profound and difficult because they place under scrutiny the fundamentals of existing models and explanations of human activity and organization.

With this background, the chapter examines the relationship between environmental protection and economic development. It does so from the vantage point of the business organization and those responsible for its management. It explores the contribution of ideas in the field of corporate social responsibility and applied ethics to an understanding of business policies and actions as they affect the environment. In particular, the chapter considers two important concepts: sustainable development and improved environmental performance. Using these concepts questions are raised about business – its context, purposes and organization, and the value systems and ethics which underpin business activities and managerial decisions.

The ethical positions considered in the chapter range from the human-centred, utilitarian perspective of economics, which sees the natural world as a set of resources or services providing for human utility or well-being, to environmentally centred perspectives, that emphasize the intrinsic value of the natural world and its right to be treated with respect through human activity. Between these extremes lie many other ethical systems and positions: positions that concern justice in the distribution of economic resources, justice in the protection and application of rights and obligations, as well as notions of duty and respect for both the human and non-human world. A key idea is that values and ethical systems are important in judging the acceptability of relationships made in, and through, business – relationships both between peoples and between people and the natural world. Finally, a conclusion is drawn about the contribution of ethics to business decisions and environmental management.

Sustainable development

The notion of sustainable development is discussed in detail by Gladwin and Kennelly in Chapter 1 of this book. What is important to establish here is the critical role that the Brundtland Report (WCED, 1987) has played in framing so much of the recent debate about sustainable development and business. Brundtland's conception of sustainable development has been subject to many subsequent interpretations (see, for example, Pearce, Markandya and Barbier, 1987). These 'rich' interpretations of sustainable development are consistent with the idea that sustainable development is a basis for individuals and organizations to examine their behaviour, as part of a continuing process involving a shared search for more sustainable forms of development. In that sense sustainable development does not provide prescriptions of how present and future generations must act (Carley and Christie, 1993). However, the notion of sustainable development, as learning and change, challenges all members of society, including business and its managers, to question the assumptions and values which underpin their purpose and responsibilities.

Values are critical to sustainable development. Brundtland clearly points to the need to integrate environmental values into economic processes, as a means to maintain environmental wealth and economic progress and to protect the earth's systems and resources; to attend to inequality in the current distribution of environmental and economic wealth and to acknowledge the importance of equity between members of this and subsequent generations; and to embark on change which recognizes the importance of longer horizons in planning and decision-making. These ideas question the assumptions of past business practices.

But, more than this, sustainable development is surrounded by a deep discourse about values. In particular, it draws attention to the tension between anthropocentric and ecocentric views of the world. This tension is characterized in Figure 2.1. The idea of tension is preferred to the opposition of values because it carries the sense of O'Riordan's (1991) conjecture that humans have deep, often contradictory relationships with nature. We can view the environment as a provider of resources to be exploited for our benefit whereas we can also value the life supporting, nurturing character of the earth and the notion of a community of interdependent forms of life of which humans are but part. Although others (Gladwin, Kennelly and Krause, 1995) have argued that approaches based on ecocentrisim, anthropocentrism or technology (technocentrism) do not lead to sustainability, preferring the normative construct of a distinct paradigm based on a nurturing approach to the earth and its processes called sustaincentrism.

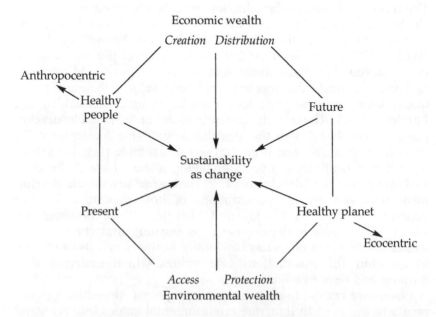

Figure 2.1 Dimensions of environmental management and sustainability

However, discussion needs to go beyond simple distinctions between different worldviews, to ask which particular philosophical system of values should be used to judge the 'goodness' or 'desirability' of changes that take place as part of the process of sustainable development? Critically, how do we judge whether we have made progress towards sustainability? Should the appeal be to notions of utility (as underpins neo-classical economics), duty (see for example Donagan, 1977), justice (Rawls, 1971), respect for the community of humans and non-human life (Leopold, 1949) or to intrinsic value in protecting richness and diversity of human and non-human life (Naess, 1993)? An excellent review of these and other alternative ethical systems together with their relationship to environmental issues is provided by Armstrong and Botzler (1993). The important point is not to advocate a particular values system but to recognize that sustainable development exists firmly within the domain of this tension around values. Indeed the concept is surrounded by competing value and ethical systems and what is needed is a process through which values are surfaced and subject to scrutiny and discussion.

Improving environmental performance

In contrast to this emphasis on values, much of the ambition of business organizations in relation to sustainable development has avoided the need to define values and ethics. For example, sustainable development for many has been translated into the more limited idea of improved environmental performance. This side-steps the fundamental issue of ethics and new values. The values underlying improvement in environmental performance are normally not discussed yet are almost always based on anthropocentric and utilitarian ethical systems. For example, 'sustainable development is a system of open, competitive markets in which prices are made to reflect the cost of environmental as well as other resources' (Schmidheiny, 1992: 14).

Characterizing sustainable development as improved environmental performance alone oversimplifies the dynamics and uniqueness of organizational and contextual change. Gladwin (1992) reminds us that improving the environmental performance of business is not easy to define. In addition, the changes that take place in organizations in response to the same contextual issues and disturbances, can assume a variety of pathways (Laughlin, 1991). This means that approaches to improve environmental performance are neither easy to practice or emulate. It also runs counter to mainstream practice. With advocates of improved environmental performance emphasizing the importance of reformed organizational relationships as preconditions for successful environmental policies – for example, by replacing hierarchical, instrumental forms of management by the empowerment of employees or the move towards more open, learning-oriented styles of management; establishing new forms of partnership between organizations to cope with organizational interdependence, or reappraising the constraints imposed by strictly interpreted organizational boundaries in the light of environmental interdependence. These ideas are also consistent with aspects of the thinking behind total quality management (GEMI, 1991); organizational learning (Senge, 1992); or strategic intent (Hamel and Prahalad, 1989) (see Hall and Roome, 1996).

Organizational change

Whether we are dealing with sustainable development or improved environmental performance in business organizational change is critical to overturn the obsolescence that arises as a consequence of the boundaries, power structure and the hierarchies of the organizational or administrative mind. However, sustainable development also touches on deep questions about the social nature of individuals, especially their relationship to societies (or, in this case, the relationship between individuals and between individuals and the non-human world as mediated through the functioning of business organizations). It raises critical questions about notions of autonomy and control, collective and individual rights, responsibilities and accountability and, yet, concerns about the relationship between individuals and business organizations have not been addressed directly in the literature on business and the environment.

Conventional analysis argues that environmental issues provoke the need for new vision, leadership and the introduction of management structures and systems which encourage environmental responsibility. It recognizes the importance of gaining commitment and support for environmental policies and programmes throughout the organization (see, for example, Fischer and Schot, 1993). However, Freeman and Gilbert (1988) are critical of approaches to organizational strategy based on such notions. They assert that relationships in business organizations should be guided by ethical systems based on, among other things, respect for individuals and their autonomy, as well as, respect for the views and involvement of the organization's stakeholders in the choices the organization faces. They argue that organizational strategy invariably ignores direct consideration of ethical systems.

Rather, strategic processes accept without question existing value systems that govern relationships within the organization.

Freeman and Gilbert's views are also relevant to the more recent ideas about environmental performance and sustainability in business. Here too there has been little account given to the ethical systems that underpin organizational relationships between employees, between employees and other human stakeholders, or between employees and non-human stakeholders. Some of these issues are explored in a conceptual form in Figure 2.2. This figure connects ideas about individual, organizational and social action from different ethical positions. The positions shown are deep green, mid-green and shallow green. The figure suggests that deep green perspectives are rooted in the core beliefs of individuals and in philosophical systems of society. These core beliefs define the symbols, structures, systems and practices used in business and social organizations and they are substantively different from those currently practised by society (Naess, 1993). This unorthodox perspective requires that a particular set of values is placed at the centre of the process of organizational change. A deep green business would use these values explicitly as a touchstone to determine the kind of relationships it should have with other businesses, society and the natural world.

Shallow green approaches, by contrast, accept existing values and work, first, through altered forms of organizational implementation and action. Only then may they operate on more deep-

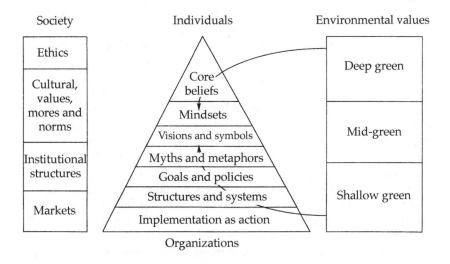

Figure 2.2 Environmental values, individuals and organizations

seated facets of organizational and individual behaviour – visions, symbols, structures and systems. An example of a shallow green approach is the marketing of products under a green banner. It is also found in organizations which simply want to comply with environmental legislation.

Mid-green perspectives are shown in Figure 2.2 as working in both directions. This can be compared to a pendulum swinging across organizational systems, structures, visions and symbols, from core beliefs to implementation as action, and back again to core beliefs. Mid-green perspectives acknowledge the importance of changed organizational values (Roome, 1992) or organizational culture (Rothenberg reported in Ehrenfeld and Hoffman, 1993; Shrivastava, 1992; Stead and Stead, 1992) in determining success in environmental performance as part of the move towards sustainable practices. Even so, the specific values which determine the ethical systems that guide managerial and business decisions are not explicitly discussed by these commentators. Instead they tend to identify accepted business concepts such as total quality (GEMI, 1991) or product safety (Ehrenfeld and Hoffman, 1993) as bridges between existing organizational culture and the culture required to support improvements in environmental performance and sustainability.

These comments enable certain tentative conclusions to be brought forward. First, improved environmental performance and sustainable development are concepts increasingly applied to the practices of business organizations. Second, business organizations appear to construct their contribution to achieving sustainable development in narrow terms related to improving environmental performance. Third, even this more limited reorientation of business is seen to require substantive organizational change, including greater emphasis on co-operative structures to complement established notions of competition. Fourth, the concepts of sustainable development and improved environmental performance are surrounded by fundamentally different values and ethical systems which influence the shape of the response by business. Fifth, improving environmental performance in business organizations, using notions of ecoefficiency, total quality or product and risk analysis endorses the anthropocentric, utilitarian ethical system implicit in much of orthodox business practice. Sixth, discussion of sustainable development and the environmental performance of business rarely examines the philosophical and ethical systems that underpin the decisions of business and managers. Finally, it is axiomatic that successful environmental management is predicated on explicit, ethical systems which guide organizational choices and the decisions of managers.

The purpose of business

The previous section establishes the important role of ethical systems in shaping the emerging relationship between business and the environment. It also identifies a reluctance by business to make ethical positions an open and clear part of organizational relationships. At the heart of these issues are questions about the purpose of business and the purpose of business managers.

The orthodoxy of neo-classical economics is that business is a collective term to describe that part of society which is concerned with the production and exchange of goods and services, in market and mixed-market economic systems. The term 'business' incorporates organizations which assume many different structures, legal identities and roles in society. It embraces the individual operating as a sole trader, the co-operative, the privately owned and limited company, the multinational corporation. At the boundaries of definition, it includes the trading arms of charities, which operate with the status of limited companies, as well as organizations which are partly state owned. What distinguishes these organizations from other sectors of society, is that their viability depends on securing profits, the excess of revenue from the sale of outputs over the costs of their production.

It follows that the principal focus of the activities of business is the market and its simple purpose is to make profit. Neo-classical economics develops this idea further, asserting the basic assumption that the purpose of the firm is profit maximization. Accepting this assumption implies acceptance of two important axioms. First, given a risk-free choice between economic opportunities, managers of business will prefer options which yield more profit to those that yield less. Second, managers involved in pure profit-maximizing decisions, will confine their frame of analysis to an assessment of the stream of revenue and costs projected to accrue to the company from alternative investments. These streams determine profitability when considered in relation to the risks associated with each alternative project.

The adequacy of the simplifying assumption of profit maximization has been questioned by many authors. Few of these concerns are new, yet they are of sufficient significance that they deserve to be rehearsed here. Schumacher's (1974) criticism of profit maximization is based on questions about the fundamental ability of economic systems to measure value. He argues that market values only partially measure value because markets are preoccupied with resources as means rather than ends.

In the case of individual business organizations Galbraith (1971) has argued that profit maximization is only one possible explanation of business behaviour. He ventures the view that market share, turnover and advertising are also valid explanations of corporate purpose. Drucker (1974) is highly critical of the idea of businesses as profit-maximizing organizations. He describes this idea as 'harmful' and goes on to define the purpose of business as 'creating a customer'. March and Simon (1958), for their part, take the view that maximization is not a realistic element of business purpose, given the complexity involved in most decisions and the limits on human capabilities, whether acting alone or in organizations. Other decision theorists (Etzione, 1967; Lindblom, 1959) take similar views about the adequacy of optimization as an outcome of decision-making but for different reasons.

Ideas current in the field of corporate social responsibility suggest that businesses are not simply given to responding to signals from markets and the economic system. The purpose of business is therefore not just connected to profits. There are a number of issues here. At the micro-organizational level, businesses can be regarded as purposeful groups of individuals who are invested with their own values which often impact on the decisions they make within the business. At the level of social organization, business is embedded in the system of legal, political and cultural structures and norms. For these reasons, Carroll (1989) suggests that there are four elements which contribute to the purpose of business. These responsibilities are: economic, legal, ethical and discretionary.

Carroll argues that the purpose of an individual business is determined by the way each organization chooses to interpret and implement these different responsibilities. Moreover, the advent of the environmental debate acknowledges that business operates as part of a yet broader set of systems and processes which, for convenience, can be described as the natural environment.

The purpose of managers

From the viewpoint of the manager in business, managerial decisions take place in a complex, dynamic and ambiguous setting. The literature here is far less dominated by the orthodoxy of economic theory. For example, Katz (1970) sees management in terms of the application of skills needed to determine what a business organization does, how it is done, and why it is done. Katz argues that management uses different skills – technical, human and conceptual – to help in the definition of organizational purpose. He regards it as important for business to be able to mobilize these skills as well as to integrate them together.

Stewart (1993) has examined the flexibility that managers have in their work. Her studies imply that managers can have considerable flexibility in their behaviour, where the level of flexibility is influenced by the demands, constraints and choices available within a managerial post. The more flexible the post the greater the opportunity for a manager to exercise discretion over their purpose and behaviour. Organizational purpose is therefore determined by managers but organizations also provide space within which managers have discretion to define their own purpose and behaviour. It is unrealistic to regard the purpose of management to be static. It is more appropriate to regard purpose as a shifting concept in a constant state of flux.

Ansoff (1979) takes the idea that managers are struggling with complexity into discussion about the managers' role in determining business strategy. He suggests that the essence of management is about creation, adaptation and coping with change. He distinguishes two types of change: change which expands or contracts the business while leaving its nature intact, and strategic change which transforms the business. This permits Ansoff to link ideas of strategic change to the idea of securing the legitimacy and survival of the organization. He ventures that the strategic concern to secure legitimacy is transformative, requiring possibly discontinuous forms of adaptation by organizations. The search for legitimacy echoes Vickers's (1970) earlier assertion that 'policy-making' entails setting relationships rather than goal-seeking. Under these circumstances the purpose of management is survival and seeking out and maintaining desired relationships through change.

Profit, in this context, can be regarded as a proxy measure of survival and a sign of reasonable or successful relationships. Rather than profitability leading to survival, it is survival that enables businesses to continue profit-making activity. Taking these ideas together, it is convenient to argue that business management involves four main elements. The administration and adaptation of human activities within the business organization; the adaptation of the business to changes in markets; the maintenance of the social relations and the legitimacy of the business; and now, critically, the adaptation of the organization in the light of changes in the natural environment as mediated through social organization. The important issues for business are the extent to which managers conceive the need for change; how they continue to balance these elements; and how the purpose of business is defined through the decisions and actions managers make. In other words, managers are ultimately responsible for defining their own purposes through their actions and behaviour around their relationship to the human and non-human world.

The implication of the idea of self-definition of purpose is that managers are responsible for determining the nature of their relationships. Management therefore does not necessarily involve instrumental or controlling forms of relationship. Management can also be seen as a process of facilitation, a process which provides others in the organization with opportunities to define their own contribution to the organization's success or survival.

Corporate social responsibility

The arguments about the purpose of business set out above indicate the important role of ideas in corporate social responsibility in helping to unravel the relationship between business and the environment. A number of authors have helped to classify the alternative positions business might adopt.

Friedman (1962) defines the social responsibility of business in a strictly limited neo-classical economic sense. He views the responsibility of business as the exploitation of economic opportunities to make profit for shareholders, ensuring that employees are suitably trained to secure efficient production while ensuring that the business conforms to the basic rules of society embodied in law and ethical custom. Beyond this, Friedman contends that managers are only bound by a responsibility to maximize the interests of shareholders.

McGuire (1963), writing at about the same time, put forward the view that social responsibility supposes that the corporation has not only economic and legal obligations, but also certain responsibilities to society which extend beyond the law. For Friedman's part, serving social purposes of this kind can only be justified if it is a means to meet the interests of shareholders.

The difference between Friedman and McGuire's views of responsibility can be explained in terms of emphasis and values. Their positions are really normative statements about what businesses ought to do, as judged from the authors' own system of values. However, both constructs are bound together by a common concern for business to operate with legitimacy. The difference between them rests with their interpretation of how legitimacy is gained. For Friedman, legitimacy stems from the legal and market obligations on managers and business. McGuire's interpretation is broader. He connects legitimacy with the values that define a businesses' social purpose.

The idea that markets and the law are the sole basis for legitimacy has been criticized for a number of reasons (Sethi, 1975). Laws lag behind social norms and are therefore slow to react to social concerns. Laws tend to define the minimum standards expected of business, they are less useful in setting out the responsibilities and duties of business to society. Law has, until recently, been concerned primarily with the narrow economic interests of business in each country within which it operates. It is less concerned with the broader impact of business on society as employer, neighbour or international producer and seller.

The gap between (narrow) legal views of legitimacy and broader interpretations based on business within society, is illustrated by Ansoff's (1979) comments on the nature of strategic decisions. He suggests that the forces influencing the strategic choices made by business have changed over the last ninety years. He identifies the pressures on business during this period and describes the trends in the shape of strategic management through the 1950s to the late 1970s and goes on to anticipate the changes that would influence strategic management in the 1980s and 1990s. His assessment is that (strategic) management has moved from the realm of technical choices about products, markets and technology; through a process involving the balance of products, markets and technology with the internal capability of the business to support the intended direction of change; and then, more recently, to a more sophisticated strategic process which seeks to balance these concerns together with a need to maintain the social legitimacy of business, in the face of constrained resources and constrained growth. He terms this last approach 'enterprise strategy'.

Ansoff therefore offers ideas which bring together apparently antagonistic views of business, by suggesting that the nature of the strategic choices confronted by business have and are shifting over time. In other words, the responsibilities of business are set by the context in which it operates so, as the values prevalent in that social context shift, then the determinants of the legitimacy of business are changed. Even so, Friedman would appeal that managers could only justifiably respond to the emergence of new factors in the social and political agenda, if there were advantages to shareholders in responding to them, before they were general legal requirements.

Authors in business ethics have also been critical of the idea that (ethical) legitimacy is derived through business positions set relative to shifting social norms. Freeman and Gilbert (1988), for example, argue that shifting norms are a form of moral or ethical relativism. And that relativism is an abrogation of management's responsibility to identify and work to a set of basic values and ethics which then operate, consistently, at the core of business.

The substantive issue, here, is not just about absolute and relativist ethics but whether ethical systems should be explicit in business organizations and what role ethics have in defining and guiding the decisions and choices of managers.

Before taking these issues further it is important to address the influence of context on the nature of business and the values to which it subscribes. At the heart of this issue are the relationships between the internal and external environment of business. It cannot be assumed that the criteria for the legitimacy of business are just determined by changes taking place in the external context of business. The idea of mutual causality, whereby the activities of business influence the context in which they operate, as well as that context influencing business, implies a more dynamic and interdependent relationship. This notion of interdependence is important, because it is a principle common to ecological and economic analysis. However, both ecological and economic analysis have difficulties dealing with interdependent models.

Interdependence, identity and values

The significance of interdependence on the purpose and legitimacy of business have been considered by Emery and Trist (1965). They advance the notion that the pursuit of narrowly conceived organizational economic self-interest, in the face of turbulence and deepening interdependence between economic and other facets of society, contributes to a yet more turbulent context of business. This leads them to argue that even large organizations cannot successfully adapt to these turbulent fields without the stabilization of their actions through recourse to values as a control mechanism over organizational behaviour. Emery and Trist advance the view that these values are necessary to the strategies, operations and tactics ordinarily employed by organizations to cope with uncertainties. Yet, critically, close examination of values and ethical systems is uncommon in the discussion of business and the environment.

The role of values as a means to stabilize actions needs to be examined further. Values are personal, organizational and social constructs. They indicate what is important and worth while. They guide the responses people make to ideas, situations, other people, actions and events. By definition individuals, organizations and society hold multiple values. These can be ambiguous and contradictory at each level and between levels. Consequently, Emery and Trist's appeal to organizational values to stabilize actions really begs the question about where and how these values arise? Trist's (1983) later work on referent organizations suggests that these questions cannot be answered by individuals or, indeed, individual organizations. They require that organizations work together to specify the values necessary to reduce turbulence.

More recently, theories of autopoiesis, developed by Maturana and Varela (1980) to describe the relationship between biological systems and their environment, have influenced thinking about organizations and organizational environments. Especially important is how this theory has been developed by Morgan (1986) as a metaphor to unravel our understanding of business organizations and their interaction with their social and environmental context. Morgan's adaptation of autopoietic theory explores the idea of businesses as systems which operate in, and relate to, a context. Not only is this relationship conditioned by mutual causality, autopoiesis argues that a business and its context are one and the same system. Consequently, it is inappropriate to regard business as the victim or beneficiary of changes in context, seizing on opportunities or constrained by events. Rather businesses are reacting, not to external stimuli, but with systems of which they are part. In this sense they shape themselves. The capacity of managers of a business to define and understand these systems is critical to organizational outcomes. Managers can choose to interpret their interaction with their system in terms of narrowly conceived purpose, such as market share or profit. In turn this reflects the manager's conception of the business's identity within the system. The unquestioning application of business orthodoxies, including the adoption of unquestioned values, also creates a businesses identity within a system.

The implication, for Morgan, is that systems and businesses survive when managers establish an identity which involves a well-developed, self-critical awareness and accepts the capability of change in that identity. Consequently, managers in organizations must understand the organization's identity, where this is determined by looking at the organization, its context and the organization's view of its context. This analysis places the issue of the identity of the business at the centre of its ability to survive within the context of which it is part. It leads Morgan to conclude that an organization's identity or self-image should be subject to considerable attention. In particular, a characteristic of long-run survival of business is put in place when managers think and act systemically, are more self-reflective and less self-centred. Part of this thinking involves more self-reflection on conventional values and ethical systems.

These ideas are important because they highlight how critical both identity, values and relationships are to the survival of business organizations. For example, Ontario Hydro is among a number of utility companies worldwide seeking to redefine their identity. Previously, as a public utility concerned to provide electricity to the consumers of Ontario they sought to pursue a purpose of providing electricity at lowest cost. This involved a policy of expanding energy supply, through large-scale energy generation projects, to match expected increases in demand.

Large-scale projects were favoured because they enabled apparent economies of scale. Demand-side management programmes were used as a means to correct short-term problems of inadequate supply. The expansion of the company's generating capacity, which grew steadily up to the mid-1980s, has now stopped. There are now a set of new pressures. These include the emergence of small-scale co-generation projects, the downturn in projected demand as well as a shift in demand away from electricity to other sources of power. In the early 1990s Ontario Hydro faced a mounting debt burden, surplus capacity and a growing concern about the environmental impacts of electricity generation and transmission.

The utility is now in the process of redefining its purpose and changing its culture, structures, systems and practices to seek out more sustainable forms of energy development and use (Ontario Hydro, 1993: ix). Many of these ideas are captured by the utility's new mission set out in 1993 'to help Ontario become the most energy efficient and competitive economy in the world, and a leading example of sustainable development'.

Ontario Hydro is therefore in the process of reshaping its identity. Where previously it believed in growth, large-scale projects and private economies of scale to bring about low rates for consumers, it is now increasingly concerned about flexibility, balancing stakeholders' and customers' needs, and meeting environmental as well as market obligations. This is brought about, in part, through a closer involvement of stakeholders in the decisions of the corporation. In part, this change is affecting the information-gathering and decision-structures of the organization which have become more complex with the greater complexity of purpose implied by an differently conceived identity.

This illustration indicates something of the idea of identity. It places emphasis on systemic wisdom, which has been so influential in the interpretation of natural environmental processes (Odum, 1971) as well as social organization (Vickers, 1974, 1983) and to the interaction between social and natural systems (Erlich, Erlich and Holdren, 1973, Frosch, 1992; Lovelock, 1987). From this perspective business is seen as an integral part of a social and physical environment, not as an entity which is separate from its environment but as something in constant interactive relationship – which arises in many different and often unpredictable ways.

In the literature Freeman and Gilbert (1988) raise the question of identity and self-critical awareness as ethical issues. They put forward the proposition that what lies at the heart of the excellent company is respect for people, where this includes those inside the business, those who depend on the business – shareholders, customers or suppliers – and those who are influenced by the activities of the business – its wider stakeholders. Similar arguments, about the design of large organizations, are found in Schumacher's ideas about how capital should be used to serve people (Schumacher, 1974).

Sethi (1975) has approached the question of identity and values from yet a different perspective, seeking to classify business practices into three distinct types. He identifies the characteristics of social obligation – where identity is defined in terms of satisfying legal and economic criteria, social responsiveness – where identity is seen as derived by requirements which go beyond current legal and market criteria; and social responsibility, which represents an identity or set of values where the business works within the dynamics of the evolving social system. Social systems that define the organization's role as well as placing self-imposed limits on its operations because of ethical standards the business sets for itself.

Other authors have ventured similar categories of corporate social responsibility, for example Tombari, Post and Davis, and Blomstrom. These, and others, are reviewed by Carroll (1989). What is interesting is that the approach these authors ascribe to the socially responsible company – anticipatory, proactive, adaptive, open, accountable, and commitment to a clear purpose and values – are similar to those regarded as important by Morgan (1986) as preconditions for organizational survival, by Schumacher (1974) in defining the need for organizations to transform to a more human-scale of operation, and by Peters and Waterman (1982) in their study of excellence in American corporations. Again they are essentially definitions of what guides the relationships businesses and managers engage in, rather than being preoccupied with goals as purpose.

Conclusion: routes for business and the environment

The aim of this chapter is to examine the contribution of ethics in the relationship between environmental protection and economic development as seen from the vantage point of the business organization and those involved in its management. The nature of the ethical systems which surround sustainable development and improved environmental performance have been examined.

Alternative views of the purpose of business and managers have been considered and related to ideas from the field of corporate social responsibility. The intent in this conclusion is to draw together these ideas and to identify the contribution of corporate social responsibility and ethics as routes to successful environmental management in business.

Figure 2.3 sets out schematically the relationship between many of the ideas discussed in this chapter. The figure works through groups of ideas that range from mindsets and thinking, in the north-west corner of the figure; through approaches to strategy in business; on through a set of organizational processes, such as management systems, collaboration and the analysis of threats and opportunities; and finally to organizational positions ranging from improved environmental performance to sustainability which are shown in the south-east corner of the figure. The figure outlines the connections between three forms of organizational strategy – strategy as the mix of products in a company portfolio, strategy as learning and strategy as change for continued legitimacy.

Anthropocentric management driven by utilitarian values dominates strategy based on product portfolios. It also makes a major contribution to ideas of strategy based on organizational learning and strategic intent. However, these variants of strategy are strongly influenced by systemic thinking and concepts found in the literature about mutual causality. This has led authors such as Morgan (1986) to imply that systemic thinking is essential in shaping the identity of organizations capable of survival; Senge (1992) to venture that thinking systemically and globally is a precondition for organizational learning. Ideas which build on Vickers's (1993) observations about human systems and his conclusion that managing relationships is the real basis for organizational survival.

Strategy as enterprise legitimacy is defined by authors such as Ansoff (1979) and Freeman and Gilbert (1988) who believe it is critical to explore the ethical systems operating within organizations and management as part of the search for legitimacy. All three strategic variants readily acknowledge the importance of organizational change in adjusting to environmental concerns. Where they differ is in the role that ethics play in determining the depth and the process of organizational change.

For example, in the case of strategy as product portfolio, ethical systems are generally implicit and unquestioned, except where products are developed or offered in ways which are designed to appeal to the values or lifestyles of particular consumer groups. The marketing and development of green products is one aspect of this approach. The very act of promoting the environmental characteristics of products to consumers may cause an organization's management to recognize a need better to align their organizational

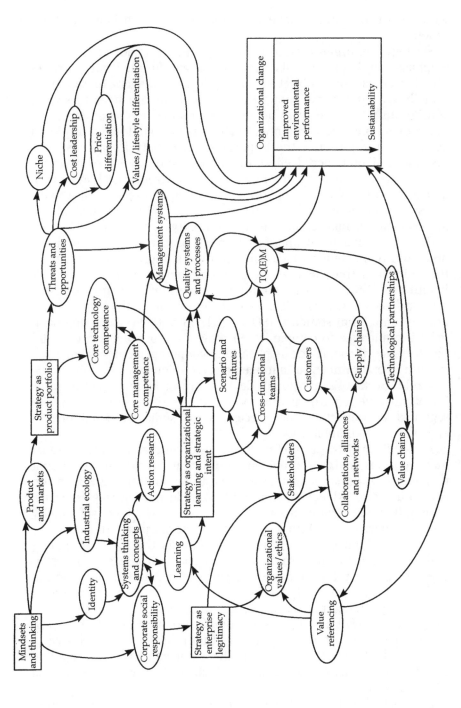

Figure 2.3 Routes to improved environmental performance and sustainability

values with the values they expect customers to associate with their products.

Strategy, as organizational learning and strategic intent, places emphasis on improvements in practice within the framework of broad organizational objectives. It requires managers to recognize that they do not know enough and that there is a need to search continuously for ideas from outside the organization in order to test the conventions and assumptions which tacitly guide organizational decisions. It emphasizes the importance of quality in management systems and managerial effort to improve the quality of products and services as well as to improve the environmental impact of activities. This involves collaborative systems and relationships with other organizations in the company's supply or value chain aimed at developing similar commitments to quality.

Quality management approaches have been transferred to environmental management. Ideas of continuous improvement underpin the guidelines that have been developed by the British Standards Institution (BSI) for the voluntary environmental management standard BS 7750 (BSI, 1992) which now provide the basis for the draft international standard ISO 14001 (ISO, 1995). This approach provides guidance to companies on ways to improve environmental performance through the application of management systems and the use of environmental management techniques.

While these organizational devices are a useful step towards improving the environmental performance of business they are regarded as important, not necessary or sufficient conditions in achieving sustainability.

A specific criticism of the extension of quality assurance management systems to incorporate environmental considerations is that this approach does not require explicit discussion and agreement on the values and ethical systems which guide managerial decisions, although it does raise questions about the importance of quality and the need to maintain procedural mechanisms that lead to assurances about quality. While this connects the issues of quality and environmental performance to the core purpose of business it does not question the fundamental purpose nor underpinning ethics and value systems of business. In that sense, the extension of quality approaches to environmental management offers a way to integrate environmental considerations into business. In contrast, an emphasis on sustainability implies that a business is interested to accommodate its activities within the environmental capacity and social expectations of the areas in which it chooses to operate and have impacts.

It is in the field of strategies for enterprise legitimacy that values and ethical systems of the organization are placed at the forefront of management thinking and practice. Enterprise strategy encourages discourse with stakeholders, employees and other organizations about both what it is appropriate for the organization to do (products and services) and how the organization undertakes its activities (values, processes and relationships). Ultimately these issues are referenced externally to see whether the organization is maintaining its legitimacy. However, if sustainable development is a continuing process of adaptation, surrounded by competing values and ethical systems, it follows that business organizations and business managers can only be part of that process, when they are prepared to entertain continuous dialogue and redefinition of the values which guide their actions; to work to more explicitly stated ethical codes; and contemplate alternative ethical systems as part of the paradigm change anticipated by sustainable development. However, even these demanding conditions are regarded as necessary rather than sufficient to achieve sustainability.

In conclusion, this chapter advances the view that the relationship between business organizations and the natural environment must be seen as part of a broader debate about an overall and more comprehensive process of sustainable development, with its agenda for both social and environmental well-being. Moreover, sustainable development, as a process of continuous change from current social/environment relationships to new sets of relationship, must itself be guided by values and ethical systems. However, there are many alternative systems that can be used to guide decisions.

No particular set of values is put forward here as essential in making progress towards sustainability. However, it is suggested that existing approaches to business and the environment, based on notions such as industrial ecology, ecoefficiency, environmental management systems and total quality management do not go far enough questioning the established utilitarian ethic which implicitly guides current business.

The utilitarian ethic – where utility is defined as a function of the quality as well as the quantity of outputs, and where the flow of utility, over time, is secured by seeking to maintain the quality and functionality of the products and services available to humanity while reducing the resource demands made through consumption – does not address those aspects of sustainability that are concerned with the intrinsic value of environmental resources and processes, the importance of human well-being and the value placed on futurity.

The utilitarian ethic therefore needs to be combined with other ethical principles. These might include respect for people as individuals, not just as means to secure utility for others; justice in the distribution of resources between segments of the present generation, or justice in the allocation of resources so that the interests of future generations are no less constrained than those of the present. It might include the judgement that the maintenance of biodiversity serves as a supreme constraint to organizational actions. In this way a business would work within these principles so that it does not engage in any actions or activities which directly or indirectly reduce the biodiversity of the earth. Examples of this approach are to be found in the principles that form the basis for the Swedish movement, The Natural Step – principles that have been adopted internationally by a number of business organizations as goals to strive towards.

Choosing a set of values to guide decision-making is therefore seen as critical to sustainability. However, it is also important that the values which shape the identity of organizations should be made explicit, as should the values which determine the relationships within organizations and between organizations and other human and non-human existence.

Only by addressing these values in clear and unambiguous terms and subjecting them to discussion and scrutiny, is it possible to secure meaningful progress towards business that contributes effectively to sustainability. Indeed, avoiding the need to address and change the fundamental values which underpin business decisions is to deny the need to contemplate the types of change necessary to secure more sustainable forms of business practice.

References

Ansoff, H. (1979). Strategy and strategic management: the changing shape of the strategic problem. In *Strategic Management* (D. Schendel and C. Hofer, eds) Little Brown and Company.

Armstrong, S. and Botzler, R. (1993). *Environmental Ethics: Divergence and Convergence*. McGraw-Hill.

British Standards Institution (BSI) (1992). *Specification for Environmental Management Systems*. BSI.

Carley, M. and Christie, I. (1993). *Managing Sustainable Development*. Earthscan.

Carroll, A. (1989). *Business and Society: Ethics and Stakeholder Management*. South Western Publishing Company.

Donagan, A. (1977). *The Theory of Morality*. University Press of Chicago.

Drucker, P. (1974). *Management: Tasks, Responsibilities, Practices*. Butterworth-Heineman.

Ehrenfeld, J. and Hoffman, A. (1993). Becoming a green company: the importance of culture in the greening process. Paper presented to the Greening of Industry Conference Designing the Sustainable Enterprise, Boston, October.

Emery, F. and Trist, E. (1965). The causal texture of organizational environments. *Human Relations*, **18**(1), 21–32.

Erlich, P., Erlich, A. and Holdren, J. (1973). *Human Ecology: Problems and Solutions*, W. H. Freeman and Company.

Etzione, A. (1967). Mixed scanning: a third approach to decision-making. *Public Administration Review*, **27**, 385–92.

Fischer, K. and Schot, J. (eds) (1993). *Environmental Strategies for Industry*. Island Press.

Freeman, R. and Gilbert, D. (1988). *Corporate Strategy and the Search for Ethics*. Prentice Hall.

Friedman, M. (1962). The responsibility of business is to increase profits. *New York Times Magazine*, 13 September, p. 12.

Frosch, R. (1992). *Industrial Ecology*. Proceedings of the Academy of Science, Washington.

Galbraith, J. (1971). *The New Industrial State*. Hamilton.

Gladwin, T. (1992). The meaning of greening: a plea for organizational theory. In *Environmental Strategies for Industry*. (K. Fischer and J. Schot, eds) Island Press.

Gladwin, T. N., Kennelly, J. J. and Krause, T. (1995). Shifting paradigms for sustainable development: implications for management theory and research. *Academy of Management Review*, **20**, 874–907.

Global Environment Management Initiative (GEMI) (1991). Proceedings of the First Conference of the *Global Environmental Management Initiative: Corporate Quality Environmental Management*, GEMI.

Hall, S. and Roome, N. (1996). Strategic choices and sustainable strategies. In *The Greening of Industry Resource Guide and Bibliography* (P. Groenewegen, K. Fischer, E. Jenkins and J. Schot, eds) Island Press.

Hamel, G. and Prahalad, C. (1989). Strategic intent. *Harvard Business Review*, May–June 63–76.

International Organization for Standardization (ISO) (1995). *Environmental Management Systems: Specification with Guidance for Use* (ISO/DIS 14001). ISO.

Katz, R. L. (1970). *Managing the Total Enterprise*. Prentice Hall.

Kuhn, T. (1970). *The Structure of Scientific Revolutions*. Chicago University Press.

Laughlin, R. (1991). Environmental disturbances and organizational transitions: some alternative models. *Organization Studies*, **12**(2), 209–32.

Leopold, A. (1949). *A Sand County Almanac*. Oxford University Press.

Lindblom, C. (1959). The science of muddling through. *Public Administration Review*, **19**, 79–88.

Lovelock, J. (1987). *Gaia*. Oxford University Press.

March, J. and Simon, H. (1958). *Organizations*. Wiley.

Maturana, H. and Varela, F. (1980). *Autopoiesis and Cognition: The Realization of the Living*. Reidl.

McGuire, J. (1963). *Business and Society*. McGraw-Hill.

Morgan, G. (1986). *Images of Organization*. Sage.

Naess, A. (1993). The deep ecological movement: some philosophical aspects. In *Environmental Ethics: Divergence and Convergence* (S. Armstrong and R. Botzler, eds) McGraw-Hill.

Odum, E. (1971). *Fundamentals of Ecology*. W. B. Saunders.

Ontario Hydro (1993). *A Strategy for Sustainable Energy Development and Use for Ontario Hydro*. Ontario Hydro.

O'Riordan, T. (1991). The new environmentalism and sustainable development. *Science of the Total Environment*, **108**, 5–15.

Pearce, D., Markandya, A. and Barbier, E. B. (1987). *Blueprint for a Green Economy*. Earthscan Publications.

Peters, T. and Waterman, R. (1982). *In Search of Excellence*. Harper and Row.

Rawls, J. (1971). *A Theory of Justice*. Harvard University Press.

Roome, N. (1992). Developing environmental management strategies. *Business Strategy and the Environment*, **1**(1), 11–24.

Schmidheiny, S. (1992). *Changing Course: A Global Business Perspective on Development and the Environment*. Massachusetts Institute of Technology.

Schumacher, E. (1974). *Small is Beautiful*. Abacus.

Senge, P. (1992). Systems thinking and organizational learning: acting locally and thinking globally in the organization of the future. *European Journal of Operational Research*, **59**(1), 137–50.

Sethi, P. (1975). Dimensions of corporate social performance: an analytical framework, *California Management Review*, Spring, pp. 58–64.

Shrivastava, P. (1992). Corporate self-greenewal: strategic responses to environmentalism. *Business Strategy and the Environment*, **1**(3), 9–21.

Stead, W. and Stead, J. (1992). *Management for a Small Planet*. Sage.

Stewart, R. (1993). *The Reality of Organizations*. (3rd edn) Macmillan.

Trist, E. (1983). Referent organizations and the development of inter-organization domains. *Human Relations*, **36**(3), 269–84.

Vickers, G. (1974). *Freedom in a Rocking Boat*, Allen Lane.

Vickers, G. (1983). *Human Systems are Different*. Harper and Row.

World Commission on Environment and Development (WCED) (1987). *Our Common Future*. Oxford University Press.

Part Two

Disciplinary Perspectives

3 Different lives, different worlds: anthropology and environmental discourse

Kay Milton

'What a wonderful place the world would be,' cry the members of each organizational culture, 'if only everyone was like us,' conveniently ignoring the fact that it is only the presence in the world of people who are not like them that enables them to be the way they are. (Thompson, 1986: 454)

Two main features distinguish anthropology[1] from the other social sciences. First, there is its traditional emphasis on 'culture' as a central analytical concept. While sociologists employ 'social theory' and political scientists 'political theory', anthropologists use 'cultural theory'. Second, there is its traditional interest in the exotic. Anthropology developed as the study, usually by scholars from the West and initially in colonial contexts, of 'other' societies. While sociologists and political scientists draw their insights from comparisons among industrial states (e.g. Jamison, Eyerman, Cramer and Læssøe, 1990), anthropologists are more likely to compare societies in Africa and the Pacific (Keesing, 1970), or hunter-gatherers in Africa, India and Malaysia (Bird-David, 1990). In this chapter I shall argue that these two features, a theoretical interest in culture and an empirical interest in the exotic, enable anthropology to make a distinctive contribution to contemporary environmental discourse. In the second part of the chapter I consider how anthropology's focus on the exotic can shed light on the familiar, how a knowledge of the ways in which non-industrial peoples understand their environment, can sharpen our awareness of the perceptions and interpretations that inform environmental debate in industrial society. In the third part of the chapter, I show how a well-known anthropological model of cultural diversity can throw light on the kinds of differences that generate and sustain environmental conflict in industrial societies. Since it is important first to establish the theoretical basis for these arguments, the first section focuses on culture as an analytical concept in anthropology, and its relevance for the study of environmental issues.

The argument that an understanding of culture has a role in environmental discourse rests on a simple observation: that environmental activists, be they radical or moderate, are essentially engaged in cultural reform. In attempting to change the ways we use our environment, they are also trying to change the values we hold, the goals we pursue, the assumptions we make. They seek to persuade us that the benefits of cleaner air and a more stable climate are worth more than the convenience offered by cars, that a living rain forest should be valued more highly than its potential harvest of timber. Some argue that we need to rethink our relationship with nature; to abandon the assumption that humanity is the centre of the universe, that the environment exists for us, and to see ourselves instead as part of a complex ecosystem in which all species and processes deserve consideration. What we do with our environment, whether we drain a wetland for agriculture or leave it for wildlife, whether we build a factory or plant a woodland, is bound up with the way we understand the world, our assumptions and values. Environmentalists assume that in order to replace destructive ways of using the environment with more benign ways, we need to change the way we think about it. To a non-anthropologist, it may not be clear how this constitutes cultural reform. For this reason, it is important to clarify what anthropologists understand by 'culture'.

What is culture?

Like most key concepts in social science, 'culture' has been defined in many ways, but one feature has remained constant: within anthropology, culture has consistently been defined in broader terms than in the other social sciences or in the public arena. The early anthropological definitions of culture, from the late nineteenth century, saw it as all inclusive. For Tylor it was: 'That complex whole which includes knowledge, belief, art, morals, law, custom, and any other capabilities and habits acquired by man as a member of society' (Tylor, 1871, quoted in Keesing, 1981: 68). Many anthropologists have continued to think of culture in these broad terms, often describing it as having three main types of component: the material, the cognitive and the behavioural (Howard, 1986: 5). Ferraro, for instance, defined culture as 'everything that people have, think and do as members of a society' (Ferraro, 1992: 18, cf. Hicks and Gwynne, 1994: 46).

But this broad concept of culture has its limitations. It was appropriate when anthropologists were concerned primarily with describing whole ways of life, when the main objective for an anthropologist in the field was to gather as much information as possible concerning a society's belief systems, social institutions and material products. In this tradition, anthropology was characterized as the study of 'other cultures' (Beattie, 1964). But this concept of culture is of little use in analysing the relationships among its components. It cannot, for instance, be used to examine how people's actions are related to their knowledge of the world, how their religious beliefs shape their political and economic activities and vice versa. Around forty years ago, anthropologists became primarily interested in precisely these kinds of relationships, and modified their concept of culture accordingly.

In order to study any relationship, it is necessary first to distinguish its components. From the late 1950s, anthropologists began to split their data into two categories: phenomena which, it was assumed, could be observed directly (what people do and say) and phenomena which were assumed to exist in people's minds (their feelings, thoughts, knowledge, and so on), and which can therefore only be inferred from what they do and say. The term 'culture' came to be confined by many analysts to the second category. Thus, for the past four decades, culture has been seen as consisting of people's perceptions and interpretations: everything they think, feel and know about themselves and the world in which they live. In this form, the concept of culture has become an appropriate tool for analysing people's activities. The relationship between culture and action is generally treated as dialectical. The way people understand the world (their culture) forms a basis for their actions, which in turn generate experiences which modify (confirm, reinforce, undermine, contradict) their understanding. This is what anthropologists mean by cultural change.

Culture and the environment

It has long been assumed (though not universally accepted) in anthropology that culture mediates in some way between people and their environment, so much so that the study of human–environment relations has often focused on the relationship between culture and the environment. Anthropologists have produced various models of this relationship. Until the 1960s, such models were dominated by 'environmental determinism', the view that human cultures are shaped by the environments in which they are assumed to have evolved. Thus Huntington (1924) sought to explain the development of human civilizations in terms of climate. Later analysts, through the approach known as 'possibilism', sought to identify the limits placed on cultural development by environmental factors (for instance, Kroeber, 1939). Still more recent approaches, such as cultural ecology (Steward, 1955) and cultural materialism (Harris, 1979), have provided more detailed interpretations of the relationships between cultural phenomena and environmental conditions. In each of these approaches, culture is seen as an ecological adaptation, as the mechanism through which people adapt to their environment in order to ensure or optimize their physical well-being and the continuation of their society.

From the 1960s, 'cultural determinism' became the prevailing anthropological model of human–environment relations. It was assumed that people define or 'construct' their environment through culture, that culture is what gives shape and meaning to the world. However, while this 'constructivist' model informed much of what has been written in the name of symbolic or semantic anthropology, it proved less useful to anthropologists whose prime interest is human ecology. In the constructivist approach, people's understanding of the world is assumed to come solely from within their own culture; thus the environment that exists outside people's understanding is denied a role in human society. This difficulty led ecological anthropologists initially to turn away from the study of culture and to focus instead on human populations (rather than cultures) as participants in ecosystems (see Rappaport, 1969), and more recently to challenge the constructivist model (Ingold, 1992, Milton, 1996).

Probably no anthropologist writing today would wish to describe the human–environment relationship as purely deterministic in either direction. The focus on ecosystems (Moran, 1990) has led anthropologists to see human populations and their environments as interacting in mutually constitutive ways. In this approach, culture is seen as mediating this relationship in such a way that it both constitutes and is constituted by the environment. It forms a basis for human activity, and therefore drives our interaction with our environment (cf. Ellen, 1986: 206), and is also shaped by the environment through human experience. People's perceptions of the world, upon which they elaborate through cognitive processes, flow directly from their active engagement with their surroundings (Ingold, 1992). Thus we can suggest that human populations have different cultures, different understandings of the world, because they engage with their environments in different ways (as hunters, farmers, industrialists), and that these cultures (by defining needs, wants, values, strategies, and so on) also shape that engagement.

The argument that its theoretical focus on culture can give anthropology a role in environmental discourse should now be clear. If culture guides the way people use the environment and shapes their understanding of it, then it can be argued that the study of culture forms an important part of the study of human ecology. And since it is human activities that are presented, in environmental discourse, as the main cause of environmental damage, the study of human ecology is essential in our search for ways of alleviating and minimizing that damage. If, for instance, we want to increase the ecological sustainability of industrial and commercial processes such as mass production and trade, it is important to understand the cultural underpinnings of these processes, to know why people engage in them, what fundamental assumptions inform them, what kinds of life strategies they support. In the light of such understanding, the potential for change and the paths it might take become clearer. I now turn to the other distinguishing feature of anthropology, its traditional interest in exotic cultures.

The importance of the 'other'

In its popular image, anthropology is the study of small-scale, traditional, non-western societies. This image has tended to create the impression that it has little to say about the issues facing the contemporary industrial world. But this impression is misleading, partly because anthropologists are increasingly focusing on the cultural aspects of industrial development (Appadurai, 1990; Miller, 1991) and technological change (Strathern, 1992), but mainly because it misses the point; anthropologists have tended to study non-western societies, not specifically because they are non-western, but because they are, to most anthropologists, exotic and unfamiliar. The exotic is, by definition, alien or foreign. It is therefore a relative concept; what is mundane in one society is exotic to another. Because anthropology, like other academic disciplines, is a product of the industrial west, the exotic, to most anthropologists, tends to be non-western and non-industrial. But what matters is not the type of culture studied, but the fact that it is different from one's own. A spell of fieldwork in a foreign society is regarded as an important part of an anthropologist's training. For a western anthropologist, this might mean living in an African village or with a band of nomadic hunter-gatherers. For an anthropologist brought up in Africa or Indonesia, the appropriate sense of 'otherness' might be experienced in a European town.

Anthropologists study the exotic because it generates a particular perspective on the familiar and, in so doing, forms a springboard for generalizations about human culture. Other cultures are used as lenses through which to view our own, and their effectiveness as such depends, to a large extent, on their 'otherness', their exotic quality. When people interact in familiar contexts they take a great deal for granted; indeed, they must do so for interaction to proceed smoothly. A visit to a friend is relatively unproblematic because much is mutually known and understood; how to dress, what sort of gift to take, and so on. In unfamiliar contexts, one proceeds cautiously; the rules of interaction are not mutually agreed and the wrong move might cause offence. Anthropologists in the early weeks of fieldwork are particularly aware of this danger. New rules are learned by setting aside preconceptions about what is appropriate and replacing them with what is observed, tested and found acceptable in the new social surroundings.

The importance of understanding diverse rules of interaction is increasingly being recognized in the commercial field. When potential business partners from the same cultural background meet, the rules of interaction – how and when to show respect, how to 'talk business' – are mutually understood. When the potential partners belong to different cultures, such as Britain and Japan or America and the Middle East, an extra dimension is added to the negotiations. There is a possibility that business might be lost because signals are not correctly interpreted, because the wrong kind of greeting is used or because hospitality is not properly acknowledged. These concerns have generated a trend in educational courses across the commercial sector, designed to familiarize business personnel with the cultures of their 'exotic' colleagues. It is interesting to note that such measures are often seen, not only as ways of smoothing negotiations, but also as ways of gaining advantage in a competitive international arena, where particular value may be placed on having made an effort to learn unfamiliar cultural rules.

But a culture consists of far more than rules. Rules of interaction imply certain values and assumptions about how the world operates. Becoming familiar with a culture therefore means more than learning how to behave; it means understanding why certain actions are appropriate or inappropriate. In an English park I would not hesitate to sit in the shade of a particular tree. In an African village I might stop to ask whether the spirits might be offended by such an action. In western culture it is understood that to take something without asking for it violates a sense of exclusive ownership. Among the Nayaka of southern India, such an action offends because it deprives the 'owner' of the right to give (Bird-David, 1990: 193). The process of learning about the exotic throws the familiar into relief, enabling us to see it more clearly, to raise questions about it, to apply 'systematic doubt' (Morgan, 1991: 224) to our taken-for-granted assumptions. Ultimately it leads to the (sometimes painful) realization that our own culture, like other cultures, is one of many ways of perceiving and interpreting the world and does not, as we had previously assumed, represent the way things are.

Cross-cultural comparison

Anthropologists have used the lens provided by other cultures to throw light on the ways in which western industrial societies perceive and interpret the environment. To illustrate this, I shall draw briefly on Dwyer's (1996) comparison between the cultures of village communities in Papua New Guinea. In western industrial society, a distinction is commonly made between the natural environment and the products of human activity. Nature is seen, among other things, as something opposed to culture, as 'space which is not human' (Ellen, 1996: 110). This separation of the human from the natural is seen by many environmentalists as the source of environmental destruction. Because humanity is seen as separate from nature, people have, until relatively recently, failed to recognize both the environmental consequences of their own actions and the consequences, for themselves, of environmental change. Dwyer raised the question of how nature might come to be seen as distinct from the sphere of human activity. A possible answer is provided by comparing the worldview of the Kubo-speaking community of Gwaimasi, in the Western Province of Papua New Guinea, with the worldview of the Siane-speaking community of Leu, in the more mountainous Simbu Province (Dwyer, 1996: 163 ff.).

In the Gwaimasi region, the human population is sparse, their gardens occupy a tiny proportion of the land, and they draw extensively on the resources of their environment, combining cultivation with sago extraction, hunting, gathering and fishing. Through these activities, they range widely over their landscape, becoming thoroughly familiar with it, endowing it with memories, gleaning from it both material and spiritual sustenance. For the Gwaimasi residents, there is no space which is not human; everything occurs 'within the landscape of human action, for there is no other place' (Dwyer, 1996: 168). Thus there is no possibility, in the Gwaimasi worldview, of developing a concept of 'nature' as something separate from and opposed to the human sphere, since the human sphere occupies the entire known environment.

The Siane-speaking people of Leu village occupy a very different world. Their population density is higher, they practise intensive horticulture and pig husbandry and obtain 90 per cent of their food from their gardens. The occasional visits to unoccupied areas, to hunt and collect fungi and pandanus nuts, are short and take up only a small proportion of their time (Dwyer, 1996: 174). The residents of Leu village have no difficulty in conceptualizing space which is not human. The manner in which they engage with their environment, by intensively cultivating some areas and rarely visiting others, creates such space.

By using these case studies, and a third intermediate example, Dwyer argued that the potential for 'inventing nature' in the western sense of something that is separate from and opposed to the human sphere, depends on whether the environment is seen as an integrated whole, or as mixture of familiar and unfamiliar, human and non-human spaces. This, in turn, is related to patterns of resource use, specifically their degree of spatial concentration. His argument is similar to that presented by Coursey (1978), who, following studies of tropical agricultural systems, suggested that an oppositional understanding of nature, which depends on a sharp contrast between human activities and natural processes, is generated by the practice of seed cultivation, which requires a more interventionist approach than vegetative cultivation.

These analyses and others have important implications for the way we understand the development of environmental knowledge within western industrial culture. Environmentalists often argue that western society's alienation from nature is the fault of the Judaeo-Christian tradition which places humanity in a dominant position over the rest of creation (Taylor, 1991: 258). But anthropological work would suggest that it derives from much earlier events such as the neolithic revolution (Coursey, 1978: 140), or the domestication of animals (Ingold, 1996). This in turn may have implications for the cultural changes advocated by some environmentalists. The call to rethink our relationship with nature may be more radical than is realized either by its advocates or by its opponents.

Understanding cultural diversity

As well as showing how an understanding of the exotic can throw light on the familiar, Dwyer's study reinforces the point made above, that people's understanding of their environment is related to their mode of engagement with it and to the experiences generated by that mode of engagement. The residents of Gwaimasi and Leu perceive and interpret their environments in different ways, not only because of the objective differences between those environments (that one area is more mountainous than the other, one more forested, and so on), but also because one community uses their whole environment extensively and experiences an easy familiarity with all parts of it, while the other uses part of their environment intensively and the remainder only occasionally, resulting in an experience of partial familiarity.

The argument is strengthened further by instances in which communities living close together have been shown to perceive and interpret their environment in fundamentally different ways. The Nayaka hunter-gatherers of South India, studied by Bird-David, see their forest as a 'giving environment', one that provides what they need unconditionally, without imposing any obligation to return. Their neighbours, the Bette Kurumba, who are shifting cultivators, experience the same forest as a 'reciprocating environment', one that provides in return for gifts already given. The Bette Kurumba make offerings when they sow their crops, to secure blessings for a successful harvest, whereas the Nayaka make offerings in thanks for what they have already received (Bird-David, 1990: 191). Bird-David noted similar differences between other hunter-gatherers (the Mbuti of Zaire and the Batek of Malaysia) and their cultivator neighbours.

These observations, and other recent work in ecological anthropology (Ellen 1996; Ingold 1992, 1996), carry implications for the analysis of environmental understanding in western industrial society. If the way people perceive and interpret their environment is related to how they engage with it and the experiences entailed therein, then we can expect a society whose members engage with the environment in many different ways to encompass a wide range of cultural perspectives on it. It is to be expected that rural and urban dwellers, farmers, teachers, scientists, tourists, manufacturers, consumers, and so on, will each hold a different concept of 'the environment'. Understanding this diversity is the key to understanding contemporary environmental discourse.

One way in which anthropologists have made progress in this direction is through the adaptation and application of Douglas's theory of culture (Douglas, 1970). Expressed simply, Douglas's theory states that culture is related systematically to social organization. In other words, people's understanding of the world varies according to the way they organize their social relationships – the degree to which they regulate each other's actions, the patterns of authority they establish, the extent to which they act in groups or as individuals. Combinations of these variables produce three main forms of social organization: market, hierarchy and sect.[2] In the market form, individual action is relatively unconstrained and group attachment is weak. This is associated with an entrepreneurial culture, which encourages people to pursue personal gain. In the hierarchical form, individual actions are constrained and attachment to groups is high. The corresponding culture values central control and collective benefit; the most admired actions are those performed within the law for the good of the community. In the sectarian form, group attachment is strong and individual action is relatively unconstrained. The culture is egalitarian; both personal gain and the rule of law are valued less than the general good.

In a western liberal democracy, market and hierarchy are central forms of organization, characterizing the major political and economic institutions (Douglas and Wildavsky, 1982); government is hierarchical while business is entrepreneurial in its cultural perspective. Sectarian organization is more typical of peripheral institutions, groups which form as voluntary associations in opposition to business and government. Douglas and Wildavsky (1982) argued that the rise in environmental concern in the United States in the 1960s and 1970s was related to an increase in sectarian organizations. They suggested that groups espousing an egalitarian ideology, characterized by voluntary commitment to the principle of communal benefit, were held together by fears of environmental threats (see Milton, 1996: 93–95).

Social organization and environmental understanding

The forms of social organization in Douglas's typology have been associated by analysts with different models or 'myths' of nature.[3] Entrepreneurs, who favour market organization, treat nature as robust; they act on the understanding that, whatever they do, the environment will recover, and so are free to pursue personal profit, unconstrained by environmental considerations. Egalitarians, who favour sectarian organization, treat nature as fragile; they fear that the environment cannot bear even the slightest additional burden, and so attempt to minimize the adverse environmental impacts of their own and others' actions. Hierarchists tend to treat nature as robust within limits; the environment will bear a certain amount of abuse but no more. They argue that our use of the environment therefore needs to be carefully controlled, and based on the best possible scientific knowledge.

This model of cultural diversity thus draws attention to the 'plural rationalities' (James, Tayler and Thompson, 1987) that underpin environmental discourse in contemporary industrial society. It can be used to expose the premises on which environmental arguments and strategies are based and can help to make sense of conflict. For example, in the summer of 1995, Shell's intention to dump the Brent Spar oil rig in the North Atlantic provoked a widespread and prolonged public protest led by Greenpeace. Despite the company's claims to the contrary, the protesters assumed that Shell was acting as if nature is robust, as if the marine environment could absorb the impact without suffering significant damage. The protesters themselves acted as if nature is fragile, arguing that, in the absence of scientific proof that the marine environment would suffer no harm, the precautionary approach of not releasing toxic materials into the sea should be taken. The conflict makes sense as a contest between fundamentally opposed cultural perspectives. Because the opposition is often fundamental, it is difficult to establish common ground in environmental disputes and to negotiate agreed solutions.

The model can also draw attention to contradictions and inconsistencies in the actions of participants in environmental discourse. The British government's environmental strategy presented the environment as a 'common inheritance' (HMSO, 1990) and stressed that its protection is a communal responsibility. As well as identifying the environmental responsibilities of central government, the document listed actions for individuals, businesses and local authorities (HMSO, 1990: 268–70), and declared that, 'We all have a part to play, however small, in conserving this common inheritance' (HMSO, 1990: 16). Such language is characteristic of an egalitarian or hierarchical system, in which the environment is seen either as fragile or as robust only within limits, and in which individuals are urged to act with caution, for fear of damaging a communal resource. And yet the same government's broad economic strategy was designed to allow entrepreneurship to flourish by giving market forces a free rein. Thus citizens were being asked to adopt egalitarian principles in an economic system designed to produce entrepreneurs, to treat the environment as, in some degree, fragile, in the context of a system which treated it as robust (Milton, 1991: 16).

To some extent, then, the argument that certain forms of social organization are associated, in a systematic way, with particular ways of conceptualizing the environment, appears to fit the observed reality, and can help analysts to make sense of environmental discourse. However, it is not difficult to find examples which do not fit the expected pattern. Some successful businesses, such as The Body Shop and Ecover,[4] have built their success on the message that the environment is fragile and needs our protection. Companies from toilet roll manufacturers to investment brokers now present themselves as environmentally responsible and use green messages to sell their products. At the same time, some environmental non-governmental organizations (NGOs), sectarian groups held together by voluntary commitment, are becoming more hierarchical in their organization (Douglas and Wildavsky, 1982: 130 ff.) and are adopting entrepreneurial approaches in their campaigns for funds and supporters.

These observations suggest that Douglas's model of cultural diversity should not be treated as a straightforward representation of reality; that if cultural perspectives on the environment are related to forms of social organization, this relationship is not simple and transparent. Douglas's model is more useful as a starting point for asking questions about environmental discourse, than as a representation of what takes place. For instance, if, according to her model, entrepreneurs can be expected to act as if the environment is robust, we can ask why some of them increasingly do not act in this way. Conversely, if the view that the environment is fragile is expected to be associated with sectarian forms of organization, we can ask why people who appear to hold this view sometimes act like entrepreneurs. I suggest that the answers to these questions lie in the plurality of western industrial culture; that it is the presence of diverse cultural perspectives, and the tensions between those perspectives, that shape environmental discourse.

Cultural diversity and cultural change

Examples of apparent environmental awareness in the commercial sector are easy to find. The use of green images in advertising has been with us for some years. Companies have become sensitive to the consequences of bad environmental practice, not least public exposure, and have sought to reduce the environmental impacts of their activities through improved technology and management. This process has been led and supported by legislative changes, such as the UK's Environmental Protection Act 1990, and an ever-growing array of environmental directives and regulations from the European Union (EU). Certification schemes (such as the UK's BS 7750 and the EU's Eco-management and Audit Scheme) have helped to promote the view that sound environmental practice is also sound commercial practice. A whole new business sector of environmental consultants has emerged to meet the needs of companies seeking to improve their environmental performance, and many companies now employ their own in-house environmental experts. The importance of public accountability is recognized in the publication, by many companies, of annual assessments of their own environmental performance.

One of the most striking features of commercial environmentalism is its use of symbolism, alongside the statistics and statements of good practice, to communicate the message more effectively. An advertisement for a certification service, which asks the question, 'Would you help save the environment if it helped your business save money?' carries a photograph of two hands cradling a seedling (SGS, 1996). Imperial Chemical Industries' (ICI's) 1993 review of environmental performance juxtaposes a series of diagrams showing how waste materials were dealt with, and an evocative photograph of two children standing hand in hand in a field of swaying grass, gazing upwards (one cannot tell whether in hope or in fear) at the gathering clouds (ICI, 1993: 12–13). The following year, ICI presented its 'she' (safety, health and environment) symbol: a sculpture of a woman's face (representing ICI staff) and hand (representing care) supporting the form of a circle (representing unity of purpose). The symbol's declared purpose is as an encouragement and inspiration for company employees (ICI, 1994: 19), but it also has a potentially powerful impact on the company's public image. It gives a soft, caring, feminine gloss, which evokes, for those sensitive to them, all the associations of femininity with environmental concern (birth and creation, nurturing, mother earth, ecofeminism), to what might otherwise be seen as the hard, masculine world of the chemical industry.

The more cynical interpretations of commercial environmentalism tend to take two forms. Either they dismiss it as 'greenwash', a purely cosmetic attempt to sell products by giving industry a green image, or they see it as an attempt to control the environmental agenda. Chatterjee and Finger (1994), for instance, interpreted the involvement of commercial interests in the Rio Earth Summit as a successful attempt to take over the green agenda from the voluntary sector, which, they argued, was marginalized in the Rio process. There is no doubt that such interpretations can help to throw light on some of the observed events, but they tend to ignore the underlying cultural conditions which both drive and are driven by environmental discourse. A cultural analysis leads us to ask why business interests should want to use green messages to sell their products, and why they should want to control the environmental agenda.

The most obvious answer is that it has become commercially important for them to do so, and the reason for this lies in the cultural plurality of western industrial society, and in the nature of the market as a form of social organization. Markets, because they are driven by an ideology of personal gain rather than personal sufficiency, depend on expansion. If they are to survive, they cannot afford to ignore opportunities, nor can they ignore threats to their sustainability. Entrepreneurs might wish to treat the environment as robust, but if a significant proportion of the population sees it as fragile, and seeks to protect it, the market cannot afford to ignore them. And a trend which might start as mere lip service, as 'greenwash', quickly becomes transformed into action, as companies compete for the custom of an increasingly critical public.

Radical environmentalist ideas can have a significant influence on this process. The activities of those who seek to protect the environment by advocating fundamental change are often highly conspicuous in western industrial society. It is difficult for the central market and hierarchical institutions to tolerate the presence of radical environmentalist groups, which are often strongly sectarian in organization and egalitarian in ideology. Their very existence is seen as a threat to central industrial and political institutions because they seek independence from market forces and replacement of the rule of law with consensual decision-making. The environmental practices of commercial companies may not be directly affected by radical environmentalist groups, whose collective membership remains small in most western democracies, but the indirect impact may be considerable. Conspicuous radical protest can strengthen public opinion against environmentally damaging activities, making the market less tolerant of those companies which continue to treat the environment as robust, and favouring those which seek genuinely to improve their environmental performance.

This argument leads to one final point about the way in which cultural diversity shapes environmental discourse. The tension between different cultural perspectives is experienced, not only among groups and institutions, but also by individuals. Douglas's model relates cultural perspectives to forms of social organization; the way people understand the world varies according to the way their activities are organized. In a complex society, an individual's actions are unlikely to conform to just one institutional pattern. Only those who truly opt out of industrial society, for instance, can live a thoroughly sectarian life guided by egalitarian principles. Most members of voluntary organizations also participate in hierarchical and market institutions. Those who belong to Greenpeace or Friends of the Earth are also consumers, teachers, civil servants, office workers, company executives, members of the legal, financial or medical profession, tradespeople, and so on. This means that the interaction between different ways of understanding and acting towards the environment does not take place simply among different sectors of society, but is played out in the lives of individuals. The same person who contributes to pollution by using a car instead of public transport might also buy a more expensive phosphate-free washing powder, and lobby the government for tighter controls on pollution. The same individual who drives to and from work along a six-lane motorway each weekday, might spend their weekends campaigning against a proposal to build such a road through their own backyard.

The fact that cultural diversity operates at a personal level, that the tensions between different ways of understanding and interacting with the environment are experienced by individuals as internal dilemmas, can have conflicting effects on environmental discourse. On the one hand, people's willingness to take action for the environment (such as conserving energy) is tempered by their reluctance to give up personal pleasures and conveniences (such as cars and well-heated homes). The environmental movement is held back by people's enjoyment of the trappings of modern life. On the other hand, the understanding that such trappings are often environmentally harmful fosters a sense of guilt and responsibility which encourages environmental activism. 'Conscience money', in the form of commercial sponsorship, personal donations and membership subscriptions, is an important source of income for environmental NGOs. Environmental discourse in the contemporary industrial world is thus a contest between different cultural perspectives on the environment which operate to influence action at both an institutional and a personal level.

Conclusion

In this chapter I have tried to show how some of the principal analytical tools employed in anthropology can throw light on the nature of environmental discourse in western industrial society. Central to an anthropological approach is the understanding that our knowledge of the environment is cultural; it is generated by the ways in which we engage with the physical world and with each other. This is demonstrated most clearly in the study of small communities in which individuals depend directly on their immediate surroundings, as we saw in Dwyer's comparison between New Guinea communities who think of their environment in different ways because they use it in different ways. The argument is just as relevant, however, to contemporary industrial society, in which, due to trade and economic specialization, individual dependence on the environment is less immediate and, therefore, less easily observed.

Once we understand the cultural nature of our environmental knowledge, we can begin to see environmental discourse as an interaction between diverse cultural perspectives. The kind of cultural diversity which, for the most part, exists *between* small, non-industrial communities, exists *within* contemporary industrial society. For instance, some non-industrial communities see their environment as 'giving', others see it as 'reciprocating' (Bird-David, 1990); still others might see it as dangerous or protective, reliable or unpredictable (see Milton, 1996: 106 ff.). Within industrial society, these kinds of perspectives exist side by side and, in the course of everyday social interaction, frequently come into contact. Douglas's model of cultural diversity has been used to identify some of the significant variations (the environment seen as robust, fragile or robust within limits), and to comment on the consequences of this diversity for environmental discourse in the contemporary industrial world.

When studying the commercial sector, we need to acknowledge that cultural diversity is a product, not only of the plural nature of 'western' society, but also of the fact that business practice and ideology have colonized many societies through the process normally referred to by social scientists as 'globalization'. The same can be said of environmentalism, which is global in its concerns and its distribution (see Milton, 1996). Thus, both business and the environment have become transcultural discourses, in which debates played out in the international arena are reflected and reproduced, in a multitude of cultural forms, at locations through-out the world. In this context, the type of understanding to which anthropology is dedicated – an understanding of the sources and consequences of cultural diversity, and of the relationship between ideas and activities – is not merely intellectually satisfying, but can be a practical tool in the pursuit of 'progress', however that conten-tious concept might be defined.

Notes

1 Anthropology is a broad discipline. Here I use the label to refer to what is called 'social anthropology' in Britain and (perhaps more appropriately) 'cultural anthropology' in America. (The differences between these fields, which are significant in some contexts, are of little importance here.)

2 In fact, Douglas's model generates four variations in organization, but the combination of a high level of individual constraint with a low level of group adhesion tends to generate a fatalist ideology which is associated with inaction; for this reason, it receives little analytical attention.

3 See Douglas, 1992; James, Tayler and Thompson, 1987; Milton, 1991; Thompson and Tayler, 1986, among others.

4 The Body Shop, which makes skin and hair care products and sells them through stores in forty-six countries, claims to use 'environmen-tally sustainable resources wherever technically and economically viable' and 'is dedicated to the pursuit of social and environmental

change' (*BBC Wildlife*, March 1995: 59). Ecover manufactures a range of environmentally friendly cleaning products.

References

Appadurai, A. (1990). Disjuncture and difference in the global cultural economy. *Public Culture*, **2**(2), 1–24.

Beattie, J. (1964). *Other Cultures: Aims, Methods and Achievements in Social Anthropology*. Free Press.

Bird-David, N. (1990). The giving environment: another perspective on the economic system of gatherer-hunters. *Current Anthropology*, **31**(2), 189–96.

Chatterjee, P. and Finger, M. (1994). *The Earth Brokers: Power, Politics and World Development*. Routledge.

Coursey, D. G. (1978). Some ideological considerations relating to tropical root crop production. In *The Adaptation of Traditional Agriculture: Socio-economic Problems of Urbanization* (E. K. Fisk, ed.), Development Studies Centre Monograph 11, Australian National University.

Douglas, M. (1970). *Natural Symbols: Explorations in Cosmology*. Cresset.

Douglas, M. (1992). *Risk and Blame: Essays in Cultural Theory*. Routledge.

Douglas, M. and Wildavsky, A. (1982). *Risk and Culture: An Essay on the Selection of Technical and Environmental Dangers*. University of California Press.

Dwyer, P. D. (1996). The invention of nature. In *Redefining Nature: Ecology, Culture and Domestication* (R. F. Ellen and K. Fukui, eds) pp. 157–86, Berg.

Ellen, R. F. (1986). What Black Elk left unsaid: on the illusory images of green primitivism. *Anthropology Today*. **2**(6), 8–12.

Ellen, R. F. (1996). The cognitive geometry of nature: a contextual approach. In *Nature and Society: Anthropological Perspectives* (G. Palsson and P. Descola, eds). pp. 103–123, Routledge.

Ferraro, G. (1992). *Cultural Anthropology: An Applied Perspective*. West Publishing Company.

Harris, M. (1979). *Cultural Materialism: The Struggle for a Science of Culture*. Harper and Row.

Her Majesty's Stationery Office (HMSO) (1990). *This Common Inheritance: Britain's Environmental Strategy*. HMSO.

Hicks, D. and Gwynne, M. A. (1994). *Cultural Anthropology*. HarperCollins.

Howard, M. C. (1986). *Contemporary Cultural Anthropology*. Little, Brown and Company.

Huntington, E. (1924). *Civilization and Climate*. Yale University Press.

Imperial Chemical Industries (ICI) (1993). *Environmental Performance 1993*. ICI.

Imperial Chemical Industries (ICI) (1994). *Environmental Performance 1994*. ICI.

Ingold, T. (1992). Culture and the perception of the environment. In *Bush Base: Forest Farm* (E. Croll and D. Parkin, eds) pp. 39–56, Routledge.

Ingold, T. (1996). Hunting and gathering as ways of perceiving the environment. In *Redefining Nature: Ecology, Culture and Domestication* (R. F. Ellen and K. Fukui, eds) pp. 117–55, Berg.

James, P., Tayler, P. and Thompson, M. (1987). *Plural Rationalities.* Warwick Papers in Management 9, Institute for Management Research and Development, University of Warwick.

Jamison, A., Eyerman, R., Cramer, J. and Læssøe, J. (1990). *The Making of the New Environmental Consciousness.* Edinburgh University Press.

Keesing, R. (1970). Shrines, ancestors and cognatic descent: the Kwaio and Tallensi. *American Anthropologist,* **72**, 755–75.

Keesing, R. (1981). *Cultural Anthropology: A Contemporary Perspective.* Holt, Rinehart and Winston.

Kroeber, A. L. (1939). *Cultural and Natural Areas of Native North America.* University of California Press.

Miller, D. (1991). *Material Culture and Mass Consumption.* Blackwell.

Milton, K.(1991). Interpreting environmental policy: a social-scientific approach. In *Law, Policy and the Environment* (R. Churchill, J. Gibson and L. Warren, eds) pp. 4–17, Blackwell.

Milton, K. (1996). *Environmentalism and Cultural Theory: Exploring Anthropology's Role in Environmental Discourse.* Routledge.

Moran, E. F. (1990). Ecosystem ecology in biology and anthropology: a critical assessment. In *The Ecosystem Approach in Anthropology* (E.F. Moran, ed.) pp. 3–40, University of Michigan Press.

Morgan, G. (1991). Advocacy as a form of social science. In *Making Knowledge Count: Advocacy and Social Science* (P. Harries-Jones, ed.), McGill-Queen's Press.

Rappaport, R. A. (1969). Some suggestions concerning concept and method in ecological anthropology. In *Contributions to Anthropology: Ecological Essays* (D. Damas, ed.), National Museum of Canada Bulletin 230, Queen's Printers for Canada.

SGS (1996). Advertisement for SGS Yarsley International Certification Services Ltd. *Environment Business Magazine,* **20**, May/June, 2.

Steward, J. (1955). *Theory of Culture Change.* University of Illinois Press.

Strathern, M. (1992). *Reproducing the Future: Essays on Anthropology, Kinship and the New Reproductive Technologies.* Manchester University Press.

Taylor, B. (1991). The religion and politics of Earth First! *Ecologist* **21**, 258–66.

Thompson, M. (1986). Commentary on 'Mythology and surprise in the sustainable development of the biosphere', by P. Timmerman. In *The Sustainable Development of the Biosphere* (W.L. Clark and R.E. Munn, eds) pp. 453–54, Cambridge University Press.

Thompson, M. and Tayler, P. (1986). *The Surprise Game: An Exploration of Constrained Relativism.* Warwick Papers in Management 4, Institute for Management Research and Development, University of Warwick.

Tylor, E. B. (1871). *Primitive Culture: Researches into the Development of Mythology, Philosophy, Religion, Art and Custom.* John Murray.

Relatively green: sociological approaches to business and the environment

4

Keith Grint

> Should not in this best garden in the world,
> Our fertile France, put up her lovely visage?
> Alas, she hath from France too long been chased,
> And all her husbandry doth lie in heaps,
> Corrupting in its own fertility.
> Her vine, the merry cheerer of the heart,
> Unpruned dies; her hedges even-pleach'd
> Like prisoners wildly overgrown with hair,
> Put forth disorder'd twigs; her fallow leas
> The darnel, hemlock, and rank fumitory
> Doth root upon, while that the coulter rusts
> That should deracinate such savagery;....
> (*Henry V*, v, ii).

From the state of nature to the end of nature

After the battle of Agincourt in 1415, at least in Shakespeare's version of *Henry V*, the Duke of Burgundy rails against the effects of war and beseeches both the Kings of France and England to look upon the battle as an opportunity for peace to prevail, to drive out the savagery of war with the abundance of peace; he longs for the lush garden of France to recover and for the rusting 'coulter' (plough) to be put back to work – to tear up the weeds of war, to 'deracinate such savagery'. Deracination – to pull up by the roots or to remove from a natural environment – embodies the traditional approach to nature in the West: without human control over it not only can nature not be exploited to the benefit of humans but nature is actually an anarchic formation which benefits only 'weeds', those parasitic, displaced things that have no place in a 'properly' ordered world. So keen were the Victorian naturalists in Britain on making sure things were in their proper place – in this case ferns in copper pots by the fireside – that many hillsides lost all their ferns to the collectors (Prance, 1996: 22).

European colonists in North America seem to have 'civilized' the 'wilderness' they 'discovered' with a similar kind of ruthless reordering of the natural world (Nash, 1983). Of course, the 'natural' world was itself, at least in part, the consequence of prior human reordering by the original human populations. For example, many of the western prairies were not naturally devoid of tree cover but were kept clear by regular burning to ensure the growth of vegetation congruent with ensuring a stock of game animals for hunting (Pyre, 1982). After the European colonization, 'naturally', the ecology would again have been altered by the invasion of alien plants, animals and diseases brought by the colonists (Crosby, 1986). The displaced ferns and the clearings of the American wilderness can, as Williams (1972) has argued, be related to several developments, all linked to the Enlightenment events that appear to be responsible for a gradual change of perspective on nature from one where society and nature were essentially intertwined to one where society succeeds in dominating nature (see MacNaughton and Urry, 1995).

Three issues are particularly important here. First, as science and the rational analysis of the material world developed so the focus shifted from explaining how humans and nature related to each other in religious terms to explaining how the various elements in nature acted. In effect, the question shifted from why the world of nature was as it was, to how it worked.

Second, political debates erupted concerning the significance of the relationship of humans to nature, not in terms of explaining the relationship but in terms of how humans were different from nature. Thus, Rousseau (1968) argued that humans in their 'natural (pre-social) state' were originally good but had been infected by human institutions. One can read here a contemporary parallel with Lovelock's (1987) *Gaia* hypothesis where the world is perceived as a living organism, previously unspoilt in its 'state of nature' but now rebelling against the destruction wrought by humanity. Hobbes (1968), on the other hand, argued the opposite: that in the 'state of nature' humans were 'naturally' evil – the 'Yahoos' of *Gulliver's Travels* – and had to be socialized by social restraints. Either way, nature was now irrevocably separated from humanity, although many early European accounts of the native populations of the Americas suggested that their state of nature provided the necessary but oppositional touchstone through which the Europeans constructed their own identity as 'civilized' people (Hall, 1992).

Third, the growth of the market economy, presaged by Adam

Smith (1974), implied that the operation of the economy was itself subject to natural 'laws'. Of course, where such 'natural' economic laws did not exist – in 'uncivilized' lands – then humans had the 'natural' right to introduce them: enter the colonies. Even those politically opposed to the imperialist developments, like Karl Marx, were nevertheless unaware of any possible limits to natural resources and considered nature merely as a resource to be exploited for the benefit of (all) humanity.

Such domination can be perceived through the relationship of humans to those animals which humans eat. Indeed, Fiddes (1991) has argued that the slaughter and eating of animal flesh is a powerful symbolic re-enactment of human domination. After all, we seldom eat animals killed by accident or killed by other carnivorous animals – they somehow seem to be 'dirty' if we accidentally run them over in our cars but 'clean' if they are wrapped in clingfilm and look as distanced from a once-living creature as possible. This is rather similar to Thomas More's identification of cleanliness with godliness in *Utopia*, where: 'There are special places outside the town where all the blood and dirt are first washed off in running water. The slaughtering of livestock and cleaning of carcasses is done by slaves. They don't let ordinary people get used to cutting up animals, because they think it tends to destroy one's natural feelings of humanity' (More, 1965: p. 81).

All of these debates have recurred within what has been termed a modernist debate, that is a debate in which the progressive domination of nature through the rational application of science is the measure of civilization. Indeed, McKibben's (1990) considera- tion that we in the West have now reached the 'end of nature' (in so far as our relationship with nature is no longer direct but always mediated by technology), is the logical end point of this approach (see also Yearley, 1992). However, even though many current Green movements are antipathetic towards such an anthropomorphic view of the world, the main attempt to limit damage to the environment has occurred through the same modernist channels. In effect, while the debates about pollution are as acrimonious as ever, the actions of most Greens have been premised upon the use of the very same scientific techniques which allegedly instigated the problem in the first place. In short, science may have polluted the world but only science has the ability to stop the pollution, and only through greater scientific knowledge can we begin to construct sustainable developments (see Hajer, 1996, on this approach). For example, drought may be caused by farming or land use patterns and it is not always possible to (re)irrigate such lands since this tends to increase the level of salinity in the soil unless the soil is well drained (an expensive option) or irrigated with relatively pure water (another expensive option). However, plant physiologists and geneticists have recently been experimenting with enzyme inhibitors to develop salt resistant strains of plants such as *Brassica napus*, a genetically engineered form of oilseed rape (*Guardian*, 18 April 1996). Eco-realists, such as Easterbrook (1996), suggest that human-induced pollution is declining through the application of science, and anyway such pollution is marginal compared to the self-destruct systems operating within nature itself. In a similar vein there have been claims for many years that information technology developments will eliminate the need for physical journeys for many, so that we can shop and work from home etc. Let us hope so because if everyone who wants a car gets one we may have to live in them.

There are several different sociological responses to this modernist approach. Arguments by the likes of Ulrich Beck (1992) suggest that we have now moved from one form of society to another in which the very foundation stone of the way we live has changed. Whereas the challenge of the eighteenth, nineteenth and twentieth centuries was to accumulate wealth, the challenge from now on will be to avoid risk, for we are now entering the 'Risk Society'. By this Beck means that disputes which were previously centred over the distribution of 'goods' are now increasingly likely to be centred over the distribution of 'bads'. Where most people used to worry about whether they had food, shelter and work, in the future they will be more concerned with whether they are eating 'mad cow' or drinking poisoned water or breathing polluted air.

As Beck argues, such risk is not new – people have always been poisoned by pollution or died in high-risk adventures – but there are differences now. First, the risk has changed from being personal to being universal. In his example, Columbus took a voluntary personal risk in his adventures but we face an involuntary and global risk from the likes of Chernobyl. On the other hand, Chatterjee and Finger (1994) and Yearley (1996) have suggested that local, rather than global, action is the only practical way forward for environmentalists – especially in the absence of meaningful and powerful transnational environmental organizations. Second, the risks have changed from visible to invisible: it was clear to all that the streets of most medieval towns were littered with filth but we cannot see the deadly viruses that infect our food and air, nor the immediate risk of pouring twenty tons of aluminium sulphate into drinking water – as occurred in Camelford, England, on 6 July 1988 – though the cluster of leukaemia in the town has generated considerable public alarm (*Observer*, 14 July, 1996). Third, previous risks were the consequences of an undersupply of hygienic technology whereas today's risks are a consequence of an oversupply of production. For example, on 28 May 1996 the UK Ministry of Agriculture, Fisheries and Food (MAFF) announced that nine unnamed brands of baby milk had been found to contain phthalates – synthetic chemical compounds – which were in excess of the EU precautionary limit but below the safety limit. Phthalates may reduce fertility if present in sufficient quantities but since, according to the government, there was 'no risk', there was 'no point in naming the brands' (Vidal, 1996).

We can add a fourth ingredient to Beck's list of differentiation and that would be that the current crop of ecological threats are not just unseen and unknowable but, by their very randomness, pose a serious question about the ability of humans to *control* nature. Thus not only are we threatened by natural mutations that appear to outstrip our knowledge of disease eradication, but we appear to be essentially unable to control nature and secure the kind of progression to a better life that science once promised us (see Vidal, 1996). The question then is can modernist science dispel modernist risks? We are, according to Beck, 'Living on the volcano of civilization' (p. 3).

We might also add a fifth form of change here to Beck's list, and that is an increasing doubt about the ability of science to generate knowledge that the public accept as true. So whether the risks are actually increasing or not, and whether they are changing in form, is compounded by an increased scepticism on the part of the public that scientists know what they are talking about with any certainty. We only have to run through the changes to healthy eating over the last two decades to know that, almost by definition, whatever is regarded as healthy today will turn out to be unhealthy tomorrow.

On the other hand there are, of course, a range of pressure groups, such as Green political parties, Friends of the Earth, Greenpeace and the like, who for several years now have attempted to influence the direction taken by governments and by businesses in an effort to persuade them to protect the environment. Many of these groups began life as protest movements and the direct action of those like Greenpeace carry resonances of these origins. However, while direct action still occurs within groups dedicated to animal rights or 'deep green' groups dedicated against the development of new roads etc., many of the more established groups have become considerably more professional and scientific in their approach to the environment. In other words, they have modernized themselves. Students of democratic parties will recognize a parallel debate here as democratic organizations take on the clothes of their autocratic opponents to engage them on a more level playing field – what Michels referred to as 'the iron law of oligarchy': all democratic institutions become oligarchical over time. Or in this (olive)green version, 'the iron law of olivarchy': all anti-modernist protest organizations become modernist over time. So what often starts out as an emotional rebellion against the consequences of 'science' is ultimately forced to take on the clothes or camouflage of the scientists if they wish to be successful. To put it another way, if you want to persuade the government to stop building nuclear plants on your doorstep then mere protest is unlikely to be effective. However, if you can garner the resources to fund a research project undertaken by legitimate scientists which proves a link between such plants and cancer among the local population then you have a much better chance of success. The morale of the tale is clear, and it is one reason why so much effort is now spent by Green protest groups in monitoring pollution in as systematic and scientific way as their resources will allow: facts count.

Now the rub. Greenpeace's scientific assessment of the dangers over dumping the Brent Spar oil rig at sea was probably wrong – but it worked in so far as Shell changed its mind. A similar controversy is currently raging through Britain at the time of writing (April–August, 1996) and concerns bovine spongiform encephalopathy (BSE) or 'mad cow disease'. In the latter case the apparent absence of leadership and responsibility mirrors that which transfixed Exxon when the *Exxon Valdez* ran aground and no senior executive talked publicly for a whole week after the disaster. In contrast, when the Piper Alpha rig blew up, Occidental's head, Armand Hammer, flew straight to the scene of the disaster and minimized the damage to the company through his public appearances. Unless those responsible for similar environmental disasters take immediate actions that exceed expectations, and unless mistakes are admitted, it seems unlikely that the crisis will wither away quietly and much more likely that the media will ferret around for further damning evidence (Pedler, 1996).

In what follows I take three different sociological approaches to the issue of environmental pollution to demonstrate not just that sociology can add something of value to the debate on the environment but to reveal some of the differences that exist within sociology. At a very general level these three sociologies encompass: an action approach, in which the focus is upon the conscious action of individuals and groups in the construction of their world; its opposite and a structural approach, in which the structures in the environment or organization coerce individuals into certain forms of behaviour. Finally, the chapter introduces social constructivism, a third way of considering the issue of explaining pollution.

Social constructivist accounts sidestep the debate of the other two approaches and concentrate more upon the epistemological areas of knowledge construction and verification.

Structural approaches

Structural approaches tend to locate the causal explanation for events in the structure of the environment or organization or whatever phenomenon is believed to lie outside the individual. Structural accounts are usually relational, that is, it is the relationship between elements that generate the motivation to act. Thus my action is determined by my place in the social order and the direction of my organization is determined by its relationship to its environment. In the most extreme form of this kind of perspective the views, interpretations and motivations of actors are deemed irrelevant to the unravelling of events. Thus, phenomena external to the protesters cause the protest to occur; excessive road-building causes road protest in the same way that increased environmental pollution generates Green parties. This 'structural' response is the equivalent of seeing trade unions and labour parties as the response to the growth of the industrial working class originally in the nineteenth century. Since the working class has now been fragmented into a myriad of different forms, and since the problems of the working class have also altered radically, the consequence is the development of new problems 'out there' and a new response, as seen in Green parties which have only a very loose identification with social class (see Scott, 1992). This particular approach has a long and substantial history of support from Marx to Dahl but it does assume a direct connection between external reality and consequent mobilization by those affected by the reality.

The focus on external causation and away from the volitional acts of individuals also implies that the responsibility for error shifts from the individual mistake-maker, and the scientific resolver of the mistake, to the institutional facilitation and resolution of crises. A persuasive account of another disaster waiting to happen: the Challenger space shuttle which blew up in 1986 killing all seven crew, can also be developed through a structural account. Conventional accounts of the disaster focus on the faulty construction of the O-rings which sat between sections of the solid-propellant rocket booster and failed to prevent the escape of gas created by the ignition. Here, a technical mistake, presumably made by an individual, leads to a catastrophe as the importance of the launch took precedence over the potential safety problem. But a space shot like Apollo 11 involved over 5.6 million parts, so even a 99.9 per cent success rate leaves you 5600 defects. Hence the system itself is problematic, irrespective of the action of individuals. And when the opportunity for large profits is added into the mixture (NASA paid $120 for nuts and bolts that cost $3.28 in the local hardware store), you have a disaster waiting to happen.

Vaughan's (1996) account of the same disaster stresses instead the way the entire NASA culture operated to normalize such problems to the extent that the management ignored advice to the contrary. It was not, then, that a rule had been broken by a deviant individual but that the organizational culture redefined what counted as a rule that could be broken. It is this 'normalization of deviance', an issue concerned with the structure of the organization, therefore, that can explain how such catastrophes regularly occur.

The opposite may also occur. That is, the scientific establishment may close ranks to ostracize those who actively challenge the norm. We can see this historically in attacks upon Galileo or in contemporary developments over Denis Henshaw's research which suggests there may be a plausible link between overhead power lines and cancer through the concentration of radon and other potential carcinogens around the cables themselves. In this case Henshaw has been accused by the public relations officer of the National Radiological Protection Board, Matt Gaines, as 'setting up his case for more (research) funding' (quoted in the *Times Higher*, March 29). Whether there is a link or not is not the point here. What matters is the consequences for the institution of its culture. In Sweden the possibility of a link has led to cautious avoidance: they do not build very close to power cables. In Britain, because there is no scientific consensus on the 'truth', building continues under power cables. If house buyers' behaviour mirrors beef eaters behaviour then the absence of irrefutable evidence should lead to a fall in the value of houses built under or very close to power cables.

Another structural way of hunting the scapegoat is to consider the extent to which political muscle encourages forms of farming that are likely to do the most damage to the environment. For instance, under the current EU agricultural subsidies the highest subsidies are provided are often for those crops which require the most chemical additives; for instance, growing linseed (£520 per hectare). Now the bizarre issue here is that the EU also pays farmers not to produce anything at all. In the set aside scheme a farmer can claim £340 per hectare for not growing anything. Why, you might be wondering, does the EU pay farmers for not doing anything? In theory it is because European farmers currently overproduce and there is no market for the resulting produce. Under almost every other system an overproduction leads to a contraction and widespread unemployment and plant closure, but in farming we insist on paying farmers compensation for overproduction and it is the structure that generates the results, not the acts of individuals.

The same has occurred with BSE. If food factories produce contaminated produce they are closed down, period. But for farmers with contaminated cows an array of compensatory payments are being devised. Thus we have a system that encourages farmers to farm as intensely as possible, using the maximum amount of chemical agents, and which encourages them to adopt novel cost reduction strategies, like feeding sheep infected with scrapie to cows. If ever there was a case for going back to less intensive farming to protect nature it is this. But the main point here is to note how the system is held responsible for the problem: we cannot blame farmers for being rational, can we? In short, the generation of the problem lies within the structure of the system and so must its resolution.

Action approaches

An alternative approach is to shift from this 'structural' to an 'action' approach in which it is the action of an individual or group which brings about the focus on the issue and not vice versa. In the social class case it could be argued that people do not have objective social class positions which determine their political response but that people come to identify themselves with a particular social class as a consequence of taking certain actions. If I consider my identity to be determined by my work then perhaps I regard myself as first and foremost a member of the working class. But in this perspective the division between social classes is not 'out there' but in academic and government papers which try – and sometimes succeed – in imposing their pattern upon the population. But if I decide that my identity actually relates to my skin colour and/or gender and/or sexual orientation then the term social class may have no relevance to me. In the Green case this would be to suggest that people do not join Green parties because the environment is self-evidently being polluted and a green response is inevitable, but that they are persuaded that the environment is being polluted – and that something can be done about it as a consequence of the actions of the Green Party.

It is, in effect, not pollution 'out there' that coerces people but people's interpretation that allows pollution to be discovered and stopped. For example, dead fish in a stream do not persuade people that the stream is polluted because it may be that God or lightning has struck all the fish dead, or that all the fish are old or that there is no explanation and therefore nothing that can be done about it. But if we are persuaded that the site of a chemical factory near the stream is the cause of the pollution then we can interpret the evidence of dead fish in a different way. The data remain the same: the fish are dead, but the explanation changes and, as a result of the changing explanation, we may decide to act. The consequences of this shift are profound because it now seems that the more Green parties and research we have the more likely we are to discover an increasing level of pollution. This is the equivalent of flooding an urban area with police and discovering a massive increase in the crime rates over the last year when previously there were no police and no means of the population alerting the police as to alleged criminal acts.

For Green activists the problem has always seemed to be that many issues are regarded as single issues: once the problem is identified and action taken the population can relax and forget about the environment. But note how this suggestion reproduces the structural account – the outside reality causes the mobilization of the population. An action approach might suggest that environmental and other social problems are related. In short, the siting of the most polluting plants are in the poorest countries, and poorest areas of a country, is not coincidental but a manifestation of a link that exists between poverty and pollution. Hence, what appears to be a single issue – pollution – could conceivably be the foundation for a politically oriented group to mobilize the local population and to *create*, not simply wait for, the agent of social change (see Szasz, 1994, on this).

Action approaches, then, tend to reject the idea of external forces coercing individuals and focus instead upon the sense-making activities of actors. Under this form of explanation it is the interpretive actions of people that explain what is going on, and not any system that determines their action. Moreover, the action approach also recognizes the responsibility of actors for their own action. Thus individuals can no longer blame the system for the problem but have to bear the consequences of individual deviance, such as a Worcestershire farmer fined £10,000 for selling cattle in 1995 without revealing that the herd had been previously infected with BSE (*Guardian*, 16 April 1996).

Much of the debate concerning BSE hinges on boundary destruction, in particular the destruction of natural boundaries by deviant individuals. If we return to the discussion about nature we will see that there is a degree of naturalness and innocence attached to the state of nature before the arrival of humans. Thus it is only when humans begin to interfere with the naturalness of the world that things go wrong. In the mad cow case the boundaries that nature imposes upon its fauna suggest that some are vegetarians, some carnivores and some omnivores. When any of these categories cross the boundaries trouble ensues. Hence vegetarians are regularly assailed by omnivorous humans for their 'unnatural' behaviour. But the most sacred boundary is not where carnivores are forced to eat vegetables but when vegetarians are forced to eat meat. Enter the sheep-eating cow complete with certain damnation written across its forehead. So we do not need all the scientists to prove any links because the problem is a simple but dastardly transgression of a moral boundary by deviant individuals.

At one level this looks like a structural explanation: the structures that divide different categories of creature are intended to ensure the replication of all, and when these structures are breached then the problem occurs. On the other hand, we have to consider the extent to which the boundaries are 'out there' in the system itself or merely a consequence of our own interpretation. For example, are humans naturally omnivores? And if they are, does this make vegetarians unnatural? If cows eat animal by-products, is this morally wrong or biologically wrong? If we could prove the practice to be safe, and a survey of all cows resulted in no objections, would this make it all right? Why is it considered unnatural to eat dogs but acceptable to eat sheep?

It is also possible that persuasive scientific evidence about risk reduction can lead to an unintentional increase in risks where the actions of individuals interpret policies in ways contrary to those intended by the systems' designers. For example, Adams (1996) has suggested that the consequence of seat belt legislation, intended to reduce accidents, may well be the opposite. If we all drive Volvos that are built like tanks and are belted and air-bagged in a cocoon of safety we may well start driving more dangerously because we think we are safer. Of course, the opposite is true for pedestrians who may be regularly mown down by such 'safe' drivers as the 'risk compensation hypothesis' kicks into effect.

What happens if no knowledge exists of the external picture? What if we are not told about mad cows or ozone holes and the like? Do pressure groups form to defend interests when there is no information that their interests are being affected? Can individuals be held responsible for their action if they literally do not know what they are doing? Since the degree of veracity with which the various proclamations about mad cows seems to correlate as much with my choice of shirt as with anything else should we look elsewhere for another way of reflecting upon the problem of the environment? In the last section I turn to a contemporary form of sociological analysis, constructivism, to see whether this may shed new light on the topic.

A constructivist approach

One way of posing an alternative approach to the modernist stance on science and the environment is to engage with a particular variant of what has been called postmodernism. This is not the place for a review of postmodernism but in what follows I develop a brief overview of what has come to be known as social constructivism (see Burr, 1995), or at least a particular variant of this called post-essentialism.

This approach adopts a sceptical attitude towards knowledge of all forms in the assumption that we can never achieve an account of the world except through language. Since language is not a mirror of the world but a producer of it we are constantly faced with developing our ideas about the world through a permanently opaque fog of words. We can, in effect, never get to the world as it is but only to an appreciation of that world through language. For example, we cannot touch mad cow disease and know that it is mad cow disease. However, we can be persuaded by experts that a wobbly cow is indeed suffering from the disease or that the tissue under the microscope is an example of BSE – but these two cases require us to be persuaded, the facts do not speak for themselves. Naturally we can dispute what the expert is saying but since we do not have an equivalent level of expertise (otherwise we would not need the expert) we are really not in a position to generate legitimate alternative explanations of the phenomenon. In other words, the things which exist do not have an 'essence' that speaks to us directly, and therefore some human has to intervene and, through the medium of language, persuade us as to the 'truth' of the matter under consideration.

This approach may seem lost in the ivory towers of academia and to have no practical relevance to mad cows, but let me suggest that the opposite is the case. On the one hand modernist accounts, grounded in 'hard' science suggest that we can know the truth about pollution and quantify the risks. But the trouble seems to be that the population at large simply do not believe the truth, as deployed by the scientists. Perhaps, then, the issue of risk ought to be relocated away from the mathematicians and towards the context in which the risk occurs. Since the truth of BSE appears to have mutated almost as many times as the disease itself, on what criteria should people heed the advice of the scientists? We know politicians are economical with the truth but the whole of the modernist era has revolved around scientific truth. In the BSE case the original research into it concluded that beef offal should not be banned from human consumption because 'it was most unlikely BSE will have any implications on human health' and because, in the words of the chair of the committee (Richard Southwood) 'We felt it was a no-goer. MAFF already thought our proposals were pretty revolutionary' (quoted in Wynn, 1996). In effect, it would appear that the scientists' policy proposals were shaped by the political realities as they perceived them, at the same time as the political realities are shaped by the scientific truth.

This is not to say that all scientists believe the same thing. Far from it, Richard Lacey, a microbiologist, suggested in the House of Commons in 1990 that a generation of people might be killed if his worst fears were realized. A comment that stung Wiggin, the chair of the House select committee on agriculture to say that Lacey was 'losing touch completely with the real world' (quoted in Wynn, 1996). Yet it may have been Lacey's comment in the *Sunday Times*, recommending that people under 50 years old should not eat beef that inaugurated the scare. What marks Lacey out from many others on the 'other side' is his refusal to fall into the 'proof' trap. As he says: 'You can't prove that smoking causes lung cancer in an individual ... what you are talking about is epidemiological association' (quoted in Wynn, 1996). This is similar to the debate surrounding the British government's attempt to overturn the export ban on beef. For the British government, because 'a definitive stance on the transmissabiliy of BSE to humans is not possible', the ban should be lifted. For the European Court of Justice, because 'the risk of transmission cannot be excluded' the ban should stay (see Macrory and Hession, 1996) In other words, the dispute surrounds the significance of scientific proof: does no evidence for a link mean that there is no link?

Political 'realities' also impeded the development of research into BSE. As Anand and Forshner (1995) argue, the intervention of politicians into the debate in a normative role is seldom constructive (Gummer, the then British Minister of Agriculture fed his 4-year-old daughter a beefburger on television at the time that we now know was probably not a good idea). Without a scientific background politicians tend to leap into action to defend scientists (when the evidence suits them) and then find themselves in a rather awkward situation when the scientific evidence is inverted. Yet the inviolable role allotted to science also means that research monies into environmental issues tend to be distributed only to natural scientists and not to social scientists who might be able to offer alternative advice to that which has, in the BSE case, landed several government ministers in the veritable mad-cow muck. As Anand and Forshner conclude:

the residual impression is one of individual competence shackled to systems which were unhelpful to the maintenance of confidence in the beef and related industries. This food scare, like the 'salmonella-in-eggs' crisis, illustrates the fact that in the absence of complete information, negotiation, and to an extent persuasion, play a key role. (Anand and Forshner, 1995: 231)

The critical issue is that the government appears to insist that such environmental problems are wholly technical and can, therefore, be resolved by scientific experts. In this case Dorrell, then the British Health Minister, insisted that he could do nothing because he was merely reflecting what the scientists said. Yet we know that the BSE problem has little to do with the technical problem because, ironically, we know that we do not actually know much about BSE. That is the problem – it is an issue of risk management not science. We need to consider what makes institutions generate patterns of action that lead to or exacerbate problems not merely find the individual culprit or ask a scientist for the true picture and assume this will persuade a rightly suspicious population who, like mad cows, seem to have been fed something rather dubious. Since opinion surveys suggest that 66 per cent of the British public already mistrust government scientists there seems little point in genuflecting towards them as an act of scientific faith (Pedler, 1996). Indeed, contrary to Wildavsky's (1995) claim that ordinary citizens can acquire a sufficient degree of scientific knowledge to participate equally with scientists in environmental debates, the issue is that most people have neither the necessary knowledge, time nor interest to acquaint themselves with the appropriate level of expertise. Moreover, since even experts profoundly disagree with each other why should we assume that ordinary citizens will do otherwise? The consequence is that we are forced to adjudicate between accounts of such problems on the basis of trust not expertise; and trust is a long way from the truth.

This is an important point because in the absence of any information, or information that we can trust, how are we to know that a problem exists? In other words, it is only through the actions of the media in some form or another that information exists and a scare is created. One implication here is that control over information is crucial for those involved in data suppression or whistle blowing – no information – no pollution scare.

Environmental action and truth

If the evidence is so subjective, so relativist, does this have any profound implications for action in the environmental arena? Keller

(1988), Kling (1992) and Winner (1985, 1993), in very different arenas, suggest that since the approach involves rejection of the possibility of establishing the truth about technology or science or anything else[1] relativism appears to be the font of moral compromise. Kirkup and Smith Keller (1992: 10) put the point forcefully: 'epistemological relativism . . . suggests that there are as many truths as individual people and that no single truth has any claim to be better that any other . . . As a position it runs counter to the aims of science (which are) concerned to remedy distortion and move closer towards a more accurate description of how things are.

Two issues are worthy of comment here. First, the authors charge that the relativist denial of a single reflective and objective truth hides realities, in this case, that environmental pollution can remain hidden through relativist approaches. Ironically, constructivists are precisely concerned to support alternative truth claims rather than necessarily siding with prevailing ones. Constructivists can enrich the debate with their critical analyses of claims to truth without automatically supporting the claims of any particular environmental lobby to be in possession of the alternative but truly 'real' truth. Do all Greens or all ecofriendly businesses claim to support the same interpretation of pollution? If not, then, in line with this kind of essentialism, it would follow that some are in possession of the truth and others not. If, as has frequently happened, constructivists are accused of siding with the powerful in such disputes, then presumably they would be guilty of siding with the powerful against the weak, and so they would still be no nearer the truth.

The second issue hinges on the assertion that constructivism surrounds itself with contending claims to truth between which it has no means of discriminating. This is only a problem if it is possible to construct a position which is free of all social context and which we know to be true for now, for ever and everywhere (see Rorty, 1982). The constructivist does not assert that all claims have equal status; instead he or she asks which claims attract the most significant support and why (see Fish, 1980). Take the example of pollution. Kirkup and Smith Keller's essentialist view would be that ecologists, like scientists, are (and should be) intent on uncovering the truth about pollution, a truth allegedly hidden from view by scientific distortion. This approach implies that research can discover the truth and that this discovery will lead, eventually at least, to mechanisms which prevent it. By denying objective truth, relativism is said to allow its adherents either to sit on the fence and procrastinate about truth claims while pollution continues to increase. The latter charge is simply wrong: assessing the strength of a truth claim through an analysis of its social construction is not equivalent to supporting that claim.

The former charge is more complex. Constructivism does leave one bereft of the certainties that might propel a Green fanatic or religious fundamentalist; for these people the truth is self-evident and the line of action follows directly from such truth. For the constructivist there may, of course, be a pragmatic legitimation of action – doubts about truth claims are fine for the university seminar but too dangerous for the real world. Does this mean there is a clear limit to the application of Kant's injunction *sapere aude* (dare to know)? Acquiescence to the politics of the real world implies not just a pragmatic boundary but an epistemological, and ultimately political, flaw.

Constructivist approaches to the environment have certainly attracted a considerable amount of hostility from social scientists of one form or another who perceive themselves to be defenders of the weak, and often defenders of the truth too, while constructivists have 'retreated into a blasé, depoliticized scholasticism' (Winner, 1993: 29). This disinterested scepticism, it is claimed, merely leaves the field open to those who are already powerful – and by definition these people appear to have problematic morals. On the other hand, the constructivist approach does, through its scepticism of truth claims, suggest that traditional accounts can be subjected to vigorous critique on epistemological grounds, rather than moral grounds; grounds that realists and traditionalists may find harder to reject.

For example, powerful industrial corporations may be charged, by radical environmental scientists (supported by realist social scientists), with polluting the atmosphere; for the realist the scepticism of the constructivist necessarily inhibits taking sides in the debate, and as a result the corporate polluters continue to pollute. Aside from the dubious assumption that the revelation of objective truth by committed social scientists is going to sway private corporate interests, the problem for realists is that the corporation is just as likely to generate alternative accounts of 'the truth' which demonstrate that the corporation is not a polluter. Where such truth prevails the realist has no option but to accept that, indeed, the corporation is innocent of the charge. But for the constructivist the issue is not which side is telling the truth – and should therefore be allowed to prevail – but why one side manages to persuade the actors who are involved in decision-making processes that their version of the truth is the only one, and why such debates have a tendency to dissolve into dualisms: truth and lies; right and wrong; good and bad. The realist concern for *the* truth invokes its opposite for all other accounts: if there is just one truth then everything else must be false. But to remain sceptical of truth claims does not imply that all such claims are truly false; rather that all such claims are subject to sceptical inquiry. This permanent question mark over the truth, then, leaves the constructivist free to maintain a scepticism whatever the evidence deployed. Hence, when a public enquiry, hearing evidence from experts, proves that pumping waste into the ocean is actually safe the sceptical constructivist is much harder to enrol into the corporation's camp than the environmental realist.

Radder, for example, argues that the upshot of a constructivist approach can lead to some clearly absurd results: if the discourse about the ozone hole ceased than 'the hole would simply disappear at the very moment we stopped discoursing about it' (Radder, 1992: 156). It is not clear in what sense this can be a valid critique of constructivism. The point might be that our knowledge of the hole constitutes the hole, and that in the absence of any knowledge about it we have no way of knowing whether it exists or not. This is not the same as saying: 'the truth is that there is no hole'. Nor is it the equivalent of saying: 'if we all stop discoursing about it the hole will disappear'; this implies that all knowledge of the hole can be erased from human memory and from its physical inscription. If this was to be the case, thanks to some fiendish alien plot to destroy the earth's atmosphere, then Radder's claim would be: 'although we have absolutely no knowledge of anything going on up there (the term 'ozone hole' would have been erased too presumably) we know there is truly a hole'. How, one is tempted to ask, can we know this to be true? It is not a question of saying it is *not* true but of asking how we know that it *is* true.

Conclusion

In this chapter I have sought to demonstrate that the relationship between the environment and humans is not something that can be taken for granted nor left to the (scientific) experts. Nature is simply too important to be left to the scientists. Using a variety of issues three different sociological perspectives have been brought to bear on the problem to suggest that the difficulties faced by those charged with protecting the environment are not simply reducible to securing a better purchase on 'reality'. Different theoretical approaches embody different epistemological frameworks and a reversion to the 'iron law of oligarchy' can only provide for a limited advance in our knowledge of the environment. Whether business is attempting to deploy an environmentally friendly strategy or Green activists are trying to inhibit the intentions of business, the problem of what *should* be done is essentially located in how we *know* what should be done. This is not to suggest that the ambiguities of knowledge impel us to take *no* action at all but to suggest that companies and individuals consider carefully the lessons of the epistemological quagmire and note how an over-reliance on the truth of scientific knowledge can itself lead to a series of actions that look remarkably like the actions of a mad cow. Or as one realist mad cow said to another: 'I can't catch BSE because I'm a sheep.'[2]

Notes

1   This section draws on a joint work with Steve Woolgar (1995). On some failures of nerve in constructivist and feminist analyses of technology. *Science, Technology and Human Values*, **20**(2).
2   On 24 July 1996 the British government announced a ban on the consumption of sheep's and goats' brain, spinal cord and spleen after scientific evidence suggested that what had previously been impossible, according to scientific research, was now possible: sheep could contract the disease from cattle.

References:

Adams, J. (1996). *Risk*. University College Press.
Anand, P. and Forshner, C. (1995). Of mad cows and marmosets: from rational choice to organizational behaviour in crisis management. *British Journal of Management*, **6**, 221–33.
Beck, U. (1992). *Risk Society*. Sage.
Burr, V. (1995). *An Introduction to Social Constructionism*. Routledge.
Chatterjee, P. and Finger, M. (1994). *The Earth Brokers: Power, Politics and World Development*. Routledge.
Crosby, A. W. (1986). *Ecological Imperialism: The Biological Expansion of Europe 900–1900*. Cambridge University Press.
Easterbrook, G. (1996). *A Moment on the Earth*. Penguin.
Fiddes, N. (1991). *Meat: A Natural Symbol*. Routledge.
Fish, S, (1980). *Is There a Text in this Class?* Johns Hopkins University Press.
Hajer, M. A. (1996). *The Politics of Environmental Discourse: Ecological Modernisation and the Policy Process*. Oxford University Press.
Hall, S. (1992). The west and the rest: discourse and power. In *Formations of Modernity* (S. Hall and B. Gieben, eds) Polity Press.
Hobbes, T. (1968). *Leviathan*. Penguin.
Keller, E. F. (1988). *Feminist Perspectives on Gender and Science*. Falmer Press.
Kirkup, G. and Smith-Keller, L. (1992) The nature of science and technology. In *Inventing Women* (G. Kirkup and L. Smith-Keller, eds) Polity Press.

Kling, R. (1992). Audiences, narratives and human values in Social Studies of Technology. *Science, Technology and Human Value*, **17**, 349–65.

Lovelock, J. (1987). *Gaia*. Oxford University Press.

McKibben, B. (1990). *The End of Nature*. Penguin.

MacNaughten, P. and Urry, J. (1995). Towards a sociology of nature. *Sociology*, **29**(2), 203–20.

Macrory, R. and Hession, M. (1996). High noon for mad cows. *Guardian*, 11 June, p. 4.

Michels, R. (1949) *Political Parties*. Free Press.

More, T. (1965 edn). *Utopia*. Penguin.

Nash, R. (1983). *Wilderness and the American Mind*. Yale University Press.

Pedler, R. (1996). Like cows to the slaughter. *The Times*, 18 April.

Prance, G. (1996). Mother nature: the classified story. *Times Higher*, 19 April.

Pyre, S. (1982). *Fire in America: A History of Wildland and Rural Fire*. Princeton University Press.

Radder, H. (1992). Normative Reflexion in Constructive Approaches to Science and Technology. *Social Studies of Science and Technology*, **22**, 141–73.

Rorty, R. (1982). *The Consequences of Pragmatism*. Harvester Wheatsheaf.

Rousseau, J. J. (1968). *The Social Contract*. Penguin.

Scott, A. (1992). Political culture and social movements. In *Political and Economic Forms of Modernity* (J. Allen, P. Braham and P. Lewis, eds) Polity Press.

Smith, A. (1974), *The Wealth of Nations*. Penguin.

Szasz, A. (1994). *Ecopopulism: Toxic Waste and the Movement for Environmental Justice*. University of Minneapolis Press.

Vaughan, D. (1996). *The Challenger Launch Decision: Risky Technology, Culture and Deviance at NASA*. Chicago University Press.

Vidal, J. (1996). Be very afraid. *Guardian*, 29 May.

Wildavsky, A. (1995). *But is it True?; A Citizen's Guide to Environmental Health and Safety Issues*. Harvard University Press.

Williams, R. (1972). Ideas of nature. In *Ecology, the Shaping of Enquiry* (J. Rendell, ed.) Longman.

Winner, L. (1985). Do Artefacts have Politics? in *The Social Sharing of Technology* (D. MacKenzie and J. Wajcman, eds) Open University Press.

Wynn, B. (1996). Patronising Joe Public. *Times Higher*. 12 April, p. 16.

Yearley, S. (1992). Environmental challenges. In *Modernity and its Futures* (S. Hall, D. Held and T. Mcgrew, eds), Polity Press.

Yearley, S. (1996). *Sociology, Environmentalism, Globalization: Reinventing the Globe*. Sage.

5 Corporate behaviour and sustainable development: the view from economics

David Pearce

Introduction: environment and the theory of organizations

An extensive literature exists on business and the environment, but most of it is devoid of a convincing model to explain business attitudes to the environment. In this chapter we investigate the economic foundations of the business–environment link. The basic aim is to explain why it is in the interests of firms to invest in environmental assets and how the costs of those investments can be minimized, and to show how corporate accounting procedures can be revised to reflect those environmental investments, as well as the environmental damage for which any firm is responsible.

The basic model is one of benefit-cost analysis. The argument is that firms will invest in environmental assets, such as clean air, clean water, amenity and nature protection, if the benefits to them of so doing exceed the costs. It is important to understand that this idea of maximizing *net* benefits need not be equivalent to maximizing the profits of the firm. Profit maximization is the standard assumption of many economics textbooks, but modern industrial organization theory stresses that firms may have not just different goals to profit maximization but a number of different (and sometimes conflicting) goals at the same time (Milgrom and Roberts, 1992). Firms may therefore seek to maximize or achieve various goals, and managers may have quite distinct views about those goals. For example, it may be that, regardless of the legal ownership of the firm, the interests of employees are ranked higher than those of shareholders. If so, maximizing net benefits may well involve giving precedence to benefits as seen from the standpoint of the employee. What it is that constitutes the goal of the firm is relevant because it defines what counts as a benefit (or a cost). As we shall see, this affects the firm's behaviour towards the environment.

While it is possible that firms will deliberately seek to achieve their goals, whatever they are, with higher resource costs than necessary, a reasonable corollary of the maximizing hypothesis is that they seek to minimize those costs. Resource costs here include labour, capital, raw materials, land, etc. The rationale for minimizing these costs is that the resulting surplus of revenues over costs per unit of output is available for distribution to meet the various goals of the firm, i.e. cost minimization becomes one of the mechanisms for achieving the goals. Note that minimizing costs is not the same as maximizing profits: a firm may decide on some profit level (to keep shareholders happy) which is not the maximum feasible profit level. It will still seek to minimize the costs of achieving that profit level.

We therefore begin with a theory of the firm that stresses the potential multiplicity of goals of the firm, and cost minimization. It is into this that we need to fit the environment. The final building block is the idea that what firms maximize need not coincide with what is 'best' for society as a whole. If firms did maximize net *social* benefits, then there would be little rationale for regulation. Some advocates of deregulation would indeed argue that firms come at least close to maximizing net social benefits in the sense that the costs to them of achieving some social goal, such as a further improvement in environmental quality, exceed the benefits to society as a whole. For the USA, Hahn (1996) suggests that in only twenty-one out of sixty-one cases of environmental regulation promulgated by the US Environmental Protection Agency between 1990 and 1995 did social benefits exceed costs. Pearce (1995) suggests that, within the European Union, several major Directives on bathing water and drinking water quality would not pass a social benefit-cost test. But there is no study for the European context similar to that of Hahn for the USA. Other studies do tend to suggest that there are still areas of environmental degradation where substantial damages are being incurred (Pearce and Crowards, 1996). The essential role of environmental regulation, then, is to close any gap between the degree of environmental control exercised by firms and the degree that would be warranted by social benefit-cost analysis.

The formal benefit-cost model

Figure 5.1 sets out the basic model. The diagram shows two curves, marginal control costs (MCC) and marginal benefits (MB). The control cost curve relates to the cost of controlling pollution through, say, the use of abatement equipment or through output losses. The term 'marginal' here simply means 'extra', so that rather than showing the total costs of pollution control the curve

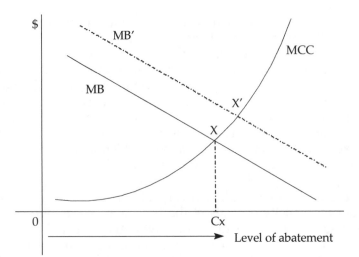

Figure 5.1 Formal benefit-cost model

shows the extra costs of control for an increment in the level of control (marginal curves are simply the first derivatives of total curves). The MCC curve slopes upwards the more abatement there is, i.e. the assumption is that the cost of preventing more and more pollution rises with the amount of pollution controlled. This fits the available evidence: for example, tertiary effluent control is markedly more expensive than secondary and primary control. Marginal benefit (MB) shows the extra benefit *to the firm* secured by implementing environmental controls. This curve slopes downwards the more control is undertaken to reflect the likely fact that the firm will place lower values on further increments of environmental improvement the cleaner the environment is. But this downward slope is not crucial to the argument: MB could, for example, be horizontal. For the moment, the second MB curve, MB′ can be ignored.

In the absence of regulation, how much investment in environmental improvement will the firm undertake? In Figure 5.1 the answer is given by point X where MB and MCC intersect. This is because to the right of X, the costs of further abatement exceed the benefits to the firm. To the left of X, benefits of further controls exceed costs. Point Cx is then the 'optimal' level of abatement from the firm's standpoint. Note that benefits are assumed to be expressed in monetary terms, which is a convenient device for diagrammatic presentation but not essential for the analysis. Note also that nothing is said about the ultimate beneficiaries: the MB curve may be reflecting benefits to shareholders, managers, employees or other stakeholders. All that is necessary is that the decision-makers within the firm reflect these concerns in their decision-making.

Armed with Figure 5.1 we can now investigate the make-up of the benefit curve.

Motivations for investing in the environment

The different goals of the firm reflect the different stakeholders in the outcome of the firm's decisions. Shareholders will primarily be concerned with profits, but some shareholders may be members of ethical investment trusts in which case a 'green image' or health and safety record may be more important than profits. Employees will also have an interest in profits because of job security, but may be just as influenced by green image or ethical stance because of the status effects of working for firms with good or bad images. Certain pressure groups may also be stakeholders in that failure to meet some of their concerns could damage longer-term demand prospects. Management is likely to be concerned with profits for job security reasons, and because of profit-sharing and bonuses, but they may also have some commitment to ethical image and doing 'what is right'. However, whatever the management objectives we have suggested above that cost minimization will be pursued. As such, management should be concerned to invest in some environmental activities which result in cost savings. This motivation will apply even without profit maximization but it is obvious that the profit maximization motive would substantially reinforce the idea of cost minimization.

How does the existence of these various motives affect the analysis in Figure 5.1? Motivations can be analysed in various ways but in what follows we produce a classification which develops that originally advanced in Pearce (1991):

1 *Cost minimization through efficiency.* Certain environmental investments will reduce unit costs, although it cannot be assumed that cost reductions continue regardless of the level of the investment. Examples include energy conservation, materials recycling, economies in the management of transport fleets, and waste minimization (i.e. the reduction of waste at source by, for example, simply using less packaging material).

2 *Stakeholder interests: pressure groups.* Costs may be reduced by avoidance of costly encounters with pressure groups such as environmental groups. The philosophy of 'engage, not enrage' can, if there is an element of truth in the pressure group's

arguments, be less expensive than confrontation, although it also seems fair to say that a number of corporations have all too willingly listened to, and accommodated, pressure group arguments. Striking a balance of judgement is difficult, but essential.

3 *Stakeholder interests: employees.* It is well known that employees have strong views on the status of the firm for which they work, and those views may not always be consistent with profit maximization. Notable among such employee concerns is the environmental profile of the company. Equally, management has a strong interest in meeting employee concerns for both profit and non-profit reasons: avoiding costly work disruption episodes, maintaining longer-term continuity of staff, especially skilled staff, avoiding the transactions costs of labour turnover (searching for, selecting and monitoring new staff), avoidance of a bad external image. Thus a complex of motives produces a positive attitude to environmental investments.

4 *The green consumer.* Just as employees may be 'green', so consumers may demand that products be 'environmentally friendly' (a misnomer for any product other than one designed specifically to enhance environmental quality or save resources). The green consumer phenomenon is well documented and meeting the interests of green consumers is consistent both with profit maximization and with 'customer loyalty', i.e. the retention of an established customer base, something that is not necessarily synonymous with profit maximization (Arora and Gangopadhyay, 1995; Ulph, 1995).

In terms of Figure 5.1, all environmentally induced cost-cutting measures, the market gains from retention of green consumers, avoidance of confrontation costs, and the stability and image benefits from meeting the concerns of employees, are all components of the MB curve. Put another way, the MB curve comes about because of these motivations. Any increase in the strength of these concerns would show up as a shift in the MB curve from MB to MB'. Note that if this does happen, more environmental investment is justified up to the point X'. We shall refer to X and X' as *voluntary optima*, because they are the levels of abatement that would come about in a purely voluntary system without regulation.

The cost reduction motive is well established (Cairncross, 1991, 1995). Some companies have 'formalized' the cost-cutting role of environmental investment in acronyms: 3M's 'pollution prevention pays' (PPP); Chevron's 'save money and reduce toxics' (SMART); Texaco's 'wipe out waste' (WOW). 3M's programme is supposed to have saved the company $500 million since 1975. The most pertinent question is why companies had to wait for an 'environmental revolution' to appreciate that unit costs could be reduced by paying attention to raw materials, energy, transport and waste disposal. One answer is likely to be that these items tend not to be major portions of cost in most industries, compared, say, to labour costs. As such, they may have been neglected until the rise of environmentalism forced attention on to these cost items. Another likely explanation is simply lack of managerial expertise in the management and control of materials and energy. This is often reflected in the fact that company accounts often do not enable anyone to determine just how much was spent on energy, raw materials, transport and waste management. Given the scale of some of the cost savings, however, there must be some doubts as to whether businessmen can always be regarded as being good cost-minimizers.

The 'green image' advantages of investing in the environment have perhaps been exaggerated. It relies on the phenomenon of 'green consumerism' and this has been shown to have some stable and sustained elements and some highly volatile elements. Cairncross is of the view that: 'green consumerism will never be the main driving force behind corporate environmentalism. For one thing, it simply does not penetrate far enough' (Cairncross, 1995: 183).

None the less, there are some important niche markets for environmentally sound products and production methods. The growth of eco-labelling for internationally traded products could be important here. The example of timber is relevant. Some developed economy companies have introduced schemes to ensure the import of sustainably managed timber only. Again, the coverage of such schemes is not likely to be very large since they again rely on the persistence of green consumerism. Some bad experiences with the use of environmental image as a market share tactic may also limit its extent. Probably the most important fact here is the wide variation in the results of life cycle analysis (LCA) of individual products, i.e. differing results as far as the environmental impact of products from cradle to grave. Apart from the technical difficulty of many LCAs, which makes them less than transparent to the uninitiated, one result has been confusion in the mind of the consumer who does not know which expert to believe.

A number of surveys of industrial workers show that employees may be a potent force for ensuring that industries take on environmental commitments. In the OECD countries this phenomenon may arise because the environmentalists of the 1970s are now the middle and upper management of industry, instilling an environmental ethos into management generally. But even if junior and senior management are separated in their concern for the environment, senior management can ill afford to alienate more junior staff even in contexts of unemployment and recession. Again, this phenomenon is currently confined to Organization for Economic Co-operation and Development (OECD) countries but given the rapid economic growth rates of companies in other regions, notably the Asia-Pacific region, it is a phenomenon that is likely to occur as the growing body of environmental NGOs becomes institutionalized in these countries.

Commitment occurs when self-interest cannot explain the decision to invest in environmental goods or assets. Commitment reflects a concern for the environment, a concern that may actually be inconsistent with the cost-minimizing or profit-maximizing goals of the firm. How far commitment explains environmental activity by corporations is open to doubt. As Cairncross puts it: 'Companies are not individuals, with a moral obligation to be good environmental citizens, even in situations where that is not in their commercial interest. They are owned by shareholders; and their overriding duty is to do what is in the long-term commercial interest of their owners' (Cairncross, 1995: 188). Business motives are not likely to vary much by world region, despite massive cultural differences. It would be expecting too much, therefore, to suppose that commitment will drive sustainable development, at least in the near future. That does not make it unimportant, but it does suggest a sense of perspective.

The analysis so far has neglected regulation, i.e. the voluntary equilibria X and X' in Figure 5.1 have been determined by environmental investment that meets the non-regulatory goals of the firm. Figure 5.2 introduces regulation into the picture. Regulators may, in principle, set regulations which produce a level of environmental investment below or above that which is brought about by the unregulated goal-maximizing behaviour of the firm. A regulation set below the voluntary equilibrium is shown in Figure 5.2 as C_{r1}, and a regulation set above the voluntary equilibrium is shown as C_{r2}. At first sight a regulation such as C_{r1} seems counter-intuitive: regulation presumably exists only because firms do not secure the *socially* desirable level of environmental control activity. But in principle there is no binding reason why the regulatory solution should improve on what firms do for themselves. Several factors explain why. First, as we have seen, firms have quite powerful incentives to adopt environmental controls based on various stakeholder interests. Second, what firms do for themselves may be a 'counterfactual', i.e. the regulation occurs first and what firms would have done if left alone is never known because regulators are not in possession of that information. Third, of course, regulators may simply under-regulate. A firm that adopts levels of envir-

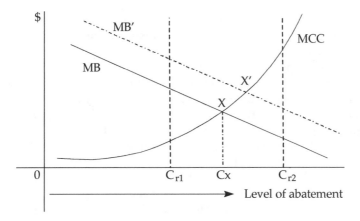

Figure 5.2 Formal benefit-cost model to meet regulatory goals

onmental expenditure above those required to meet a regulation is said to *over-comply*.

A firm with a voluntary optimum less than the regulation is, of course, *under-complying* and that situation would not prevail for long in a regulatory regime where there is adequate monitoring and enforcement of environmental law. The explanation for under-compliance would simply be one of profit maximization: the firm judges that the expected value of a fine for non-compliance (the probability of being found out multiplied by the money value of the fine) is less than the cost of installing control measures to meet the standard. As argued above, however, non-compliance can be very expensive where the prevailing industrial culture is one of trading off stakeholder interests. This explains why environmental awareness programmes and education campaigns are important: they effectively make it more expensive for polluters not to comply with regulations, as well as providing further driving forces for high levels of voluntary environmental expenditures. Over-compliance is explained by the driving forces for voluntary expenditures. Some illustrations are provided in the next section.

The phenomenon of over-compliance

The basic reason that firms may over-comply is that the levels of expenditure necessary to meet their voluntary goals exceed those implied by the regulatory standard. There are two contexts for over-compliance: where over-compliance results in lost profits for the firm and where this does not occur. The basic difference between these cases turns on the potential to extract a 'green premium' in market prices. It is well known that consumers are willing to pay a premium on prevailing market prices if they can secure assurance that the product is environmentally friendly. If so, firms may charge this premium and adopt cleaner technologies and/or cleaner products than required by a regulation, the revenues from the premium sales offsetting (and perhaps more than offsetting) the costs of the higher environmental standards. The situation in which profits are lost because of over-compliance is more complex. Here, management may be looking to 'green image' to secure a longer-term profit at the expense of short-term profits; or they may be anticipating future regulation which they feel they can avoid by 'putting their own house in order' now; or there may be a situation of genuine 'commitment', i.e. management may actually have as one of its goals the improvement of the environment.

Detecting commitment is extremely difficult, so much so that some commentators doubt its existence at all. It requires that voluntary equilibria exceed the regulatory standard, and that the over-compliance be for reasons other than profit maximization. The former is comparatively easy to measure. The latter is extremely difficult. The extent to which firms over-comply in order to avoid the threat of future regulation is also complex. Delayed expenditures will be less costly due to the effects of interest rates, i.e. the 'discounted' value of the expenditure is less the further it occurs in the future. On this basis one would expect 'anticipatory compliance' to be minimal (Baumol and Oates, 1988). But there are good reasons for supposing that anticipatory compliance is a fairly strong phenomenon. The regulatory process is one in which the regulator and the regulated interact. 'Regulatory capture', whereby firms actually influence the nature and extent of regulation is extensive. Hence firms can quite legitimately expect to influence future legislation by over-compliance now. A European example would be the industrial lobby against the introduction of environmental liability laws in the European Union. It is well known that industry considers the introduction of such legislation (already present in the USA) to be extremely expensive and it is perhaps not a matter of chance that voluntary environmental agreements have begun to proliferate in Europe at this time. Yet another reason for over-compliance arises from the lumpiness of pollution control investments, particularly where 'best available technology' (BAT) is the basis of the regulation. BAT may well produce reductions in emissions and effluent over and above regulatory requirements. Other motives for over-compliance have been suggested. One that assumes a high degree of sophistication and risk-taking on the part of industry is that over-compliance is designed to force regulators to raise regulatory standards which in turn raises barriers to entry for new firms (Barrett, 1991; Salop and Scheffman, 1983). A variation on this theme – the Porter hypothesis – is considered later.

The discussion so far suggests that over-compliance will have its foundations in:

1   anticipatory compliance, i.e. attempting to 'capture' the regulatory process so as to avoid future regulations;
2   entry forestalling behaviour;
3   indivisibilities in pollution abatement technology, especially BAT;
4   a pure commitment motive.

Voluntary agreements and over-compliance

Over-compliance has been detected in the USA where voluntary environmental agreements are a growing force in overall environmental regulation. A voluntary agreement is simply an agreement between the regulator and the firm to meet a given environmental objective, but without that objective being enforceable by the regulator. Of course, in terms of Figures 5.1 and 5.2 over-compliance can exist even without any form of agreement with the regulator, but the motivations to over-comply with the law are almost certainly the same whether a voluntary agreement exists or not. The United States Environmental Protection Agency (EPA) runs a number of voluntary environmental agreements such as the 33/5 Program (on toxic chemicals) and the Green Lights Program (on energy efficient lighting). The US government also relies on voluntary agreements to meet the US year 2000 greenhouse gas target under the Framework Convention on Climate Change. There is also strong interest in Europe in voluntary agreements. In the UK they go under the name of producer responsibility obligations (PROs) but motivations appear to vary for firms to enter such agreements, and the success of the agreements also seems to vary significantly between industries and between countries.

Arora and Cason (1995a, 1995b) analyse the US EPA's 33/50 Program which was aimed at reducing emissions of seventeen highly toxic chemicals between 1988 and 1995. The Program is voluntary and some of the motives for participation fit the cost-minimizing hypothesis above, since some of the chemicals can be replaced by substitutes which have a lower cost. In other cases the chemicals would have been reduced anyway to comply with the Montreal Protocol on ozone (layer) depleting substances. Arora and Cason (1995b) test the proposition that firms' participation in the

Program is due to longer-term expected profit increases, even though short-term profits may suffer (see above). Factors thought likely to determine participation were

1   closeness to consumers: the closer the industry to the consumer the more public recognition and 'green image' it gets;
2   levels of research and development expenditures which make it easier to afford over-compliance;
3   the degree of concentration in the industry: the more concentrated the more firms are able to pass on over-compliance costs to consumers;
4   the opposite of 3 above, that low concentration firms need to differentiate their products by establishing a green competitive edge;
5   that participating firms would have made the reductions anyway;
6   that firms with poor compliance records will join the Program to mask their failure to comply otherwise;
7   that firms with good compliance records will join the Program so as not to sully their compliance record;
8   that those who participate in one voluntary agreement are more likely to join another such agreement.

Econometric analysis of participation in the Program served to refute hypotheses 5 and 6, whilst hypothesis 1 receives most support. Over-compliance, then, would appear to be due to the market loyalty and market size arguments linked to the existence of green consumers.

In Europe, voluntary agreements are also known as producer responsibility agreements. There is less evidence that these agreements involve over-compliance. Indeed, the origin of PROs in several countries is one of legislative threat: either the industry enters a voluntary agreement or there will be regulation. In this sense, many European voluntary agreements fit the model of anticipatory compliance above, i.e. a preference for self-regulation over regulation by diktat. In Germany, the Packaging Ordnance, for example, enables the packaging industry to set up its own recycling and recovery schemes to meet national targets, but failure to do so carries the explicit threat of the enforcement of legislation which would force the targets to be met by other means.

Similarly, in the United Kingdom PROs have made the most advance in the packaging waste sector, but the obligations in question assume a legal status, so that the voluntariness of the agreement lies more in the process of setting up the environmental objectives than in carrying them out, although a good deal of self-reporting is involved in the latter. In the UK, PROs are legally enabled under the Environment Act 1995. Draft regulations were formulated in 1996 to achieve recycling of specific tonnages of packaging waste. The PRO applies to packaging raw material manufacturers, those who convert the raw material to actual packaging (the convertors), those who pack or fill packages with produce, and those who sell the packaged product. Firms within this 'packaging chain' may then meet the targets themselves, or join a 'compliance scheme' which would take over the responsibility to meet the targets. Whichever is chosen, firms must be registered with the UK Department of the Environment either themselves or via the compliance scheme. The major compliance scheme is known as VALPAK, and consists of a consortium of firms within the packaging chain. Individual targets have been set for raw material manufacturers, convertors, packers/fillers, sellers and importers of transit packaging. Along this chain, obligations to recover range from 6 per cent (raw materials) to 47 per cent (sellers) and 100 per cent for transit packaging importers. The targets are then legal obligations: the issue of over-compliance can only arise in this case if individual firms choose to go beyond the obligations. While the obligations are legal, procedures for monitoring them and securing accreditation are largely voluntary. Other PROs in the United Kingdom relate to tyres, vehicles, batteries, electronic goods and newspaper but, interestingly: these have developed without the legal obligations built into the packaging agreement. The reason for this is that the packaging industry felt it could not self-regulate without there being 'free riders', individual firms and even industries that would take little action, leaving the obligation to be met by others. A legal requirement was necessary to ensure that the industry would set up the necessary schemes (UK Department of the Environment, 1996). The Europe-wide legislative context for packaging is also more well defined, there being a Packaging Waste Directive which sets targets for recovery and recycling of packaging waste throughout the European Union.

The Porter hypothesis

One of the arguments explaining over-compliance was based on the idea that it would encourage regulators to set even higher environmental standards which in turn would act as a deterrent to new entrants to the regulated industry. This is an anti-competitive motive for over-compliance: limits on entry act as a protective barrier which keeps profits high. Much the same argument has been advanced in the context of international trade. High environmental standards in one country can be used to discriminate against imports which fail to meet those standards. If this is correct, we should expect to find industry being in favour of tougher environmental standards, rather than opposing them on the grounds that they raise costs and impair competitiveness. This view has achieved some prominence because of the work of Michael Porter (1990, 1991), although Porter's argument rests on very different grounds to the protectionist view. The Porter hypothesis says that firms can secure a competitive advantage by embracing higher environmental standards which have the effect of inducing cost reductions and innovation. The 'win win' nature of the hypothesis is obviously attractive: it implies that industry can expand, economic growth can be stimulated, and the environment can be conserved all through one mechanism.

But not just any form of environmental regulation will bring about the gains to competitiveness. Porter is a little vague about what the right forms of regulation are. They appear not to embrace command-and-control measures such as standard-setting based on best available technology, but they do embrace market-based instruments such as environmental taxes and tradable pollution permits. They involve pollution prevention but not clean-up schemes. As Oates, Palmer and Portney (1994) note, this last distinction is curious since clean-up is 'big business' in the USA and will become so as liability laws extend through Europe and elsewhere, i.e. there are competitive gains to be had from the growth of this market (see later on for the size of the compliance market).

Even with these restrictions on the right kind of regulation, the Porter hypothesis is not wholly persuasive. First, the prevailing forms of regulation, even in the USA, still favour command-and-control type regulations, although major advances have been made in the introduction of tradable pollution permit schemes for sulphur dioxide controls in recent years. Hence the hypothesis would only have validity in terms of current practice if industry was successful in persuading regulators to adopt more market-based approaches and less command and control. The relevance of market-based approaches to the Porter hypothesis arises because cleaner technology avoids the tax or cost of a pollution permit, so that adopting cleaner technology has a cost which may be offset by the reduction in tax or permit cost.

Second, meeting tougher regulations assumes that the abatement technology to achieve those new standards is feasible. If so, then firms must be able either to buy that cleaner technology 'off the shelf' or to invest in research and development to secure the new technology. Either way, if they choose not to pursue the new technology it must be because they see higher profits (or any other maximand) staying where they are. If they choose to pursue the new technology it must be because they see higher profits in so doing. In the latter case, it is unclear why they require regulators to legislate to achieve the new cleaner technology. The obvious exception to this conclusion would be if firms were unaware of the potential gain in profits from adopting the cleaner technology, and that the tougher regulations make them realize this potential is there. While this potential for 'surprise' seems inconsistent with the assumption of the rational, objective-maximizing firm, the business and environment literature is replete with examples of firms that secured cost-reductions by environmental action on energy consumption and waste management. If these examples are credible, it must mean that firms have not been cost-minimizing in the past: they have costs above what they could be. This situation is in fact quite realistic and is known as 'X inefficiency' (Leibenstein, 1966). There do appear to be unexploited cost-saving measures that firms can adopt. Conventional explanations stress problems of communication with the firm and lack of expertise in, say, energy efficiency as explanations for X inefficiency. We return to one source of this information problem later, namely environmental accounting.

Third, the Porter hypothesis requires that tougher regulation is the means whereby the cost savings and innovations are secured. This suggests a somewhat odd strategy on the part of firms, for it argues that firms encourage the tougher regulations to secure cost reductions. But this in turn implies that they know the cost reductions are available, in which case why engage in the risky strategy of effectively inviting tougher regulations to achieve something that could be achieved anyway? It seems more likely that Porter sees the regulatory process as being independent of firms' behaviour, i.e. regulators regulate and firms respond, only to find that the tougher regulations are to their advantage.

Finally, is there any empirical evidence to support the Porter hypothesis? His own evidence is fairly casual but in accord with the perceptions of many: Germany and Japan have strict environmental regulations and are competitively very successful. But while this is a popular perception, it also has limited validity since Germany and Japan spend less of their GNP on environmental expenditure than the USA (Oates, Palmer and Portney, 1994), although there has to be some question about the efficiency of these expenditures. Nor are market-based instruments any more prominent in Japan and Germany than they are in the USA (indeed, less so), so in all cases we are looking at the wrong kind of environmental regulation, the kind Porter finds constraining of innovation and cost cutting. What limited statistical evidence there is suggests that environmental regulations probably have a modest and negative effect on competitiveness, contrary to the spirit of the Porter hypothesis (although not conclusively a refutation since, again, the regulations in question are generally command and control) (Jaffe, Peterson, Portney and Stavins, 1994).

Overall, the Porter hypothesis is attractive to environmentalists and perhaps to some politicians, but like so many 'win win' arguments, it has little to recommend it.

The size of the environmental compliance market

Much of the business and environment literature is concerned with the costs of complying with regulations. But compliance involves technology and the technology has to be supplied by other industry. It is important therefore to see compliance as a market opportunity. The *compliance market* is the market for environmental technologies and services needed to meet environmental standards. This market has the potential to be supplied by environmental supply industries (ESIs) anywhere in the world and, clearly, some world regions have developed a comparative advantage in the supply of specialized pollution abatement equipment. The compliance market extends across a whole range of activities. A European Commission (EC) definition of this compliance market is that it is covered by 'eco-industries' which 'may be described as including firms producing goods and services capable of measuring, preventing, limiting or correcting environmental damage such as the pollution of water, air, soil, as well as waste and noise-related problems . . . [and] clean technologies where pollution and raw material use is being minimized' (European Commission, 1994: 5). The EC definition excludes renewable energy, biotechnology and green consumer products. Its inclusion of 'clean technology' is problematic for measurement since it is not easy to see how expenditures on clean technologies can be calculated. Clearly, the extent to which any individual region gains from compliance depends in part on whether the industries supplying this compliance demand are indigenous to the region or not. A region's overall sustainable development gains will be larger if the demands are met from indigenous supply.

Allied to the compliance market is the market for abatement based on what firms voluntarily undertake – the voluntary equilibria in Figure 5.1. But whereas it is possible to secure some 'first order' estimates of the size of the compliance market the size of the voluntary market is far more difficult to assess.

Table 5.1 The global environmental compliance market, 1990–2010 (US$ billion)

Region	ETDC		EBI		ECOTEC		
	1990	*2000*	*1992*	*1998*	*1992*	*2000*	*2010*
North America	125	217	145	199	100	147	240
Latin America	—	—	6	10	2	4	15
Europe	78	213	108	159	65	98	167
Asia-Pacific	46	138	30	49	85	63	149
Rest of world	6	12	6	9	0	7	0
Total world	255	580	295	426	252	320	571

Note: ETDC = Environmental Technologies Development Corporation (of Canada) – see Higgins (1994).
EBI = Environment Business International (of USA) (EBI, 1994).
ECOTEC Research and Consulting (of UK) (ECOTEC, 1994).
Source: OECD (1996).

Estimates of the size of the *global* compliance market are fairly consistent, but there are wide differences of view as to the composition of this market. Table 5.1 reports the available evidence. The important features of Table 5.1 are:

1 By the year 2000 the global compliance market will be of the order of $500 billion per annum, or around 2 per cent of entire world gross domestic product (GDP) at that time. This is in line with other estimates: OECD estimates that the market will be around $300 billion by 2000 (OECD, 1996), and the International Finance Corporation (IFC), using a broader definition for the industry, estimates it will be about $600 billion by 2000 (IFC, 1992). It is worth noting that 2 per cent of GDP approximates levels found for environmental expenditures in the rich world.
2 While the rich OECD countries account for the bulk of the current market (around 67 per cent of the entire market), the Asia-Pacific region accounts for 10 per cent up to 18 per cent of the current global market, but could increase in importance to some 24 per cent of the market in the year 2000. Latin America accounts for perhaps a modest 2 per cent of the world market currently, and this might increase to around 3 per cent in 2010.
3 While the regional estimates for Europe and North America are consistent across the different studies, there is a substantial difference between the estimates on the future size of the compliance market in the Asia-Pacific region. Table 5.2 shows a

Table 5.2 The Asia-Pacific environmental compliance market, 1990–2010 (US$ billion)

Area	ETDC		EBI		ECOTEC		
	1990	*2000*	*1992*	*1998*	*1992*	*2000*	*2010*
Japan	24	65	21	31	30	44	72
Australia/NZ	2	4	3	5	—	—	—
Taiwan	5	30	—	—	—	—	—
Hong Kong	—	3	—	—	5*	12*	50*
Rest of Asia-Pacific	14	28	6	13	—	—	—
China	—	—	—	—	2	5	20
India	—	—	—	—	1	2	7
Korea, Republic	1	8	—	—	—	—	—
Total	46	138	(30)	(49)	(38)	(63)	(149)

*Figures for E and SE Asia generally.
Note: ETDC = Environmental Technologies Development Corporation (of Canada).
EBI = Environment Business International (of USA).
ECOTEC Research and Consulting (of UK).
Source: OECD (1996).

more detailed breakdown for the Asia-Pacific region, suggesting that by the year 2000, the environmental compliance market will be $100–150 billion, emphasizing the role that compliance will play in the rapidly developing Pacific Rim countries as a means of competing for the richer markets of Europe and North America.
4   Adding the China estimates to the ETDC estimates in Table 5.2 suggests that Japan may account for some 40 per cent of the Asia-Pacific market in 2000 and Taiwan for a little over 20 per cent.

While these data are undoubtedly crude given the varying definitions of the environmental compliance market, the estimates are sufficient to establish that there will be a substantial global compliance market by the turn of the century. Moreover, the rate of growth of expenditure on environmental compliance is likely to be faster than the rate of growth of gross national product (GNP).

What role will the markets in developing countries play? While the data are poor, ECOTEC's 2010 forecasts suggest a developing country share of perhaps 3 per cent now rising to 9 per cent, and if Eastern Europe is included the relevant figures are 5 per cent and 13 per cent. Thus, while the bulk of the compliance market remains in the OECD countries, a rapidly growing proportion of it will be in developing countries.

Overall, while the figures vary significantly, the overriding conclusion is that the compliance market is a huge industry now and is likely to become very much larger in the next two decades, reflecting the momentum that environmental improvement has as a driving force.

Accounting for sustainable development

Many businesses now issue environmental reports and statements, as well as the environmental (impact) assessments that may be required of them for development projects. However, few attempts have been made to incorporate environmental impacts into company accounts, partly because methodologies have not been agreed. But where suggestions have been made on accounting reform, none of them appears to be based on a rigorous approach to the meaning and measurement of sustainable development. We first review, very briefly, the economics of sustainable development and then derive a measure of sustainability that can be incorporated into company accounts.

The World Commission on Environment and Development (WCED) (the Brundtland Commission) provided several definitions of sustainable development. Probably the best known is that it is: 'development that meets the needs of the present without compromising the ability of future generations to meet their own needs' (WCED, 1989: 8). The implication of this definition is that a path of economic and social development should not seek to maximize gains for this generation if in so doing it reduces the capacity of future generations to provide for their own wants and needs. The capacity to meet needs depends on the available stock of assets available to each generation. Call these assets 'capital'. Then the capacity of future generations to meet their needs will definitely be compromised if they have less of these assets than are available to the current generation. It follows that each generation should leave for the next generation a stock of capital assets no less than the stock it has available. This has come to be known as a 'constant capital rule'. But what is meant by 'capital'? It is very important to understand capital in its broadest sense. Traditionally, capital referred to man-made assets such as machines, roads, factories, houses, vehicles, and so on. As early as 1960, however, economists had begun to recognize that education was important in explaining economic development, so that the definition of capital was expanded to include human capital. It is only in the last decade that proper recognition has similarly been afforded to the environment as a source of economic development (Pearce and Warford,

1993). Environmental capital, or 'natural capital', comprises the full array of environmental assets, from oil and gas in the ground, to forests, the stocks of groundwater and river water, the quality of the air, the quality and quantity of soil, and so on. At the global level these stocks include the atmosphere and its temperature regulating activities, the ozone layer and its role in regulating ultraviolet radiation, the various biogeochemical cycles that regulate hydrological and nutrient flows, and which provide the very life support systems on which we all depend.

We can now use the 'constant capital' requirement for sustainable development to develop an indicator of sustainability. We adopt an intuitive approach here – formal proofs are given in Pearce, Hamilton and Atkinson (1996). No business is sustainable if it lives off its capital. The same is true for nations. Both companies and nations therefore need to put aside revenues as savings to offset the depreciation on their capital. This gives a very simple rule for sustainability in the form of a 'savings rule':

$$S/Y > d/Y \qquad (5.1)$$

where S is savings, d is depreciation and both are expressed as a percentage of business or national income (Y).

Now, as noted above, capital must include not just the normal types of capital in company and national accounts, but environmental capital as well. Environmental capital yields a flow of functions and life support services. It is in that sense no different to other capital. Hence the savings rule above can be expanded to become:

$$S/Y > d_m/Y + d_n/Y \qquad (5.2)$$

where d_m is depreciation on man-made capital, and d_n is depreciation on man-made capital. This can be reinterpreted as an index of sustainability by which countries could be ranked. To do this simply write the index of sustainability (Z) as:

$$Z = S/Y - d_m/Y + d_n/Y \qquad (5.3)$$

Gray (1993) has summarized recent surveys of environmental reporting. His results suggest that environmental disclosure is on the increase, and that it is still confined to large corporations.

Gray (1993) also suggests that the quality of environmental reporting is low and that there is little by way of sound quantification. To correct for this the business sector might try to emulate economics by securing socially quantified environmental accounts for companies (a suitable acronym would be SQUEACs).

A few examples of embryonic SQUEACs exist. Bebbington (1993) draws attention to the accounts of BSO/Origin, a Dutch company specializing in information technology and consultancy (BSO/Origin, 1990). Those accounts show company value added gross and net of monetized environmental impact. The basic equation is:

$$gVA = VA - (D - E) \tag{5.4}$$

where gVA is green value added (or net value added in the accounts), VA is conventional value added, D is the monetary value of environmental damage, and E is company expenditure on pollution abatement. BSO/Origin refer to $D - E$ as 'value lost'. They value D as the sum of clean-up and abatement costs borne by others (Co) and the costs of reducing residual damages (Cr) left over after the company's own abatement costs (E). The use of abatement costs, which are measured by what it costs to achieve given environmental standards, rather than the economist's approach which would be based on willingness to pay to avoid damages, is likely to understate $D - E$ if the standard is less than the optimal level of environmental quality, and overstate it if the standard is above the optimum. The resulting equation is then:

$$gVA = VA - (Co + Cr - E) \tag{5.5}$$

For 1990, the results are

$$
\begin{aligned}
VA &= 255.6 \text{ mDfl} \\
-(Co + Cr) &= 2.2 \text{ mDfl} \\
+E &= 0.2 \text{ mDfl} \\
\hline
& 253.6 \text{ mDfl}
\end{aligned}
\tag{5.6}
$$

Environmental accounting makes little difference to BSO/Origin's accounts presented in this way. The adjustment is less than 1 per cent. There are two reasons for this. The first is that the company itself is hardly a major polluter. The second, however, is that this way of presenting adjusted company accounts is never likely to result in significant adjustments. But if the figures are re-expressed in terms of the savings rule outlined above, the likely picture is different.

Company savings are best thought of as being measured by undistributed profits, although, of course, distributed profits might also be turned into savings by shareholders. But, from the standpoint of company sustainability and environmental impact, what shareholders do with their dividends should not be relevant. The value of d_m can be read from company accounts. In BSO/Origin's case, for example, it is 10.4 mDfl. Total depreciation is therefore $d_m + d_n = 10.4 + 2.0 = 12.4$ mDfl. Company savings are more complex in this particular case due to various acquisitions during the financial year. However, if one takes recorded net income, the figure is 21.0 mDfl net of d_m or 31.5 mDfl gross of d_m. Dividends were 8.3 mDfl. This suggests that the comparison should be between gross profit ( ) minus dividends (V) and the sum of the two depreciation elements. Sustainability requires:

$$(-V) > (d_m + d_n) \qquad (5.7)$$

which is met in the BSO/Origin case since

$$(31.5 - 8.3) > (12.4) \qquad (5.8)$$

But now the picture looks far less trivial than it does if the adjustments are made to value added. Moreover, the figure for d_n may be too low in the BSO accounts for the reasons stated.

We conclude that company accounts can be modified for environmental impacts and that the most appealing approach is (a) to monetize the impacts at least as far as is possible, and (b) to place those impacts in a savings rule context. In this way the company sector may be due for as many surprises as the application of the savings rule has so far produced for nations (see Pearce, Hamilton and Atkinson, 1996).

Conclusions

Adequate theories of the links between business and the environment are still lacking. As a result, the vast literature on business and the environment is informative but unstructured. This chapter has suggested a way of imposing structure on the information by placing environmental investment decisions into a benefit-cost framework, but without assuming that profit maximization is the only goal of the firm. Such a framework enables a better understanding of the phenomenon of over-compliance and regulatory capture. It also casts some light on the Porter hypothesis that firms should deliberately embrace higher environmental standards in order to improve competitiveness, a hypothesis that tends not to be supported by experience or by an analysis of motivations in the firm. Finally, we show how the literature on the economics of sustainable development can be brought to bear on the problem of environmental accounting reform for business. Adoption of a 'savings rule' offers potential insights into the sustainability of company activities which have so far been missing in the literature on environmental accounting.

References

Arora, S. and Gangopadhyay, S. (1995). Toward a theoretical model of voluntary overcompliance. *Journal of Economic Behaviour and Organization*, **28**(3), 289–309.

Arora, S. and Cason, T. (1995a). An experiment in voluntary environmental regulation: the participation in EPA's 33/50 program. *Journal of Environmental Economics and Management*. **28**, 271–86.

Arora, S. and Cason, T. (1995b). Why do firms overcomply with environmental regulations? Understanding participation in EPA's 33/50 program. Discussion Paper 95-38, Resources for the Future, Washington, DC.

Barrett, S. (1991). Environmental regulation for competitive advantage. *Business Strategy Review*, Spring, 1–15.

Baumol, W. and Oates, W. (1988). *The Theory of Environmental Policy*. (2nd edn) Cambridge University Press.

BSO/Origin (1990). *Annual Report 1990*. BSO/Origin.

Cairncross, F. (1991). *Costing the Earth*. Pinter.

Cairncross, F. (1995). *Green, Inc.* Earthscan.

ECOTEC (1994). *The UK Environmental Industry: Succeeding in the Changing Global Market*. HMSO.

Environmental Business International (EBI) (1994). As reported in Wilkes, A., Minoli, D. and Findlay, L. (1995). *The World of Opportunities for the Environmental Industry*. Environment Industries Commission.

European Commission (1993). *The Future of Industry in Europe*. European Commission.

Gray, R. (1993). Current practice in environmental reporting. *Social and Environmental Accounting*, **13**(1), 6–8.

Hahn, R.W. (1996). *Regulatory Reform: What Do the Government's Numbers Tell Us?* American Enterprise Institute.

Higgins, J. (1994). *Environmental Industry Overview*. Environmental Technologies Development Corporation (EDTC).

International Finance Corporation (IFC) (1992). *Investing in Environment: Business Opportunities in Developing Countries*. IFC.

Jaffe, A., Peterson S., Portney, P. and Stavins, R. (1994). Environmental regulation and international competitiveness: what does the evidence tell us? Discussion paper 94-08, Resources for the Future, Washington, DC.

Leibenstein, H. (1966). Allocative efficiency vs 'X efficiency'. *American Economic Review*, **56**, June, 392–415.

Milgrom, P. and Roberts, J. (1992). *Economics, Organization and Management*. Prentice Hall International.

Oates, W., Palmer, K. and Portney, P. (1994). Environmental regulation and international competitiveness: thinking about the Porter hypothesis. Discussion Paper 94-02, Resources for the Future, Washington, DC.

Organization for Economic Cooperation and Development (OECD) (1994a). *The OECD Environment Industry: Situation, Prospects and Government Policies*. OECD.

Organization for Economic Cooperation and Development (OECD) (1994b). *Environmental Industry Background Report*. Meeting of Experts on the Global Environment Industry, Washington DC, 13–14 October. OECD.

Organization for Economic Cooperation and Development (OECD) (1996). *The Global Environmental Goods and Services Industry*. OECD.

Pearce, D. W. (1991). *Corporate Responsibility and the Environment*. British Gas.

Pearce, D. W. (1995). Current economic costs of not using risk assessment in environmental policy at the European Community level. Centre for Social and Economic Research on the Global Environment, University College London and University of East Anglia, mimeo.

Pearce, D. W. and Crowards, T. (1996). The health costs of particulate pollution in the United Kingdom. *Energy Policy*, **24**(7), 609–20.

Pearce, D. W., Hamilton K. and Atkinson, G. (1996). Measuring sustainable development: progress on indicators. *Environment and Development Economics*, **1**(1), 85–102.

Pearce, D. W. and Warford, J. (1993). *World Without End: Economics, Environment and Sustainable Development*. Oxford University Press.

Porter, M. (1990). *The Competitive Advantage of Nations*. Free Press.

Porter, M. (1991). America's green strategy. *Scientific American*. 168, April.

Salop, S. and Scheffman, D. (1983). Raising rivals' costs. *American Economic Review, Papers and Proceedings*, **73**, 267–71.

Ulph, D. (1995). A Theory of Green Consumerism. University College London, Department of Economics, mimeo.

UK Department of the Environment (1996). *The Producer Responsibility Obligations (Packaging Waste) Regulations: A Consultation Paper*. UK Department of the Environment.

World Commission on Environment and Development (WCED) (1989). *Our Common Future*. Oxford University Press.

Part Three

Regulatory Frameworks

6 Government environment policy: European dimensions

Richard H. Williams

Introduction

This chapter is based on the proposition that a key prerequisite for successful extension of business operations beyond 'home territory' is to understand the logic of the legal and regulatory context in which it is intended to operate, to appreciate the perspective of the people with whom it is necessary to negotiate, or whose regulations it is necessary to adhere to or interpret.

This chapter seeks to develop the reader's capacity to think in supranational terms, and to appreciate the differences that may occur, even within a common framework of supranational law, in the ways in which authorization of development and environmental regulation operate in practice. Much of the material is drawn from the author's work on land and property markets in Europe, and on European Union (EU) policy-making.

Environmental problems are, by their nature, transnational and there are a number of international agreements concerning environmental regulation. A transnational nature means that, in the light of the experience of the EU, it is also possible to suggest that environmental problems are a natural subject for legislation by a supranational jurisdiction. The EU sees itself as being in competition with two other economic power blocs, north America and east Asia. The former has an embryonic supranational structure in the form of North American Free Trade Area (NAFTA) and the latter is also confronting issues of regional co-operation as one trading block. The parallels between the EU and both USA and NAFTA are developed in Meyer, Williams and Yount (1995).

The EU now has substantial powers over environment policy under the Treaty. Understanding the EU environment policy context and its underlying principles is therefore central to this chapter. This is important not only for those operating within EU member states: the wider European scale encompasses countries with widely differing experiences of environment policy regimes, for most of which EU environment policy is actually or potentially applicable through enlargement, association agreements or technical assistance programmes. Given the enormous scope of this subject, the aim can only be to provide signposts and guidance through its complexities and indicate sources of information, reference and further reading.

The discussion of environment policy is linked with land use planning and project development, using illustrative case studies from different EU member states. This is because land use planning procedures can provide the vehicle for environment policy measures, and because any business seeking to take advantage of the four freedoms of the European single market (free movement of goods, services, capital and labour) often needs to undertake development in a country other than its base.

Detailed consideration of the state of the environment itself is not possible here, but is well covered by Stanners and Bourdeau (1995) in their recent audit of Europe's environment. The initiative to undertake this was taken at the first pan-European Conference of Environment Ministers, held in Dobris Castle near Prague in June 1991: hence the title by which the study is commonly known, the Dobris Assessment. Similarly, for a comprehensive guide to the whole range of environmental policies and programmes, the institutions and officials responsible, and the non-EU bodies and pressure groups active in this sector, the guide published by the EU Committee of the American Chamber of Commerce in Belgium (AmCham, 1995) is very useful, while Haigh (1995) offers a detailed account of each item of legislation and its significance for the UK.

The strategic framework: treaties and powers

The authors of the EU's founding treaty, the Treaty of Rome of 1957, saw no need to refer to the environment (Wurzel 1993). Article 2, which states the task of the then European Economic Community (EEC), called for promotion of 'continuous and balanced expansion'. By 1972, public and political opinion was more aware of the environmental costs and pollution implications of economic growth, and a number of environmental measures had already been adopted. The Paris summit of 1972 therefore took the decision to establish an environmental policy sector. The question of whether the Treaty needed to be amended was also discussed, but at that time the view taken was that the Treaty was sufficiently flexible to provide the necessary powers without amendment (Haigh, 1996).

During the 1980s, there was growing acceptance that the Treaty of Rome provided insufficient powers for the action required. It was not until the passage of the Single European Act of 1987, which paved the way for the Single European Market (SEM), that an explicit legal basis for EU environmental legislation existed in the Treaty. By this time, over one hundred environmental measures had been enacted (Wurzel, 1993).

Although it started slowly, environment policy had become a rapidly growing and influential policy sector by the early 1990s, with a high political profile. The need for collective environmental standards throughout the EU received greatly increased emphasis with the adoption of the programme to create the SEM by the end of 1992. It was recognized by this time that varying standards of pollution control among member states could result in unfair economic advantage which would constitute distortions of the SEM through the creation of pollution havens (Williams 1986) or differing levels of liability for pollution costs. Therefore, in order to ensure its successful implementation and operation, harmonized environmental standards throughout the EU were seen to be necessary.

More recently, the Treaty of European Union, agreed at the Maastricht summit in December 1991 and in force since 1993, has enhanced still further the scope for intervention in the environmental field. The Treaty of European Union or Maastricht Treaty is clear about the place that environmental considerations must have in all EU policy instruments and EU legislation.

Title XVI of the Treaty, the Environment Title, sets general objectives to which EU policy on the environment must contribute:

1 reserving, protecting and improving the quality of the environment;
2 protecting human health;
3 prudent and rational utilization of natural resources;
4 promoting measures at international level to deal with regional or worldwide environmental problems.

It goes on in the second paragraph to state that, *inter alia*,

Community policy on the environment shall aim at a high level of protection . . . shall be based on the precautionary principle and on the principles that preventive action should be taken, that environmental damage should as a priority be rectified at source and that the polluter should pay. Environmental protection requirements must be integrated into the definition and implementation of other Community policies. (Article 130r, EC Council, 1992: 58)

All member states can therefore be said to have accepted, when they ratified the Treaty, the obligation to give high priority to the environment, to seek high environmental standards and to accept the incorporation of these in all other EU policies. Some commentators go so far as to assert that this obligation over-rides the exercise of all the other competencies given to the EU. However, as a matter of practical reality this interpretation does not always prevail (EEB 1994; Williams, 1996).

The Treaty on European Union reinforces the decision-making procedures for environmental legislation first established by the 1987 Single European Act. It does so by introducing three major changes to environmental policy-making at the EU level: introduction of Qualified Majority Voting (QMV); a stronger role for the European Parliament; and creation of the Cohesion Fund.

Application of QMV is intended to make the adoption of new environmental measures easier, but this is limited by the retention of unanimity (i.e. national vetoes) in some environmental sectors of significance in relation to pollution control. The European Parliament's stronger role, with powers of co-decision and of initiation of environmental legislation, is noteworthy because it has taken a strong role in promoting environmental policies and has earned the reputation for being the most environmentally concerned of all the EU institutions (Barnes, 1995).

The Cohesion Fund is potentially of great significance in respect of environmental and infrastructure improvement projects in the areas to which it applies. It was introduced in the Treaty as a measure to achieve greater economic and social cohesion within the EU. Its fundamental purpose is to enable the poorer member states to prepare for economic and monetary union, and meet the eligibility criteria, by promoting economic development through financial support for transport and environmental projects. The Cohesion Fund benefits only those member states whose per capita GDP is less than 90 per cent of the EU average. Four countries have been eligible on this basis since it came into operation in 1994: Greece, Ireland, Portugal and Spain, known colloquially as the 'poor four'. Quite substantial financial resources are made available for projects within these countries, ensuring that implementation of environmental legislation should not be held up for lack of public finance, and also that in these countries at least, the programme of trans-European networks is also funded (AmCham, 1995; Williams, 1996).

It may also be argued that the 1995 enlargement, with the

accession of Austria, Finland and Sweden, has important implications for the development of EU environment policy. Finland and Sweden have the highest environmental standards of the fifteen member states in a number of respects, and have clearly stated that they do not intend to allow environmental protection standards already set in their national legislation to be eroded as a result of adopting common EU standards. They can therefore be expected increasingly to perform the role of environmental pusher-states, pressing for the adoption of the highest standards.

Beyond this, progress on the environmental front is likely to be assisted by the establishment in Copenhagen in 1994 of the European Environment Agency. This is an EU institution, although it is also open to non-members. It is expected that it will not only work with national governments, but the numerous international organizations with environmental concerns, including the OECD, the International Energy Agency and the United Nations Environmental Programme. Currently, its main role is to provide technical and scientific support to the EU and its member states in the area of environmental protection and implementation of environmental policy. It was envisaged in 1990 that it would take an enforcement role in EU environment policy, but this has not yet been accepted in practice. The Agency has also been involved in reporting on the state of the environment across the whole of Europe, and has published the most comprehensive report and audit currently available, the Dobris Assessment, on the state of Europe's environment throughout Europe (Stanners and Bordeau, 1995).

At the intergovernmental level, the momentum for environmental protection has developed appreciably since the late 1980s. What must also be noted is that movement in this direction is by no means always smooth, as attitudes to the sustainability concept well illustrate. One of the single most influential events in the environmental discussion was the OECD conference in Oslo in 1987. This introduced and defined the concept of 'sustainable development' in the context of the developed world, and highlighted the need for international action to tackle problems such as climate change, ozone depletion and diminution of biodiversity (Brundtland 1987). In line with this new perspective, at the 1991 Inter-Governmental Conference on political union, member states accepted the argument that Article 2 of the Treaty should be amended to replace 'continuous expansion' with 'sustainable development' was accepted. In contrast, the separate Inter-Governmental Conference (IGC) on monetary union wanted to amend the same article so that it called for 'sustainable non-inflationary growth' (Haigh, 1996). Although Haigh suggests that the intention was to incorporate the Brundtland concept of sustainable development (Brundtland, 1987), the final version contains elements of both formulations: 'balanced development of economic activities . . . sustainable and non-inflationary growth respecting the environment' (EC Council, 1992: 11). The end result is a rather equivocal commitment to sustainability, highlighting the continuing tension between economic growth and environmental protection. Understandably, at the time of writing the environment lobby is pressing for the 1996 IGC to adopt once again the term 'sustainable development' (EEB, 1995).

Central and Eastern Europe

The former communist party states of central and eastern Europe present a very different picture. All have had the experience of regimes which have paid no attention to concerns over pollution, air and water quality, or conservation of the natural environment. The Görlitz-Usti-Katowice triangle in the border regions of the former German Democratic Republic, Silesia in Poland and northern Bohemia in the Czech Republic contains some of the worst polluted environments in Europe, if not the world.

The EU already has some experience of accommodating this situation and addressing it in policy development, following German reunification in October 1990, when the EU acquired a new geography and a whole set of new problems, environmental as much as political and economic.

Transition of the German Democratic Republic from a separate communist party state to membership of the EU took under one year. Institutional changes necessary for the introduction of democracy and a market economy took place very quickly, but the behavioural and attitudinal changes necessary to function in conformity with the principles of democracy and a market economy have taken much longer. This is an issue for environmental policy: not only is the task of bringing environmental standards up to those of the EU an enormous and expensive task, but a prerequisite for the adoption of such standards is a transformation of attitudes towards the environment on the part of the business community and society as a whole in the countries concerned.

Differentiation between Central and Eastern Europe in respect of political economy and EU relations is increasing. Several central European countries have the explicit goal of EU membership by early in the twenty-first century. Detailed negotiations are due to start in 1997. Key issues will include political and economic reform, and the application of EU environmental and regional development policies. The implications for the overall EU budget are enormous, especially if all the Central European countries pursue the aim of EU membership.

For membership to be agreed, these countries will need to clean up their environment and adopt a programme leading to acceptance and implementation of the standards and regulations governing the environment that apply within the EU. A number of EU aid and technology transfer programmes have been put into operation under the overall title PHARE (Pologne et Hongoire Assistance pour la Restructuration économique, so-named after the first two former communist countries to benefit from EU aid). Environmental technology and recovery projects form an important part of the PHARE programme. The territorial extent of PHARE has now extended to include all the former communist party states of Central Europe including Estonia, Latvia and Lithuania, but excluding the other countries of the former Soviet Union.

The latter have not been offered the prospect of EU primarily because the extent of transformation and economic restructuring needed is so great. They also have areas of environmental degradation as severe as in Central Europe, as well as severe economic problems.

Principles of EU environment policy

Certain basic principles have been laid down in successive statements of policy. These are that the polluter pays, that prevention is better than cure, and that action should take place at the appropriate level of government. That the polluter should pay is widely accepted in principle though sometimes difficult in practice. The greatest challenge to it comes in the area of former communist countries where the polluter may no longer exist (e.g. state enterprises of the former German Democratic Republic) or have no possibility of being able to pay the sums necessary to overcome the environmental legacy of years of neglect. For this reason there is interest in the US Superfund concept (DoE, 1994; see also Meyer, Williams and Yount, 1995) although the 1980 US legislation was not wholly successful and is to be revised.

The principle that prevention is better than cure, or the 'precautionary principle', has been an aspiration since 1973, although many of the earlier measures responded to the need to give priority to remedial action against existing pollution. Adoption of this principle is made explicit in Article 130r(2) of the Treaty. For a detailed discussion of the implications of this principle for decision-makers see O'Riordan and Cameron (1994).

The logic of prevention and the precautionary principle led the Commission to seek, when formulating directives, a sufficiently early part of the decision-making process so that the need for any preventative measure required on environmental grounds could be assessed and, if necessary, imposed by condition. This logic led the environment directorate to focus attention on the land use planning process, since all systems have a procedure for the authorisation of development which takes place at an appropriate stage of the decision-making process.

The Environmental Assessment Directive of 1985, which is integrated with the land use planning process, is an excellent example of the application of this logic (see Cameron and Mackenzie, Chapter 7 in this volume).

Policy vehicles

The Commission has, since 1973, adopted the practice of setting out a multiannual environment programme in the form of successive Action Programmes on the Environment. There have now been five of them. Although these programmes, containing reviews and statements of policy development intended for the period covered, are non-binding, many proposals have been adopted as law. Haigh (1989) listed over 200 items of European environmental legislation, and the rate of adoption has increased from around twenty per annum in the 1980s to over thirty per annum (Williams, 1990: 202).

The current 5th Action Programme, for the period 1992–2000, is entitled 'Towards Sustainability' (Commission, 1992a). This is the most comprehensive to date and is published in three volumes. It highlights as target sectors industry, energy, transport, agriculture and tourism, and develops the theme that industry should be seen as part of the solution rather than only as a source of problems, emphasizing subsidiarity and the need for bottom-up policy development.

The Commission also adopts the practice of issuing 'Green Papers' to indicate policy thinking on which consultation and reaction is sought. A far-reaching example is the *Green Book on the Urban Environment* (Commission, 1990) setting out urban planning principles that would meet environmental and energy-efficient objectives. In the same vein is the Green Paper on the impact of transport on the environment, proposing an EU strategy for sustainable mobility (Commission, 1992b). These set out longer-term visions which do not always get reported with sympathy or understanding by the British media, the technical and professional press included.

However, vision is often translated into policy, at least in part, and these documents should therefore be given due attention.

Compliance and implementation

Compliance is the term used to refer to the notification required by the Commission from member states stating that any necessary legal or administrative procedures are in place enabling a directive to be brought into operation. It is possible to distinguish between formal and practical compliance. The former is a legal process enforced by the Commission. The latter is beyond the scope of the Commission to monitor or enforce, as it does not have its own inspectorate capable of undertaking this task. The new European Environmental Agency was intended to perform this role. However, member-state governments have ensured that, initially at least, its role will be confined to monitoring and data collection, and fall short of policing and enforcing EU environment policy.

Meanwhile, considerable differences between member-states are apparent in formal compliance and the extent to which directives have been implemented. Wurzel (1993) noted that Denmark (DK) is the only member state whose compliance rate for environment directives is better than the average rate for all directives, and that other countries with good rates included Germany (D), The Netherlands (NL), Spain (E) and Portugal (P), with Italy (I), followed by Greece (GR) having the worst records, and the UK is in a middle group with Belgium, France, Ireland and Luxembourg.

Table 6.1, based on implementation data given in AmCham (1995) for 132 items of legislation for all fifteen member states, presents slight differences. Denmark has a 100 per cent record, followed by Ireland (IRL), France (F) and Luxembourg (L). The low figures for the three new member states of Austria (A), Finland (SF) and Sweden (S) reflect lack of data on the process of assimilating EU legislation after accession, not lack of willingness to comply with environmental legislation.

Relationship with employment and economic development

The Treaty of Rome of 1960 formally created a European Economic Community. The European Coal and Steel Community, the first of the three European Communities based on the Treaty of Paris of 1957 was also essentially an economic as much as political initiative. Why then should an 'economic' community be concerned with environment policy? Given the international and cross-border

Table 6.1 Implementation of EU environment legislation

	A	B	DK	D	E	F	GR	IRL	I	L	NL	P	S	SF	UK
F	9	101	132	106	103	118		120	89	116	122	103	23	36	108
N	9	22	0	13	20	1	22	5	30	11	3	24	0	7	16
*	20	6	0	11	7	5	1	5	11	3	5	3	22	9	8

F – fully implemented.
N – not implemented.
* – partially implemented.
Source: author's calculation from data in AmCham, 1995: 185–191.

nature of many environmental issues and their high political salience, the principle that the EU should have environment among its competences does not cause widespread surprise or dispute nowadays, but in early statements and action programmes on the environment it was felt necessary to address this question. The argument is worth outlining here as an aid to understanding the logic and priorities of EU environment policy.

Essentially, the rationale for an environment policy in an economic body such as the EU is based on three sets of arguments: (a) the competition argument; (b) the quality of life argument; and (c) the economic benefit argument.

The competition argument is based on the fact that the Treaty of Rome set out to create a 'common market' within which all forms of economic activity can take place free of distortions of competition due to tariff and non-tariff barriers. This is sometimes expressed by the metaphor of creating a level playing field. Variable environmental and pollution control standards between different member states are a form of non-tariff barrier, capable of creating distortions of competition resulting from the presence of pollution havens and thereby cheaper operating costs in some locations compared to others. Harmonization is the keyword associated with measures designed to overcome such distortions.

The quality of life argument can be expressed in either social or economic terms. Those emphasizing the social viewpoint argue that the EU does not exist solely to benefit business and governments, that all EU citizens are entitled to enjoy the benefits of a high standard of living, and that high environmental standards are an essential part of this. The economic emphasis is based on the argument that quality of life criteria affect location decisions made by entrepreneurs, whether or not the industrial or commercial activity being undertaken is directly dependent on a clean environment, since the decision-makers would choose to locate, other things being equal, in cities or regions with an attractive environment offering good living conditions.

The economic benefit rationale is based on the argument that in certain sectors of the economy, attainment of satisfactory operating conditions is directly dependent on high environmental quality, or that the markets for certain manufactured products or services are stimulated by the requirement of government or the expectation of society that high environmental standards should be adopted.

Which are the sectors of economic activity most dependent on a clean environment? Clearly, the prime categories are fishery, forestry, tourism and agriculture, although the latter is often accused of being the source of EU-subsidized pollution as a result of run-off from chemical fertilizers entering watercourses. Secondly, anyone concerned with the location and development of business parks and commercial property development designed to attract occupiers in modern new-technology industries must give priority to maintaining high environmental standards and offer attractive working conditions and quality of life in order to attract high-quality firms and maintain property values. Beyond high technology sectors, many mobile sectors of both manufacturing and service industry base locational decisions on quality of life criteria and a positive environmental image of an area not only for the immediate benefit of the workforce but also to attract or retain top staff and their families.

The member states

Member states play a crucial but not necessarily consistent role in environment policy. In every case there is a substantial body of national environmental legislation and policy reflecting their own needs and the political salience of the environment issue in each country's national politics. European law needs to be integrated with national law, and directives in particular allow scope for different interpretation in the manner in which they are incorporated into national legislation. Therefore, the activities of national and sub-national government in each of the fifteen member states represent an essential element in understanding European environment policy as a whole. For a comprehensive review of environment policy in the then twelve member states, the reader is referred to the *European Environment Yearbook* (DocTer, 1991).

National systems of environmental policy-making

Every member state has a body of law and policy to which the label 'environment' may be attached. This may place more emphasis on either the natural or the built environment. Every member state also has a system of land use planning. These have originated before there was any suggestion that the EEC or EU should have competence to adopt any legislation on these matters, or at least before its present extent was established. Consequently, they have all developed independently of each other, reflecting the political priorities and cultures of each country. In some cases, environment and land use planning legislation are closely integrated, in others they are quite separate codes of legislation.

For many people, it is easy to make the mental adjustments necessary to encompass the range of environmental situations and appropriate responses in terms of the dimensions of policy development in one's own country, even though this may contain considerable variety of natural environment. European Union policymakers have to acquire the ability to think European, and make these mental adjustments in respect of the EU as a whole. Anyone seeking to interpret attitudes and policies towards the natural environment in other European countries must acquire a similar skill. They must learn to think of the EU, with all its environmental variety, as one jurisdiction.

It may be helpful to indicate some dimensions of this complexity, in order to assist with the process of learning to find one's way around the system in unfamiliar countries.

First among these is the structure of governmental responsibility, respective roles of national or federal government departments, national agencies with environmental responsibilities, and subnational government. In the case of the latter, it is important to look out for the extent to which powers to legislate as well as to implement or enforce policy are held at the regional or upper tier of subnational government, as well as the controls exercised at the local or municipal level.

Second, there is the question of what approaches have been adopted to pollution control. The two classic alternatives are to set environmental quality standards or set emission standards. A commonly accepted oversimplification is that the UK insists on the former, setting environmental quality standards individually, whereas all other member states seek to set uniform emission standards. There are in fact several different principles which are used in EU legislation, and their merits are discussed in Haigh (1989).

Third, the geographical situation of each member state must not be overlooked, since national environmental priorities often reflect traditional popular attitudes towards the immediate environment, as well as the climate and ecology found in each country. Thus, concern about acid rain emissions is at its greatest in countries where wooded areas are important for recreation (for example, the Germans traditionally attach great importance to the *Stadtwald* or town forest) or where forestry is an important sector of the economy, such as Sweden and Finland. Concern for the protection of green spaces is often emphasized in countries with very high densities of urbanization, where green areas that may appear to others as quite undistinguished are afforded full protection. The importance which the Dutch attach to the so-called *Groen Hart* (green heart) of the country, i.e. the relatively undeveloped core of western Netherlands surrounded by the *Randstad* cities, is so central to their thinking that its protection has become a central doctrine in Dutch planning (Faludi and van der Valk, 1994).

Two of newest member states, Finland and Sweden, will also call into prominence another planning issue concerning the natural environment, that of shoreline development. In order to preserve the sensitive environments of both lake and sea shores, special planning procedures apply. These will need to be enhanced in order to withstand the additional pressures for development to be expected when restrictions on property ownership by non-nationals from other EU member-states can no longer be legally imposed.

Following from the geographical context is the question of practices that are popular, or at least widely condoned, in some countries but regarded as being unacceptable in others. Different forms of hunting could be cited, ranging from whaling in the Faeroes and Norway to bird trapping and shooting in Italy and Malta. In the latter case, lead shot in the soil is becoming a problem.

Perhaps more conventionally, different attitudes and traditional practices towards discharge of untreated sewage or foul effluent into open water, or of gas emissions into the atmosphere, may also be a product of geography. The high level of acceptability in the UK of discharge of untreated sewage into tidal waters, for example, is not surprising in an island but nevertheless puts the UK at odds with other member states and EU policy. The fact that Lisbon is a city with clean air, while Athens is notorious for air pollution, is also a product of geographical situation and cannot simply be attributed to national attitudes.

Fourth, is the land use planning system based on legally binding plans or on discretionary principles? Broadly, systems of planning in the Roman law countries are based on the concept of legally binding plans. Typically, their planning law requires development plans, usually at a very local and detailed scale (e.g. *Bebauungsplan, bestemmingsplan, plan d'occupation des sols*), to be adopted before proposals for development can be authorized and take place. Development proposals cannot be refused if they correspond with the provisions of the plan, and conversely they cannot be approved if the do not correspond. Authorization of development proposals is therefore purely an administrative process. Of course, the rigidity of this basic model would be unworkable in practice, so such systems do allow some scope for negotiation and a flexible response to unanticipated proposals.

Among Roman law systems, those in countries where the legacy of the code Napoleon applies tend to adopt the most codified approach, whereas others such as Sweden may have an overlay of common law. Matters which in the UK would be regarded as matters of planning policy may be embodied in law, for example by incorporation within the *code d'urbanisme* in France. Development plans and environmental designations in Germany are not, as they would be in Britain, adopted in accordance with the law: instead they are the law. Any challenge or dispute, therefore, is a legal challenge to be pursued through the law courts. In The Netherlands, the principle of *Rechtstaat*, whereby each citizen is considered to be entitled to legal certainty, applies to the planning system as to other sectors.

The two member states with discretionary planning and policy-making systems are the UK and the Republic of Ireland. In each case, the system allows scope for authorization of development proposals on the basis of consideration of their merits, or of 'material considerations', which may involve a decision to depart from the approved development plan. Both are in principle common law countries, although Scottish law is in fact based upon Roman law principles.

Fifth, there is the rather delicate issue of national political cultures and policy-making styles. What may appear to some as rather dubious forms of patronage, influence or behind-the-scenes negotiations may be accepted as perfectly normal elsewhere. It may be possible to have a totally accurate account of national regulations and policy-making procedures, and at the same time to fail completely to convey a true sense of the actual processes at work.

Environmental principles in business development: some case examples

In order to illustrate some of the above dimensions and try to convey a sense of how environmental considerations are valued by the business community, some examples of business park and industrial estate developments from France, The Netherlands and Germany are briefly outlined.

Meylan ZIRST, Grenoble, France

The first example, the Meylan ZIRST, (Zone pour l'Innovation et les Realisations Scientifiques et Techniques), Grenoble, France, is an example of a technological park first planned in the early 1970s. It is a successful science park of 110 ha, with around 200 enterprises and 5000 jobs, in Meylan commune adjacent to Grenoble and close to the universities. Grenoble is a regional centre of 400 000 population with a strong scientific base: in addition to its universities it is host to CERN (Centre européen de recherche nucléare), the main European facility for particle physics research.

Development of the project and letting of individual premises was undertaken by a private real estate company working in a public–private partnership with the municipality. This company pursued three main objectives: to develop a high technology park with innovative enterprises; to maintain the highest environmental quality; and to submit proposed developments to the severest quality constraints. It was recognized that, in order to attract the quality of enterprise necessary for a successful development, enterprises needed to be confident that the value of their investment would not be put at risk by the possibility of dirty or polluting neighbours.

Some prospective occupiers were not happy with being required to comply with such high standards. However, the developers responded by arguing that all would benefit from maintaining a very positive image and reputation as a green high technology park. The current high levels of prosperity, employment, tax base and property values in the area would seem to justify this argument. For firms that were not convinced, however, the commune used its land use planning powers to enforce the required standards. The majority of companies in ZIRST (60 per cent) were founded there. The main businesses are computers (21 per cent), sensors (17 per cent), industrial electronics (17 per cent), software, automation, robotics and artifical intelligence (Acosta and Renard 1993: 141–147).

Brainpark, Rotterdam, The Netherlands

The second example is that of Brainpark, Rotterdam, Netherlands. This is a project about 3 km from the centre of Rotterdam. It was felt that services, office-type industry and high technology businesses were under-represented in the local economy. The location of this project is close to Rotterdam's Erasmus University and Business School, which is why the name Brainpark was chosen.

Dutch environmental planning is reflected in the fact that the site is on a transport node with metro, bus, tram, park-and-ride and a motorway junction close by. In spite of the latter, car-dependency for employees and visitors is minimized. The objective was to attract high quality businesses, offices and firms which used office-like buildings, and firms linked to the university; to create a high-quality environmental design; and to diversify local employment opportunities.

Although most enterprises expect to offer high salaries and most employees are car owners, planning policy was designed to ensure maximum use of environmentally friendly modes of transport such as rail transit or cycling. This contrasts with the situation in many comparable projects in other countries.

Brainpark I (the first phase) started in 1987 and was fully let by 1990 to thirty-one firms. These included commercial services, consulting firms, traders and construction contractors and computing firms but not as many high technology firms as was hoped for. Nor were there many with functional links with the university. It was the site and accessibility factors rather than the proximity of the university which was the major attraction for the incoming firms. The second phase (Brainpark II) is going ahead with stricter planning and design controls (Needham, Koenders and Kruijt, 1993: 193–197).

Hansa Park, Düsseldorf and Technologiepark, Dortmund, Germany

Düsseldorf is a prosperous commercial city of about 570 000 population, adjacent to the industrial *Ruhrgebiet* but not part of it. Its location within Europe, as well as its accessibility to a large share of Germany's domestic market, makes Düsseldorf a highly desirable location for many firms from all over the EU. The problem is that there is a shortage of suitable land, and of course there is also pressure to direct development to the industrial cities of the Ruhr where unemployment is higher and land supply easier, such as Dortmund. However, many potential sites throughout this region are contaminated. In Düsseldorf, the pressures for development and the consequent land values are such that the costs of cleansing contaminated land can be borne without subsidy by the original owner either directly or by a reduced, but still profitable, sale price.

In the case of Hansa Park, located on 8.4 ha of land formerly occupied by the Thyssen steel company 6 km from the centre of Düsseldorf, the original owner was bound by contract to bear the cost of demolition and removal of contaminated soil, which involved removing it to a depth of 30 cm. This applied throughout the scheme, although 25 per cent was kept as green space, 25 per cent for road space and only 50 per cent for industrial building. Thirty-three firms were established, mainly in computing and communication electronics, employing 1500 people, which compensates at least quantitatively for the number of jobs lost with the closure of Thyssen (Dieterich, Dransfeld and Voss, 1993: 204–213).

Dortmund is a manufacturing city of about 600 000 population at the eastern end of the *Ruhrgebiet*. As part of its economic development programme to overcome the loss of its traditional heavy industry employment base, it has devoted considerable effort to environmental improvement programmes, frequent cleaning of all public and central spaces in the city, and of public monitoring of air quality. Through these, and associated publicity, a positive environmental and cultural image has been created. Dortmund is actually cleaner than cities such as Stuttgart which traditionally have been regarded as more attractive to modern business.

The Technologiepark in Dortmund is located on a greenfield site of 19.5 ha adjacent to the university and about 5 km from the city centre, with direct access to the motorway network. It is also served by the S-Bahn suburban rail system. It is therefore a relatively attractive site since much of the land available for industry elsewhere in the Dortmund area is in severely contaminated brownfield sites. However, the location was controversial as the site of the Technologiepark formed one of Dortmund's clean air corridors protected by the regional plan. This corridor was intended to remain undeveloped in order to ensure an undisturbed flow of air into central parts of the urban area. While the Technologiepark will not pollute the air, it may disturb the flow and does compromise the policy of protecting the corridor.

The project is still under development. It is attracting technology orientated firms in microchip production, materials and environmental technology, as well as specialist service and consulting firms. About half the space is occupied by production firms, the rest by office-type development. Links are maintained with the university, a concept developed in the first place and promoted by the chamber of industry and commerce rather than the university itself (Dieterich, Dransfeld and Voss, 1993: 173–188).

Language

Language is a vitally important issue, but one whose potential distorting effect is not always appreciated by those inexperienced in working in any language other than their own. It is a complication not only in the obvious sense, but also because the dictionary or glossary approach to the translation of technical terms often fails to draw attention to the fact that equivalent words convey quite different underlying concepts, or are attached to quite different policy designations in the different countries. For fuller treatment of the implications of this, see Williams (1996: 55–62).

Interpreting legal and professional terminology in national environmental and planning policy in all the different official languages, and ensuring that the same understanding is conveyed to speakers of these languages, is therefore a notoriously complex issue. The use of the standard translations in legal instruments do not always convey exactly the same sense or meaning to those professionally engaged in planning and environment policy in each EU member state. Thus, not only do the rules, regulations and underlying legal principles differ from member state to member state, but also the true meanings of the words used to express them differ significantly since the words in the languages quoted above are not exact translations of each other and do not convey the same meaning to users of the respective languages.

The word policy itself poses another problem. Several other European languages make no distinction between policy and politics (*politique, das Politik*) in the way English does, although they may distinguish between policy in the political sense and policy in the sense of policy instruments, measures (*Massnahmen*) or management and administration of policy (*beleid*).

English is of course very often the language in which policy-making discourse takes place. Within the European Commission, English and French predominate in the key working parties, and documents or texts are prepared and most precisely drafted in these languages. Users of other languages may have to wait for final translations, and may find some ambiguities. Use of English is not, however, an unqualified advantage for native-speakers of English. Although the language may be English, the underlying thought patterns very often are not, and the proposals under consideration may come from other jurisdictions. English words are used, therefore, to convey non-British concepts. In doing so, they may be capable of confusing or misleading monolingual English speakers. This form of English, which may be called Euro-english, is as evident in environmental discourse as elsewhere. A phrase which may serve to illustrate the point comes from the aspiration, in a Commission document, to ensure 'the rational management of space'. This refers, of course, to land use, not satellite technology.

Conclusion

Environmental policy-making and the adoption of higher environmental standards will be a fact of life of ever-increasing significance to anyone seeking to operate business in Europe. New institutions such as the European Environment Agency, new powers for existing bodies such as the European Parliament, enlargement of the EU and, above all, continuing political pressure will ensure that this is so. Recognition of the positive economic effects of such an emphasis, and of the sectors of the economy where these are most pronounced, will therefore potentially be a key foundation of long-term business success.

The aspirations of the Commission are sometimes expressed in terms which often strike pragmatic British managers as being rhetorical and visionary. The response should not be to ignore or disparage them, assuming that nothing of practical significance will come from such statements. Instead, such policy documents should be treated as advance notice of an agenda of policy initiatives some of which will attract strong political support and develop their own momentum. Business opportunities, whether in environmental cleansing technology, energy efficient transit systems or whatever, may be spotted by those who learn to think European, while businesses in any other sector must recognize both the extent that European law frames local environmental regulation and the political and commercial pressure for high standards that is a feature of several countries.

References

Acosta, R. and Renard, V. (1993). Urban land and property markets in France. In *European Urban Land and Property Markets* (H. Dieterich, R. H. Williams and B. Wood, eds) (vol. 3) UCL Press.

AmCham (1995). *EU Environment Guide 1996*. EU Committee of the American Chamber of Commerce in Belgium.

Barnes, P. (1995). Environmental Policy, Discussion Paper 14, Jean Monnet Group of Experts, Centre for European Union Studies, University of Hull.

Brundtland, G. H. (1987). *Our Common Future: World Commission on Environment and Development*. Oxford University Press.

Commission (1990). *Green Book on the Urban Environment*. COM (90) 218, European Commission.

Commission (1992a). *5th Action Programme on the Environment – Towards Sustainability*. COM (92) 23, European Commission.

Commission (1992b). *The Impact of Transport on the Environment – A Community Strategy for Sustainable Mobility*. COM (92) 46, European Commission.

Department of the Environment (DOE) (1994). *Paying for our Past*, Department of the Environment and Welsh Office consultation paper.

Dieterich, H., Dransfeld, E. and Voss, W. (1993). Urban land and property markets in Germany. In *European Urban Land and Property Markets* (H. Dieterich, R. H. Williams and B. Wood, eds) (vol. 2) UCL Press.

DocTer (1991). *European Environment Yearbook*. Institute for Environmental Studies.

EC Council (1992). *Treaty on European Union*. Office for Official Publications of the European Communities.

European Environment Bureau (EEB) (1994). *EEB Twentieth Anniversary*, EEB.

European Environment Bureau (EEB) (1995). *Greening the Treaty. A Manifesto for the Inter Governmental Conference from UK members of the European Environment Bureau (EEB)*. EEB.

Faludi, A. and van der Valk, A. (1994). *Rule and Order: Dutch Planning Doctrine in the Twentieth Century*. Kluwer.

Haigh, N. (1989). *EEC Environment Policy and Britain*. Longman.

Haigh, N. (1995). *Manual of Environment Policy: The EC and Britain*. Institute for European Environment Policy, Cartermill Publishing.

Haigh, N. (1996). Sustainable development in the EU Treaties. *International Environment Affairs*, **8**: 1.

Meyer, P. B., Williams, R. H. and Yount, K. R. (1995). *Contaminated Land Reclamation, Redevelopment and Reuse in the United States and the European Union*. Edward Elgar.

Needham, B., Koenders, P. and Kruijt, B. (1993). (H. Dieterich, R. H. Williams and B. Wood, eds) Urban land and property markets in Netherlands. In *European Urban Land and Property Markets* (vol. 1) UCL Press.

O'Riordan, T. and Cameron, J. (1994). *Interpreting the Precautionary Principle: A Principle for Action in the Face of Uncertainty*. Cameron May.

Stanners, D. and Bordeau, P. (1995). *Europe's Environment: the Dobris Assessment*. European Environment Agency, Office for Official Publications of the European Communities.

Williams, R. H. (1986). EC environment policy, land use planning and pollution control. *Policy and Politics*, **14**(1), 93–106.

Williams, R. H. (1990). Supranational environment policy and pollution control. In *Western Europe Challenge and Change* (D. Pinder, ed.) pp. 195–207, Belhaven.

Williams, R. H. (1996). *European Union Spatial Policy and Planning*. Paul Chapman.

Wurzel, R. (1993). Environmental policy. In *The European Community and the Challenge of the Future* (J. Lodge, ed.) pp. 178–99, Pinter.

7 Essential environmental law for good management

James Cameron and Ruth Mackenzie

Introduction

Three interlocking systems of international, European Community (EC) and national environmental law provide the framework in which business in Europe must operate. Domestic environmental legislation in the UK is driven not only by purely domestic concerns over environmental protection, but is increasingly a vehicle for implementing obligations undertaken by government through its participation in international negotiations and agreements, and through membership of and participation in the European Community. The interlocking nature of the system results in a variety of instruments and approaches being employed in order to achieve the goal of environmental protection. These instruments and approaches set limits and impose conditions on action of which business managers must be aware, but they also, and increasingly, provide scope and incentives for new types of activity, marketing and innovation. Business will readily appreciate that in the environmental context, as in any other, it is advantageous to be proactive rather than reactive, and to help shape the framework in which it will operate. However, involvement in the environmental law-making process need not be restricted to merely seeking to limit regulatory interference or restriction on industrial activity. In order to participate fully in the process business managers need an awareness not only of what the law is, but also of the principles and processes which underlie existing and, most importantly, prospective legislation. It has been frequently recognized that environmental concerns can be turned to competitive advantage by triggering early upgrading, investment and innovation.

The sources of environmental law

Public international law

Essentially, public international law governs relations between states. Treaties between states are the primary source of international law in relation to environmental protection. In addition to formal sources of international environmental law, also of particular relevance in the environmental context are so-called 'soft law' rules which may take the form of non-binding declarations of international organizations or conferences, or codes of conduct adopted for specific sectors. While not binding in themselves, these rules may often point to the development of future binding treaty obligations, and may represent the establishment of acceptable norms of behaviour.

International law may seem a distant source of obligations for business managers. It provides for obligations among *states*, but it is also evident that in many instances, and perhaps especially in the realm of environmental regulation and protection, these international commitments can only be met by states in turn imposing obligations and regulations at the national level (or increasingly, as the EC becomes party to international conventions, at the EC level), so that the obligations ultimately fall upon national industry. International environmental law will therefore be of relevance to business if only to the extent that it may indicate future (and often imminent) new domestic or European obligations.

International law has, furthermore, become increasingly concerned with setting more detailed standards and targets in relation to emissions from various industrial sectors or into particular environmental media. For example, the Montreal Protocol on Substances that Deplete the Ozone Layer of 1987 (26 ILM 1541, 1987) prohibits the production and use of certain man-made chemicals, and sets stringent phase-out limits for others. These internationally agreed measures have been implemented at EC level, with the EC in some respects taking more stringent action than that required under the Protocol (Regulations EEC No 594/91, OJ 1991 L 67/1, 14 March 1991; EEC No 3952/92, OJ 1992 L 405/41, 31 December 1992. See also Commission, 1993a).

The international environmental agreement which may prove of most significance to the operation of business is the United Nations Framework Convention on Climate Change signed at the United Nations Conference on Environment and Development in Rio de Janeiro in June 1992. The ultimate objective of the Convention is to stabilize greenhouse gas concentrations in the atmosphere 'at a level that would prevent dangerous anthropogenic interference with the climate system' (UN Framework Convention on Climate Change, Article 2). Although the Convention is only a framework for future co-operation among states which does not impose specific targets and timetables at this stage, it is likely to have profound implications for the future energy choices of business. It is probable that the Convention will be followed by the adoption of protocols providing for more specific regulation of certain sectors and the adoption of more specific targets and guidelines. This has been the case with previous framework international legislation, such as the 1985 Vienna Convention on the Protection of the Ozone Layer, and the 1987 Montreal Protocol.

The Convention also provides a good illustration of the linkage between the international, regional (e.g. EC) and national law, since the signing of the Convention has led to the adoption of measures at the European Community level (see, for example, Commission, 1992; EEC. 1993b), and the development of the 1994 UK national programme on climate change. Additionally, the World Trade Organization (WTO) will be increasingly influential on the environmental regime. Decisions taken in the World Trade Organization could limit the options available to environmental decision-makers in that regulatory intentions in the marketplace to protect the environment could be judged unnecessarily restrictive on trade.

European Community law

Business should be aware that the entry into force of the Treaty on European Union (the Maastricht Treaty) is likely to have a significant effect on future Community environmental protection action. The Maastricht Treaty places the environment at the centre of the European Community's objectives and policies. Amended Article 2 of the EEC Treaty provides that the Community shall have as its task, by establishing a common market and an economic and monetary union:

to promote throughout the Community a harmonious and balanced development of economic activities, *sustainable and non-inflationary growth respecting the environment*, a high degree of convergence of economic performance, a high level of employment and of social protection, the raising of the standard of living and quality of life, and economic and social cohesion and solidarity among Member States.

Environmental measures are generally adopted at EC level as either Regulations or Directives. The type of legislation determines its effect in member states. Regulations apply directly in the member states, and are therefore binding on member states and private individuals and companies *without further implementing action*. Directives are binding upon member states as to effect only, and the manner of implementation is left to member states subject to a deadline by which the Directive must be implemented.

The majority of Community legislation on the environment is adopted by way of Directive, and thus even where the purpose of the measure may be to achieve a degree of harmonization across member states with regard to the protection of the environment, differences in the manner (and extent) of implementation are likely to mean that certain variations still persist. Thus, even where Community harmonization measures exist it will still be necessary for business to check *national* environmental laws if operating in other member states. To the extent that variations in implementation are perceived to discriminate against businesses of other member states, the manner of implementation by a member state may be subject to challenge. Differences in national legislation across the EC may be further exacerbated by an apparently emerging trend in EC environmental policy which could allow certain member states to introduce environmental standards over a longer period of time, and by provisions in the amended European Economic Community (EEC) Treaty, such as Article 130t, allowing member states to introduce more stringent measures in certain circumstances.

Legislation is adopted at EC level through a lengthy process which generally includes consultation processes and consideration of proposals by the Commission, European Parliament, Economic and Social Committee and the Council of Ministers. In order to influence EC environmental legislation it is therefore important for business to be aware at an early stage of legislative proposals (which are published in the *Official Journal* of the EC) and, if likely to be affected, to make its voice heard in the consultation procedure and legislative process.

National law

As stated above, even within other EC member states, it will always be necessary to be aware of the national environmental legislation of the state in which a business is operating. Wide differences exist in the types and scope of environmental legislation and the extent to which, for example, prior authorizations may be needed for particular activities.

In the UK, environmental protection legislation has been adopted on a relatively *ad hoc* basis but much of the relevant legislation is now comprised largely in two Acts of Parliament, the Environmental Protection Act 1990 and the Water Resources Act 1991, and in regulations made thereunder. Certain provisions of the Control of Pollution Act 1974 remain relevant. Planning legislation remains important to environmental protection in relation to, for example, development consents, environmental impact assessments and the keeping of hazardous substances. There will also be some EC legislation, adopted in the form of Regulations, which will be directly applicable under national law. Relevant health and safety and consumer protection legislation should also be considered. The 1995 Environment Act created a unified Environment Agency for England and Wales, to carry out functions previously the responsibility of numerous entities such as Her Majesty's Inspectorate of Pollution, the National Rivers Authority, and local councils. The 1995 Act also contains important provisions on contaminated land.

Current trends in principles and processes

Early environmental law in the UK and other jurisdictions were aimed at reducing the acute effects of pollution from large, visible sources through 'command and control' legislation. While those policies were successful in improving the environment, they have become quite expensive, and are not equipped to address the diffuse, subtle, and transnational environmental problems of today. In response, a new breed of environmental policy is emerging which is more flexible, cost efficient, and streamlined. These environmental law-making and policy trends have their most obvious manifestation in recent and proposed EC legislation on the environment. Moreover, measures taken at EC level may well provide a precedent or basis for future international action.

In the United States, for example, the Next Generation Project at the Yale Center for Environmental Law and Policy is researching the environmental policy instruments which feature economic incentives, and which are integrated with other public development concerns (such as transportation and economic policy). The intention is to identify policy which delivers more 'environmental value' to the public – policy which is not only protective but is also efficient.

Perhaps the dominant overarching trend is the search for sustainable development. The general principle calls for a balanced economic and social development which respects both the environment, the needs of future generations, and the needs of the world's poor. Definitions also refer to the idea of maintaining environmental capital and 'living off interest'. Orienting law to this end is a tremendous challenge. In the US, however, the Next Generation Project is examining innovative ways to encourage sustainable development by replacing the US's rigid technology-based pollution laws with new policy tools which encourage good environmental practices, channel the investment of private capital into sustainable development products, and support technology innovation.

It is not intended to give here a detailed account of environmental legislation in force in the UK and EC, nor of the rapidly increasing body of international law rules in this area. Rather, a number of the emerging trends will be noted and their application in existing and proposed/prospective legislation outlined. The most marked trends appear to be:

1   the use of economic instruments;
2   use of environmental impact assessment for prevention and planning;
3   extension of access to information;
4   adoption of integrated pollution control/industrial ecology techniques;
5   extension of criminal and civil liability/responsibility for environmental harms;
6   policy integration;
7   precautionary instruments.

Economic or market-based instruments

The move towards the increased utilization of economic instruments in order to achieve environmental goals is most apparent at EC level. It is specifically stated in the European Community's *5th Action Programme on the Environment* that in order to achieve sustainable development Community policy now requires a broader range of instruments and the involvement of a wider range of actors than previous regulatory measures. The Programme states that market-based instruments will serve to sensitize both consumers and producers towards responsible use of natural resources and the avoidance of pollution and waste by internalizing external environmental costs. Recent moves in this direction include the adoption of Regulations on eco-labelling and eco-auditing, the wide-ranging discussion regarding liability for environmental harm in the Community, and proposals for a carbon/energy tax as part of the Community programme to meet its commitments under the Climate Change Convention.

The UK government has itself expressed a strong preference for the use of economic instruments as opposed to regulatory measures where possible, and has even proposed some deregulation, emphasizing that market-based measures are more flexible and cost effective (HMSO, 1990; 1992).

Other jurisdictions, such as the US, have also successfully implemented several market-based instruments in domestic environmental laws. The US Clean Air Act, for example, provides for emission fees, tax credits for clean companies, and tradable emissions allowances.

Ecomanagement and ecoaudit regulation

The EC's voluntary ecomanagement and ecoaudit scheme (EMAS), (Council Regulation EEC No 880/92), came into force in 1995. As a Regulation, it is directly applicable in member states. The objective of the scheme is to promote continuous improvements in the environmental performance of industrial activities by the establishment and implementation of environmental policies, programmes and management systems by companies in relation to their sites; the systematic, objective and periodic evaluation of the performance of such elements; and the provision of information on environmental performance to the public. The scheme is applicable to particular *sites* where an industrial activity is performed, not to the company as a whole. A company wishing its site to participate in the scheme must fulfil a number of requirements, including adopting a company environmental policy aimed at reasonable continuous improvement of environmental performance, and introducing an environmental management system at the site. The management system should commit the company to assessing the environmental impact of activities at the site, and should also require regular audits to establish whether the activities meet the requirements of the management system and policy (Salter, 1992).

Provision is made for the coexistence of the EC scheme and national schemes such as BS 7750 (see below, and Chapter 11 in this volume), in Article 12 of the Regulation, which provides that, subject to certain conditions, companies implementing national schemes shall be regarded as meeting the requirements of the Regulation. International standards also exist for environmental management in the form of ISO 14001 approved by the International Standards Organization in July 1996. Other standards being developed in the ISO 14000 series concern environmental performance evaluation and life cycle assessment.

Despite the costs of implementing and maintaining participation in schemes such as EMAS, BS 7750, and ISO 14001, participation should also bring potential benefits to the company, including reduced exposure to environmental litigation or regulatory prosecution, lower operating costs (through, for example, clean technology and the minimization of waste), and reduced insurance costs.

Moreover, participation in these schemes can act as a signal to potential consumers and investors of the environmentally sound management of the company.

Eco-labelling

The EC EcoLabel Regulation (Council Regulation EEC No 880/92) was launched in June 1993. The objective of the scheme is to promote the design, production, marketing, and use of products which have a reduced environmental impact during their entire life cycle, and to provide consumers with better information on the environmental impact of products. The scheme does not apply to food, drink or pharmaceuticals.

Ecological criteria have been set for assessing the environmental impact of products, with criteria to be specified for separately identified product groups. The criteria has adopted a 'cradle to the grave' approach. Both the range of product groups and the criteria will be subject to periodic review.

An ecolabel can be awarded to products which meet the objectives of the Regulation and the product group criteria, and which are in conformity with Community health, safety and environmental requirements. The application for the label must be made to the national competent body in the appropriate member state, and use of the label can only commence after the execution of a contract between the successful applicant and the competent awarding authority. Thereafter, the applicant will be able to display the ecolabel on the product in respect of which it has been awarded, and may refer to the ecolabel in advertising that specific product. The label will be awarded for a fixed production period only.

Criteria remain to be set for a large number of product groups under the scheme, which appears to have got off to a slow start. Some confusion is also likely to remain over the coexistence of individual national schemes which have been set up by some member states.

Proposals for a carbon/energy tax

The proposed carbon/energy tax (Commission, 1992) was intended to form the main pillar of EC efforts to meet its obligations under the Climate Change Convention (to which the Community, as well as the twelve member states, is a party), and to achieve its stated commitment to stabilize aggregate greenhouse gas emissions across the Community at 1990 levels by the year 2000. The proposed tax would have been split 50/50 between carbon dioxide

emissions and the energy content of fuel used and the fundamental effect of the proposal would be to progressively impose a
tax per barrel of equivalent oil rising from $3 in 1993 to $10 in
2000. The proposal would obviously have implications for the
energy choices and costs of industry, and the EC proposals were
put forward conditionally subject to the proviso that other OECD
countries should take similar measures so as not to undermine the
competitiveness of EC industry. However, it now seems unlikely
that the tax will be introduced in the form proposed. The
proposals met with various objections from the UK, France and
the southern EC member states and, although certain member
states attempted to link ratification by the EC of the Framework
Convention on Climate Change with the adoption of the carbon/
energy tax, in fact the EC proceeded to ratify the Convention.
Moreover, the US and Japan have failed to introduce comparable
energy taxes so that the conditionality principle in the proposal
has not been met.

In summary, it can be seen that a wide range of measures fall
under the general description of 'economic instruments'. What they
have in common is that rather than requiring compliance with
given rules or limitations, for example as to the types of activities
which can be carried on or the types/levels of permitted emissions,
they instead provide incentives for companies or individuals to
adopt different and less environmentally damaging behaviour. The
range of instruments employed may eventually extend to include a
wider range of fiscal incentives and disincentives, emissions charges,
and tradable emissions permits, on a national, EC or possibly even
international scale. Increasing attention is also being given in the
EC to the EC and in certain Member States to the use of voluntary
agreements.

Environmental impact assessment

The Environmental Assessment Directive (Council Directive 85/
337/EEC) entered into force in 1988. Impact assessment is very
much a current theme in environmental law, both at the EC and
national level, and increasingly at the international level. Despite
delays, most member states have now incorporated environmental
impact assessment (EIA) into their domestic laws.

The EC Directive makes EIA mandatory for certain types of
projects, while other classes of projects may be made subject to an
assessment where member states consider that their characteristics
so require. To this end member states may set criteria or thresholds
or specify particular types of non-mandatory projects which will be
made subject to assessment. Major discrepancies in the implemen-

tation and application of the Directive particularly in relation to non-mandatory projects have arisen between member states (ENDS, 1993).

Implementation of the Directive across the Community has proved problematic, and non-implementation or maladministration of the Directive has been the subject of a large number of complaints to the Commission. None the less, the Directive is significant in that it specifies particular projects for which prior assessment is appropriate and it specifies the types of information which a developer must provide prior to consent for the development being granted.

In the UK, the EIA Directive has been implemented principally through the Town and Country Planning (Assessment of Environmental Effects) Regulations of 1988 (SI 1988/1199). A person or company wishing to apply for a planning consent may seek a preliminary view from the local planning authority as to whether the proposed development would fall within the scope of the Regulations. Where an assessment is required, the developer must supply an environmental statement. In compiling the environmental statement the developer may collect relevant existing information from statutory consultees and from the local planning authority (Salter, 1992; Sheate, 1994).

The Secretary of State for the Environment has wide powers in relation to environmental assessments, and may, for example, overrule a local planning authority by requiring that an assessment be provided. Moreover, the Secretary of State can require environmental impact assessment for projects needing planning permission other than the mandatory projects listed in the EC Directive (Section 15, Planning and Compensation Act, 1991).

The Commission has recently put forward a proposal for a directive on the assessment of certain plans and programmes on the environment, which would require environmental protection to be taken into account at the land-use planning stage rather than only in relation to specific projects (Commission, 1996a). Proposal for a Council Directive on the assessment of the effect of certain plans and programmes on the environment. COM (96) 511.

In the international context, the scope of the application of EIA procedures has been extended in the 1991 UN Economic Commission for Europe Convention on Environmental Impact Assessment in a Transboundary Context (30 ILM 802 (1991)). This Convention goes beyond the 1985 EC Directive in terms of its potential geographical application and the nature of its obligations, and applies to a range of activities which are likely to cause significant adverse transboundary impact.

Provision of and access to environmental information

Access to environmental information is particularly relevant in a context which increasingly requires companies to provide information to regulatory authorities, for example when applying for authorizations and as a continuing condition of those authorizations (see further below). Of primary significance in Europe is the 1990 Freedom of Access to Information on the Environment Directive (Council Directive EEC 90/313). The Directive is intended to ensure freedom of access to and dissemination of information on the environment *held by public authorities*. Access to such information can be refused on certain grounds, including commercial or industrial confidentiality. Industry has pressed for restrictions on access to monitoring (i.e. emissions) information on the grounds that access to emissions data would allow competitors to deduce production processes used. However, there are signs that the commercial confidentiality exception may be construed strictly in the future.

It seems likely that provisions regarding the availability of information to the public will form part of the substance of many future EC legislative proposals on the environment. For example, the Directive on Integrated Pollution Prevention and Control of 1996 (see below) provides that without prejudice to the Access to Information Directive, Member States shall take the necessary measures to ensure that applications for permits for new installations or for substantial changes are made available for an appropriate period of time for comment by the public. Results of monitoring of releases under any permit conditions held by the competent authority must also be made available to the public (Article 15). The provision of information provides part of the rationale behind the ecolabel and ecoaudit schemes discussed above, with the ecoaudit scheme in particular requiring audits to be summarized in an environmental statement for the public. Access to information will also have implications for the enforcement of EC and national environmental law as the public or environmental groups will be able more effectively to measure the environmental performance of companies against their obligations and also the enforcement performance of the regulatory authorities.

In the UK, the Access to Information Directive has been implemented through the Environmental Information Regulations 1992 (SI 1992/3240). In addition to the implementation of the EC Directive, UK national law also contains several specific provisions which allow the public access to environmental information on companies held by public authorities. For example, a registry is maintained regarding applications for and grants of authorizations, notices issued, convictions and such other matters relating to the carrying on of prescribed processes or pollution of the environment caused thereby as may be prescribed. Unlike the US, the UK does not at the present time have a Freedom of Information Act.

International law can be said indirectly to impose reporting and monitoring requirements on companies. Monitoring and reporting requirements have now become a common feature of international environmental conventions. Although it will be the responsibility of the state to collate and report the requisite information to the supervisory body of the relevant Convention, it will be necessary for the information, e.g. with regard to industrial processes/emissions, first to be provided by industry. Much of this information will be collected through national prior authorization and monitoring procedures. The increasing number and scope of international instruments means that industry can expect to be required to provide more and better information on a wider range of its activities.

Integrated pollution control/industrial ecology

Integrated pollution control is designed to address the problem that reducing pollution in one environmental medium may have negative implications for another. It is being applied to an increasing range of activities in the UK and other jurisdictions. The Next Generation Project at Yale University refers to this principle as 'Industrial ecology', which seeks to understand and protect the natural environment by managing all resources utilized in any human activity. Industrial ecology focuses on systems-oriented decision-making, attention to materials flows, and the role of industry and technology to form a more comprehensive approach to environmental policy. The desire is to eradicate the rigidness and compartmentalization of current policy (which addresses air, water and waste separately).

In the UK, the principal obligations derive from the Integrated Pollution Control (IPC) and Air Pollution Control (APC) regimes provided under the Environmental Protection Act 1990 (EPA), and from the requirement for discharge consents in respect of controlled waters under the Water Resources Act 1991 (WRA).

As its name suggests, IPC is an *integrated* system, whereby emissions from the most pollutive process to all environmental media, i.e. air, water, soil etc., are controlled. Under IPC every prescribed process has to be authorized (s.6, EPA, 1990). Authorizations are granted subject to conditions and emissions limits, and the aim of the conditions must be to ensure that Best Available Techniques Not Entailing Excessive Cost (BATNEEC) are employed to prevent or minimize pollution. The Department of Environment has published a series of Guidance Notes setting out emissions limits and providing some clarification of what constitutes BATNEEC for various prescribed processes, but it must be noted that BATNEEC is a self-adjusting standard, which requires improvement over time as technology advances. Approximately 5000 industrial processes fall within the scope of the IPC regime, with another 27 000 subject to APC. It has been noted that the requirement for an IPC authorization imposes costs on a company in three principal ways: costs of preparing the application; fees payable to the Environment Agency (formerly Her Majesty's Inspectorate of Pollution); and the costs of meeting conditions of the authorization (Castle and Harrison, 1996; ENDS, 1994). Conditions may also be attached to statutory consents for discharges into water.

The prior authorization theme has been taken up at EC level with the introduction of a directive on Integrated Pollution Prevention and Control (Commission, 1996b). The directive is similar to the UK IPC system but with some significant differences. The concept of best available techniques is retained but without the 'not entailing excessive cost' qualification. None the less, some element of cost-effectiveness and economic viability is retained in the definition of 'best available techniques' in the Directive (Article 2(11)). Under the Directive Member States are to require that installations carrying out certain activities in Annex I to the Directive do not operate without a permit. The permit is to set out conditions for operation including emission limit values for pollutants. Since the Directive allows competent authorities in Member States to issue permits and set emission limits, it is likely that discrepancies between the levels of emissions permitted among the Member States will persist.

Liability/responsibility

The question of liability for environmental harm is perhaps the most complex and the most pertinent for business. This section focuses on UK law, but the principles are remarkably consistent from state to state.

Criminal liability

Legal systems all over the world are extending the scope of environmental crime. In the UK, the EPA creates a number of criminal offences, such as carrying on an activity without the appropriate licence or in breach of conditions attached to a licence. The penalties for such offences are potentially high. Space only permits that a number of the principal offences are noted here.

1 *Statutory nuisance*. Under s.80(4) EPA, it is an offence to contravene an abatement notice served by a local authority in respect of a statutory nuisance. Statutory nuisances include premises in such a state as to be prejudicial to health or a nuisance; smoke, fumes or gases emitted from premises so as to be prejudicial to health or a nuisance; and any dust, steam, smell of other effluvia arising on industrial, trade or business premises so as to be prejudicial to health or a nuisance.

2 *Air pollution*. The principal offences in relation to air pollution fall under the IPC/APC regimes in Part I EPA, the most significant of which is carrying on a prescribed process without an authorization or in breach of a condition of an authorization. The Clean Air Act 1993 further outlines offences relating to chimney, boiler and furnace emissions. However, there are already proposals to repeal certain provisions of the Clean Air Act 1993. Note also that the Act does not apply to IPC or APC processes regulated under Part I EPA.

3 *Water pollution*. Under s.85 WRA 1991, a person commits an offence if he or she causes or knowingly permits any poisonous, noxious or polluting matter or any solid waste matter to enter any controlled waters. In effect, s.85 creates two separate offences: 'causing' and 'knowingly permitting' water pollution.

4 *Waste*. Under Part II EPA, s.33, it is an offence to deposit, treat, keep or dispose of controlled waste or to knowingly cause or knowingly permit controlled waste to be deposited, treated, kept or disposed of in or on any land or by means of any mobile plant, except under and in accordance with a waste management licence. Additionally, an offence is created of treating, keeping or disposing of waste in a manner likely to cause pollution of the environment or harm to human health, regardless of whether a waste management licence is held.

Section 34 EPA introduces a new duty of care in relation to waste. Any person who imports, produces, carries, keeps, treats or disposes of controlled waste, or who has control of such waste as a broker, is under a duty to take all reasonable steps to prevent contraventions by any other person of s.33 (above), to prevent the escape of waste from his control or from that of any other person, and to ensure that waste is only transferred to an authorized person or to persons authorized for transport purposes.

Hazardous waste is subject to the basic provisions on waste discussed above, and also to additional Regulations: Special Waste Regulations 1996 S.I. 1996 No 972 as amended by S.I. 1996 No 2019. Essentially, hazardous waste (special waste) is subject to a consignment note procedure. Failure to comply with the Regulations is an offence.

Finally, under the Control of Pollution (Amendment) Act 1989, it is an offence for any person who is not a registered carrier of controlled waste to transport controlled waste. Applications for registration must be made to the relevant waste regulation authority. The Act also provides for the seizure in certain circumstances of vehicles which have been used for disposing of waste illegally.

5   *Genetically modified organisms.* Under Part VI EPA, s.118 it is an offence to import, acquire, keep or release certain genetically modified organisms (GMOs) without a consent from the Secretary of State. In relation to other GMOs, there must be an assessment of the environmental risks and notification to the Secretary of State who will determine whether a consent is required. In all cases (i.e. whether a consent is required or not), a duty is imposed on those involved with GMOs to use BATNEEC to keep GMOs under control and prevent them causing damage to the environment.

6   *NB Liability of directors and officers.* It should be noted that in relation to environmental offences, in certain circumstances, individual officers of the company may themselves be held criminally liable. For example, under s.217(1) WRA 1991, where a company is found guilty of an offence under the WRA and it is proved that the offence was committed with the consent or connivance of, or was attributable to neglect on the part of, any director, manager, secretary or other similar officer of the company (or any person purporting to act in such capacity), then that person may also be prosecuted and subject to the penalties provided in the Act. A similar provision is contained in s.157 EPA 1990. Moreover, where the affairs of a body corporate are managed by its members, then the same principle applies in relation to the acts or default of a member in connection with his functions of management as if he were a director of the body corporate.

One example of liability under statute in the UK is the *National Rivers Authority* v. *Alfred McAlpine* case. The defendants (McAlpines) were building houses on a residential development which was intersected by a stream. The stream became cloudy downstream of the development, and was inspected by the National Rivers Authority. McAlpines was charged with causing wet cement to enter the stream contrary to the Water Resources Act 1991.

The Divisional Court held that McAlpines did not escape liability by showing that those at head office did not determine the design of the construction which caused the pollution. Liability was established by showing that the pollution was caused by employees acting within the scope of their employment. Further, the court stated that there was no reason why the legislature should not place responsibility for environmental protection on companies as a matter of public policy. Companies were in a position to ensure through training supervision and maintenance that pollutants were not discharged into controlled waters.

Clean up costs

In addition to facing criminal penalties companies may also, or alternatively, find themselves liable under the EPA and WRA for the costs of cleaning up environmental damage. Such clean-up costs may exceed any fine imposed. Section 73(6) EPA provides that where any damage is caused by waste which has been deposited in or on land, then any person who deposited it or knowingly caused or permitted it to be deposited so as to commit an offence under s.33 (above) or under s.63(2) is liable for the damage except where the damage was due wholly to the fault of the person who suffered it or was suffered by a person who voluntarily accepted the risk of damage being caused.

Civil liability

The question of civil liability for environmental harm, i.e. liability for damage caused to third parties, is dealt with under English law in the context of the traditional common law rules. A plaintiff might be most likely to bring an action for environmental damage under the head of private nuisance or under the rule in the case of *Rylands* v. *Fletcher*. Negligence may also be available as a cause of action (Pugh and Day, 1996). Broadly, nuisance involves interference with a person's use and enjoyment of land, and thus a plaintiff would need an interest in the land affected in order to found a claim, and would additionally need to show fault or unreasonableness on the part of the defendant. The rule in *Rylands* v. *Fletcher* incorporates strict liability in relation to escapes from land and establishes that where a person brings, collects or keeps on his land anything likely to do mischief if it escapes, he will be liable for any damage which is the natural consequence of its escape. However, the application of the rule has been somewhat restricted by the interpretation that it applies only to 'non-natural' uses of land and to a restrictive interpretation of that phrase.

An example of strict liability under common law is provided by the Cambridge Water Case. The Cambridge Water Company (CWC) brought an action for damages against Eastern Counties Leather Plc (ECL) for the contamination of water at CWC's borehole. The contamination was caused by perchloroethane (PCE), an organic chloride used by ECL in the tanning process at its works in Sanston near CWC's borehole.

The decision by the House of Lords (House of Lords, 1993) stressed the importance of foreseeability in establishing liability in nuisance. Under criteria laid down in UK Regulations issued in response to an EEC Directive, the water drawn from CWC's borehole contaminated by PCE (which has never been held to be dangerous to health) was not 'wholesome' and, since 1985, could not lawfully be supplied as drinking water. The judge at first instance found as a matter of fact that the groundwater contamination had taken place before 1976. Consequently, at the time of the contamination no one at ECL could reasonably have foreseen the resultant damage to CWC. The defendant's appeal was, therefore, allowed.

At the EC level, a wide ranging discussion is under way regarding remedying environmental damage, particularly the possible imposition of strict liability for certain types of damage or for damage arising out of certain activities. A Commission Green Paper on this subject was published in March 1993 (Commission, 1993b), and effectively superseded a proposal for a directive on civil liability caused by waste. The reasons stated in the Green Paper for looking at the question of liability at Community level include public demand for systems of accountability and compensation, and the possibility that the use of different national systems and standards of civil liability for remedying environmental damage among member states could lead to distortions of competition. According to the Green Paper, the fundamental starting point for a harmonized system would be the universal principle that a person should rectify damage that he causes, and hence the principle of prevention and the 'polluter pays' principle set out in the Environment Title in the EEC Treaty.

At least in relation to certain more dangerous activities, the Green Paper appears to favour strict liability, on the grounds that this would increase incentives for better risk management and thus maximize prevention. Where the polluter cannot be identified the Green Paper suggests a form of joint compensation fund, with contributions sought from the economic sector most closely linked to the type of damage in question. The European Commission decided in January 1997 to call for a white paper on environmental liability.

A Council of Europe Convention on Civil Liability for Damage

Resulting from Activities Dangerous to the Environment was opened for signature in June 1993. The Convention is the first international legal instrument to establish general principles for civil liability across a broad range of activities in the area of environmental law, and is based upon the principle of strict liability. The Convention applies only to activities defined therein as 'dangerous' and postulates that an individual acting in a professional capacity and carrying out a dangerous activity is responsible for any risks inherent in the activity, regardless of the level of care taken. An injured party need not therefore prove fault, only establish a causal link.

So far there appear to be only a limited number of signatories to the Convention and the EC has not yet indicated whether any prospective EC scheme would follow similar lines. However, a number of EC states, such as the UK, Ireland, and Germany, have said that they will *not* sign the Convention (*BNA International Environmental Reporter*, 1996c). The EC has still not produced any legislation on liability. It is clearly time for governments to agree on common civil liability standards for environmental law. The UN International Law Commission (ILC) has been working on a liability Convention, but progress has stalled because the ILC does not believe it would be accepted by UN member states. It is expected that this Commission could complete an international treaty concerning transboundary pollution within two or three years.

Lender liability

The debate raised by the Council of Europe Convention, the EC Green Paper and by developments in UK law (as well as by experiences in the US and Canada) has drawn attention to a further issue, namely the possibility of lender liability for environmental damage. The scope of liability under the EPA (both criminal and for clean-up costs) could potentially be wide enough that lenders could incur direct liability – of crucial importance will be the way in which the courts interpret certain 'trigger terms' in the legislation (Jarvis and Fordham, 1993). The trigger terms under the legislation relate principally either to the relationship a person has to an activity or to a piece of land. The types of issues which can arise concern whether, for example, a lender could in certain circumstances be held to be an owner or occupier of land, or what degree of control a lender may have over particular activities. Furthermore, a number of more indirect concerns arise. The imposition of liability for environmental harm may affect the capacity of a business to service its debts, particularly if an EC strict liability scheme is adopted. These concerns will affect the credit assessment procedures employed by lenders. Moreover, lenders will be concerned lest any clean-up costs imposed under the legislation are held to take priority over other debts of the company.

Insurance may also prove more problematic if a scheme such as that envisaged in the EC Green Paper is adopted. Insurance has in any event proved problematic in relation to environmental damage. Many policies exclude gradual pollution, covering only sudden and accidental pollution incidents. Limitations in cover may be written into a policy so that, for example, cover does not extend to paying clean-up costs on the insured's own land. Where policies are written on an 'occurrence' basis, since there is likely to be some delay before claims arise, it may be difficult to determine in which period of insurance (and hence under which underwriter) the occurrence took place. By contrast, policies written on a 'claims made' basis cover claims made in the policy period regardless of the date of the relevant occurrence. Specialized environmental impairment liability policies covering gradual pollution damage have become available to meet some of these difficulties. Such policies are generally on a claims made basis and are site-specific, requiring a site survey prior to providing cover (Lockett, 1996; Salter, 1992).

With regard to these types of concerns, it may be that by adopting environmental management policies and techniques such as those envisaged in the EC ecomanagement and ecoaudit regulation and BS7750 described above, companies may be able to offer comfort to potential lenders and insurers.

An example of lender liability in the US is provided by the Fleet Factors Case (*US* v. *Fleet Factors Corp.*, 821 F.Supp. 707, (S.D.Ga.) 1993). Swainsboro Print Works (SPW) operated a cloth-printing facility in Georgia, which declared bankruptcy in 1981. Fleet Bank (Fleet), as SPW's secured lender, took possession of the contaminated facility to foreclose on the equipment and left the premises 'broom clean'.

In 1984 the Environmental Protection Agency inspected the facility and found $400 000 in environmental damage on the site. The plaintiff brought an action against Fleet (among others) under the Comprehensive Environmental Response Compensation and Liability Act (CERCLA) under which the *current owner and operator of a facility* or any person who owned or operated the facility at the time of the disposal of hazardous substances is liable for the response costs of remedying a release or threatened release of those substances.

After a lengthy appeals process, the Federal District Court ultimately held Fleet liable for clean-up costs at the SPW premises as 'owner or operator' at the time of the hazardous waste disposal. The court explained that lender liability was established by Fleet's 'capacity to influence' the treatment of SPW's hazardous waste. Fleet demonstrated this capacity when it arranged for the removal of known hazardous substances from the SPW site.

Integration

The Treaty on European Union introduced into the EEC Treaty the requirement that environmental protection requirements be integrated into the 'definition and implementation of other Community policies', under Article 130r(2). This integration requirement may be seen as a reflection of the growing awareness that environmental considerations can no longer be considered apart from their broader economic context (and vice versa). Although the new move may seem to signal a greener Community, integration may prove difficult to achieve, as was demonstrated by early opposition within the Commission to proposals to extend environmental impact assessment procedures to policies and programmes.

The theme of integration has also been taken up in the *Second Year Report* of *This Common Inheritance* (Britain's 1990 Environmental Strategy), which emphasizes the importance of integrating environmental considerations into every level of decision-making processes and, significantly, acknowledges that this may involve changing organizational structures and procedures. Within the UK Government itself, the issue of co-ordination of environmental policies has arisen, with a Ministerial Committee on the Environment and designated 'Green Ministers' within each Department (HMSO, 1992: 3.20–3.27). This co-ordination, and guidance from the Department of the Environment, is designed to assist Departments in assessing the environmental implications of *all* their policies although, as at the EC level, it may be that this remains only a theoretical commitment for some time to come.

Precaution

The precautionary principle has emerged as a component of international legal instruments on the environment since the 1980s, and in the Maastricht Treaty has been added to the EEC Treaty, at Article 130r(2), as one of the principles on which Community policy on the environment shall be based. The core meaning of the principle is expressed in Principle 15 of the Rio Declaration adopted at the United Nations Conference on Environment and Development in 1992: 'Where there are threats of serious or irreversible damage, lack of full scientific certainty shall not be used as a reason for postponing cost-effective measures to prevent environmental degradation.'

Reference to precaution, in similar but not always identical terms, has now been made in numerous international instruments, including the Climate Change Convention and the Montreal Protocol. At the level of domestic legislation and business management the precautionary approach may have a number of practical implications. For example, the precautionary approach would support the extended use of environmental impact assessment techniques, and the primacy of clean production methods as opposed to end-of-pipe clean-up or regulation methods. The precautionary principle is likely to be instrumental in future Community proposals for environmental protection measures.

Again, the UK strategy document, *This Common Inheritance* (HMSO, 1990: para. 1.18), made reference at least to precautionary action being appropriate in certain circumstances, where there are significant risks of damage and where the balance of likely costs and benefits justifies precautionary action, or where irreversible effects may follow if action is delayed.

An example of the application of the precautionary principle in Australia is the Leach Case (*Leach* v. *Director General of National Parks and Wildlife and Shoalhaven City Council*, Land and Environment Court of NSW, 23 November 1993). This case involved a merit appeal against a decision by the National Parks and Wildlife Service to grant Shoalhaven Council a licence to 'take or kill' endangered species (including the giant burrowing frog and the yellow-bellied glider) during the construction of a road. It was submitted on behalf of the applicant that the available scientific material relating to the giant burrowing frog in general, and its presence at the proposed site in particular, was insufficient to allow an accurate estimate of the impact of the grant of the licence on the species both locally and regionally. Accepting this, Justice Stein held that the matter was one in which it was, therefore, appropriate to apply the precautionary principle.

Although the National Park and Wildlife Act does not expressly allow for the application of the principle, Judge Stein held that the precautionary approach was relevant to his decision. The Judge stated:

While there is no express provision [in the Act] requiring consideration of the 'precautionary principle', consideration of the state of knowledge or uncertainty regarding a species, the potential for serious or irreversible harm to an endangered fauna and the adoption of a cautious approach in protection of endangered fauna is clearly consistent with the scope of the Act.

He stated that it would be permissible to conclude that the state of knowledge was such that one should not grant a licence to 'take or kill' the species until much more was known. Further, the Judge held that the Council had not sufficiently analysed possible alternative routes. The licence was, therefore, refused in so far as it sought to permit the taking or killing of the giant burrowing frog.

Conclusions

There is currently a mood of frustration bordering on contempt for regulation concerning the environment. Market mechanisms it is said are more responsive to the needs of economic development out of which wealth, innovation and business solutions to environmental problems emerge. There are some dangerous delusions here along with a lot of good sense. Market mechanisms very often require law to make them effective even if they do not always require specific regulation. People do not seem to be attracted to taxes any more than standard setting rules. However the idea that there is too much regulation, too many rules that appear removed from the real life of business and industry is readily understood. We may need less law but better law.

It is ironic to observe that the more complex our society becomes the less able our complex legal rules seem up to the task of guiding behaviour. Increasing complexity seems to require broader principles for action followed by a considerable amount of space for the actor to select the correct solution for the particular problem. Ultimately, we need to trust our human, fallible ability to judge environmental management issues. Environmental law provides a language for judgement, no more. We need to be humble about the power of the law to solve environmental problems and confident enough to declare that law is essential.

Notes

1   The authors wish to thank Tanya White for her assistance in researching and editing this chapter.
2   Introducing a new s.71A into the Town and Country Planning Act 1990.

References

Bureau of National Affairs International Environmental Reporter (1996a). **19**(13): 544.

Bureau of National Affairs International Environmental Reporter (1996b). Special Report. 12 June: 525–527.

BNA International Environmental Reporter (1996c). **19**(11): 434.

Castle, P. and Harrison, H. (1996). *Integrated Pollution Control*. Cameron May.

Commission (1992). *Proposal for a Council Directive Introducing a Tax on Carbon Dioxide Emissions and Energy*. COM (92) 226 Final, Brussels, 30 June.

Commission (1993a). *Proposal for a Council Regulation on Substances that Deplete the Ozone Layer*. COM (93) 202 Final, Brussels, 9 June.

Commission (1993b). *Communication from the Commission to the Council and Parliament and the Economic and Social Committee: Green Paper on Remedying Environmental Damage*. COM (93) 47 Final, Brussels, 14 May.

Commission (1996a). Proposal for a Council Directive on the assessment of the effect of certain plans and programmes on the environment. COM (96) 511.

Commission (1996b). Council Directive 96/61 concerning integrated pollution prevention and control, OJ (1996) L257, 10 October.

European Economic Community (EEC) (1993a). *Towards Sustainability: A European Community Programme of Policy and Action in Relation to the Environment and Sustainable Development*. OJ 1993 C 138/1, 17 May.

European Economic Community (EEC) (1993b). *Council Decision of 24 June 1993 for a Monitoring Mechanism of Community CO2 and Other Greenhouse Gas Emissions*, 93/389/EEC, OJ 1993 L 167/31.

Environmental Data Services (1993). *Taking Stock of Environmental Assessment*. 221 Report 20, June.

Environmental Data Services (1994). *IPC – The First Three Years*.

Her Majesty's Stationery Office (HMSO) (1990). *This Common Inheritance: Britain's Environmental Strategy*. Cm 1200, September.

Her Majesty's Stationery Office (HMSO) (1992). *This Common Inheritance: The Second Year Report*. Cm 2068, October.

House of Lords (1993). *Cambridge Water Company* v. *Eastern Counties Leather*. 2 AC 264 [1994] 1 All ER 53, [1994] 2 WLR 53, [1994] 1 Lloyd's Rep 261, 144 NLJ 15, 9 December.

Jarvis, J. and Fordham, M. (1993). *Lender Liability*. Cameron May.

Lockett, N. (1996). *Environmental Liability Insurance*. Cameron May.

Pugh, C. and Day, M. (1996). *Toxic Torts*, 2nd edition. Cameron May.

Salter, J. (1992). *Corporate Environmental Responsibility: Law and Practice*. pp. 160–162, Butterworths.

Sheate, Wil. (1994). *Making an Impact*. Cameron May.

Part Four

Management Approaches

8 Business strategy and the environment

Pratima Bansal

Environmental matters are 'management responsibilities that rank equally with health and safety; finance; marketing and personnel' according to the Board of Directors of P&O (see Figure 11.3). This level of expressed commitment to issues of the natural environment is becoming increasingly commonplace. It can be attributed in part to the heightened level of awareness of the strategic implications of the natural environment. By leveraging the opportunities created through early adoption of environmental concerns firms can enhance profits; whilst failure to comply to environmental concerns can put the health and livelihood of the company in jeopardy.

The natural environment has presented new opportunities to gain competitive advantage; opportunities which arise from changes in cost and production conditions, and through changes in consumer demands. As the prices of resources respond to shifts in resource supply and demand, so too do the cost conditions under which firms operate, permitting firms opportunities to gain cost-based competitive advantages. Similarly, as customer values adjust to changing social concerns, firms are able to gain competitive advantage by differentiating their products in ways that reflect these shifts in values.

On the other hand, a firm's success is potentially threatened as new environmental legislation is enacted and as stakeholders impose new standards of acceptable operation practices. Non-compliance with these standards threatens the legitimacy of the firm and jeopardizes its very survival. As resource conditions and constituent values change, the opportunities and threats generated by the natural environment become more cogent. Consequently, firms become more responsive to eco-environmental pressures.

This chapter considers the business and environment relationship from the perspective of strategic management. In the first part of the chapter, a corporate environmental strategy is defined and the main strategic changes within an organization are identified. The second part of the chapter addresses the ways in which firms can gain a strategic advantage or avoid a strategic disadvantage by responding to the opportunities and threats exposed by the natural environment.

Defining environmental strategy

Managers consider a range of strategic issues in their planning activities spanning areas such as health and safety, marketing, human resource management and environment. While firms, particularly smaller ones, do not mandate policies in all of these areas, larger firms often will write policy statements in order to reduce ambiguity and anarchy, which can be destabilizing in large organizations. Hence, larger firms more frequently than smaller firms, often define a corporate environmental strategy. A well-defined environmental strategy, often expressed as a corporate environmental policy statement, ensures that a framework is established which will guide the organization when other conflicting issues absorb its attention.

An environmental strategy is a plan which aims to mitigate the environmental effects of the firm's operations and products. Environmental effects include those related to the depletion of natural and scarce resources, to waste accumulation and emissions, and to side effects from material use and unhealthy environments. Although the ergonomic environment in which people work can also be considered part of the natural environment, it is commonly subsumed under the area health and safety. These issues will not be considered explicitly in this chapter.

A firm's corporate environmental strategy can influence organizational change at three levels: policy, process and product. Although a corporate environmental strategy requires only a change to policy, it often has implications for processes and products. The greater the scope of the change across these three levels, the greater the level of organizational commitment to environmental concerns.

In a policy change, all processes and products are scrutinized in order to achieve environmental standards. These changes involve all aspects of the organization's processes and products; they are not limited to specific departments. Specific activities which reflect changes in policies include installing an environmental management system, articulating a corporate environmental policy statement, imposing a corporate environmental audit or engaging in an environmental impact assessment, the training of staff about the environmental impacts of the firm, and imposing guidelines for the suppliers of products. Although environmental policy changes tend to be wide ranging, they do not necessarily require a reduction in environmental effects. These activities suggest the intention of the firm to mitigate its environmental impacts but do not necessarily reflect actions.

Changes in processes and products, on the other hand, reduce environmental effects but their scope is more limited than policy changes. Changes to processes influence the way in which firms do business; that is, they reflect changes in the operations of the company. For example, a firm could reduce the amount of waste it generates by intensifying processes, it could install end-of-pipe solutions so that there are fewer environmental effects, or it could engage in research and development exercises to encourage more environmentally benign processes.

Product level changes can occur at two stages of the product life. First, fewer materials or more environmentally benign materials could be used in assembling the product. For example, food manufacturers are reducing the amount of outer packaging provided with goods, such as yogurt containers, which helps to reduce input, transport and disposal costs. Second, firms can encourage the consumer to dispose of the waste associated with the product in a more environmentally responsible manner. Car manufacturers have been taking greater leadership in designing cars so that they can be more rapidly designed for disassembly and some of the parts recycled. Xerox has been rebuilding photocopiers for decades which has reduced the number of machines going to landfill sites, and has reduced their costs.

Figure 8.1 illustrates the three levels of organizational change pertaining to environmental strategies.

Reasons for an environmental strategy

In an extensive study of fifty UK and Japanese companies, firms provided three reasons for adopting an environmental strategy (Bansal, 1995):

1 to gain a strategic advantage (leveraging opportunities);
2 to avoid a strategic disadvantage (mitigating threats);
3 to act responsibly (feeling good).

When firms aim to build a strategic advantage, managers sense the opportunities exposed through changes in cost and demand conditions, and use these opportunities to build competitive advantage. Activities such as housekeeping measures to lower costs, green marketing, negotiating greater market power or building resource-based competencies fall into this category.

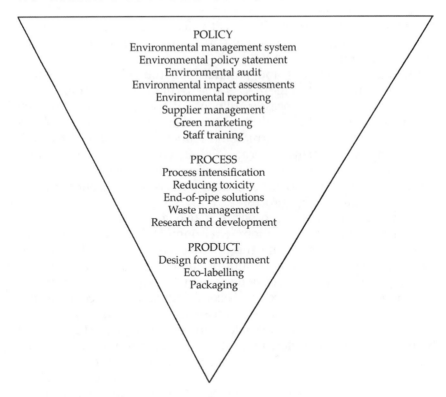

Figure 8.1 Operationalizing environmental strategies

By avoiding a strategic disadvantage, managers recognize that non-compliance will lead to a loss of support by stakeholders for the firm so that the firm's long-term survival could be threatened. Stakeholder management has often been the frame of analysis used in the discussion of corporate environmental management. It is argued that a firm must appease its powerful stakeholders if it is to remain legitimate and secure its survival. The firms must comply to rules and regulations in order to maintain its licence to operate and avoid fines and penalties, build community relations to foster trust in case there is an environmental accident in the future, and appeal to employees to use their best efforts.

When firms act responsibly, they do so out of concern for social interests and are willing to compromise profits in an effort to do what is right. As a result, individual members act out of a sense of values and responsibility rather than strictly a concern for profits. While it is arguable that these actions actually enhance the long-term profit making potential of the firm, individuals engage in

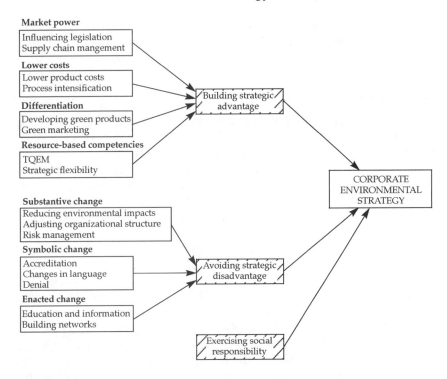

Figure 8.2 Strategic reasons for a corporate environmental strategy

responsible activities sometimes to feel good about the corporation rather than for strategic considerations. They do so for ethical reasons. Nigel Roome discusses the issues of corporate social responsibility and ethics more fully in Chapter 2, so they will not be given further consideration in this chapter.

Firms adopt an environmental strategy for at least one of these reasons. Figure 8.2 illustrates the methods by which firms build strategic advantage and avoid a strategic disadvantage. Each of these methods is discussed in more detail in the remaining part of this chapter.

Building strategic advantage

This section suggests that the natural environment opens up opportunities so that firms can build strategic advantage. Opportunities for strategic advantage are exposed by shifting resource conditions so that the firm can lower its costs, by changing customer prefer-ences so that the firm can differentiate its products, by unveiling new core competencies, and by permitting the firm to build market power. Each of these will be discussed in this section.

Lower costs

Responsible environmental management is logically consistent with low costs. If the quantity of inputs is reduced (including materials, energy, labour) for the same level of output, then waste and emissions will also be reduced if all else remains equal (process intensification). Furthermore, cost savings can be realized through greater care in the procurement and disposal of products. By improvements to processes or products, firms may be able to realize significant cost savings.

There is significant evidence of the potential to lower costs through an environmental strategy. Through the use of voice mail and other office measures, the Quaker Oats Company (Canada) Ltd saved over C$287 000 per year (NRTEE, 1992). Through waste reduction, 3M, through its Pollution Protection Pays programme, saved the company US$500 000 from the period 1975–1989 (Schmidheiny, 1992). Dow Chemical's 'Waste Reduction Always Pays' programme has saved millions of American dollars since the programme began in 1986. Glaxochem Ltd saved £1 million by reducing losses in volatile organic compounds (Hill, Marshall and Priddey, 1994).

Lower product costs

There are two ways in which to lower costs: changes to products and changes to processes. Products can be designed for the environment which not only serve an environmental responsibility objective but also serve to lower costs. Some of the tools which can be used include:

1   reducing toxic substances in the product which lowers disposal and handling costs;
2   substituting materials from non-sustainable sources with products from sustainable sources;
3   reducing the weight of the materials used so that transportation and handling costs are reduced;
4   concentrating the product or providing it in bulk quantities so that handling and packaging costs are reduced.

Levi Strauss, the jeans manufacturer, sold their denim scrap cheaply to Watson Paper of Albuquerque, New Mexico where it was used to produce denim-looking paper which became a marketing success and an innovative way to source supply. A company which started producing polyethylene fencing entirely from recycled resins was able to lower prices because of its lower costs and which led to a 50 per cent increase in sales (Newall, 1990).

Process intensification

Not only can organizations reduce costs through lower product costs, but also through improvements to processes. If an organization is perceived as loosely coupled systems, concern for the natural environment forces firms to more closely examine the connection of those systems. Developing a corporate environmental strategy compels firms to tightly link their operations. This will encourage them to intensify processes in order to gain new efficiencies. Process intensification, however, is not merely an end-of-pipe activity, it requires adjustments to engineering technology. Some examples of process changes which are environmentally sensitive while also serving to lower costs are provided below:

1 just-in-time manufacturing which reduces inventory handling costs and creates less unwanted product;
2 closed loop systems for water use which reduce energy costs and water costs;
3 closed loop systems for product use so that users of products bring them back to manufacturer for reuse or recycle which reduces input material costs;
4 industrial ecosystems where the by-products of one firm's activities serve as inputs into another firm's processes;
5 development of global packaging standards so that less disposable packaging is required;
6 lower energy use manufacturing facilities;
7 paper and packaging recycling which will sometimes raise revenues by selling the waste;
8 reducing toxic waste in processes which reduces hazardous waste removal costs.

Many of the savings realized so far by companies have been achieved by picking low hanging fruit, the housekeeping measures (Hart, 1995). Simple initiatives such as energy, water, and waste reduction have been effective in lowering costs. During the oil price increases of the 1970s, many firms focused their attention on reducing energy consumption. Similarly, the environmental movement also directed firm attention to reducing waste and energy consumption, and since it was anticipated that such activities would lower costs, these initiatives were quickly embraced by businesses. These initiatives included turning off lights, moderating air conditioning, and reduced paper use and recycling paper waste. Not only were firms able to realize cost savings, they were sometimes even able to generate a revenue by recycling some of the waste. Concerns of due diligence have focused attention on the costs associated with poor waste management and the potential to save costs because of the need to monitor and record the generation and movement of these wastes. While it is possible, however, to realize some easy gains through housekeeping measures, most activities which intensify processes require an investment in research and development, or new capital.

There are several examples of firms that have profited through process improvements. For example, a chemical plant formerly sent 6 million pounds of waste nylon to landfill sites each year at a cost of 2 cents a pound, or US$120 000 a year (Newall, 1990). This waste nylon is now recycled into engineering polymers, used to produce parts for office furniture and kitchen utensils. Dutch greenhouses now use water and rock wool in which to grow flowers. This water can be recirculated, which lowers material costs and lowers the risks of infestation which reduces the need for fertilizers and pesticides as well as improving the yield (Porter and van der Linde, 1995).

Differentiation

Cost advantages are not necessarily sustainable because they are based on technologies which can be copied. Product differentiation better helps to secure sustainable competitive advantage. Given the increasing concerns of society for environmental issues, firms are positioned to differentiate their product to appeal to this heightened concern. By differentiating their product offering along dimensions which are meaningful and valued by consumers, firms are able to charge more for their products and services and, therefore, improve profits. Differentiation can be cultivated by making substantive changes to the product or service (green products), or to the branding of the product (green marketing).

Green products

Consumers are becoming increasingly aware of environmental issues in their product purchases. A survey undertaken by Nielsen shows that from 1991 to 1993 80 per cent more consumers were buying environmentally friendly products (Stern, 1994). Through this heightened interest, firms can develop environmentally friend-lier products. IBM was the first to develop an environmentally sensitive laptop computer, the PS/2E, and profitably differentiate the product from that of some of its competitors (Bansal, 1995). Areas which have been particularly receptive to environmentally sensitive product offerings have been in household products such as laundry detergents, toilet paper, tissues, nappies and household detergents. A French disposable nappy manufacturer pioneered the use of nappies made from pulp that is bleached without using toxic chlorine gas (Tully, 1989). The move helped the company to increase its share of the British market from 10 to 13 per cent.

Firms need not only limit themselves to existing markets, they can also seek new markets. Ricoh, the photocopier manufacturer, has been developing a prototype which will 'uncopy' a piece of paper so that a printed page comes out blank. This reverse copier will be a less expensive alternative to producing recycled paper (EIU, 1993).

Green marketing

Green marketing communicates to the potential buyer the ecological attributes of the product. It is an important tool to differentiate products. Green marketing includes all activities related to the product, the presentation of the product or the exchange of the product so that environmental concerns are elevated. Its purpose is to raise the consumer's awareness of the environmental position of the organization. Such practices include:

1 a marketing plan which considers environmental impacts;
2 market research which considers the demand for products which are more environmentally benign;
3 the communication of the environmental aspects of the products.

Communications strategies include advertising, promotion, public relations and consumer affairs. Advertising is achieved in four ways: public service announcements, image advertising, labelling and product-related advertisements.

Food retailers have been particularly effective in marketing their activities as being environmentally sensitive through the deployment of several initiatives such as:

1 offering ecologically friendly brands;
2 offering customers recycling facilities including bottle banks and other recycling banks;

3 upgrading derelict buildings rather than the development of out-of-town hypermarkets on greenfield sites;
4 developing a profile or image which appears ecologically concerned, ethically oriented, and caring through the use of wide-scale and point-of-sale advertising campaigns;
5 eco-labelling.

The Body Shop is often touted as an ideal example of a firm which has successfully differentiated itself through its green marketing. By 1996, it had 1500 shops worldwide in forty-six countries. A more detailed discussion of green marketing is provided by Ken Peattie in Chapter 9.

Resource-based competencies

A firm may be able to secure sustainable competitive advantage by applying its own resources in a combination that can exploit any opportunities available in the organizational environment. An essential aspect of competitive advantage is the development and application of a firm's core competencies. A core competence represents the collective learning of an organization which usually involves the integration of several processes and skills (Prahalad and Hamel, 1991). The natural environment offers a number of ways in which to foster core competencies because of the unique way in which it requires that skills be coupled.

Total quality environmental management

A responsible environmental management system requires a systems approach to manufacturing processes. Environmental engineers must understand how processes inter-relate so that when changes are made to one process, the repercussions on subsequent processes can be estimated. This integrative view of the organization assists management in building core competencies because they will more closely examine areas of efficiency and weakness. They will evaluate the organization not only under the existing lenses of manufacturing and management accounting systems, but under a new lens of environmental management. These core competencies can be developed by installing a total quality environmental management (TQEM) system or by seeking strategic flexibility. By doing so, the firm is more likely to secure a sustainable competitive advantage.

Total quality environmental management (TQEM) system is supported by three pillars: avoiding end-of-pipe pollution control measures, encouraging continuous improvement and discouraging the shifting of environmental effects to another user. By seeking improvements in operations rather than end-of-pipe solutions, long-term costs are reduced and stakeholder satisfaction and loyalty nurtured. By taking cradle-to-grave responsibility for products, proponents of TQEM ensure greater quality in the product that they produce. Continuous improvement ensures that the concerns of stakeholders are met and hopefully exceeded, on an ongoing basis.

A group of twenty-eight companies banded together to develop the Global Environmental Management Initiative (GEMI) which aims at seeking environmental management sustainable development. GEMI has taken the TQM principles and applied them to environmental management by implementing the Business Charter for Sustainable Development developed by the International Chamber of Commerce. Members of GEMI have noted some improvements in the speed at which they respond to environmental reporting requirements, reduced violations on fines and reduced waste generation (GEMI, 1991).

Strategic flexibility

Responsible environmental management practices help firms increase their strategic flexibility. Strategic flexibility is the ability of the firm to respond quickly to events which may influence its performance. It ensures that organizations not only fit with their environment, but that they can adapt to changes by becoming more flexible through appropriate management structures.

Industries which are prone to problems, such as the chemical and pulp and paper industries, must manage their environmental risk. Firms in these industries must address issues pertaining to hazardous waste management and unwanted discharges of effluents. A disaster could be fatal. Strategic flexibility builds awareness and disaster control capabilities within the firm (Shrivastava, 1995). These capabilities permit the firm to practice proactive risk management, risk communication and liability management.

Market power

Finally, firms are able to build strategic advantage by altering market conditions so that they are able to secure greater profits. In this way, competition is altered in a manner in which the firm's low cost leadership, differentiation, or core competencies are emphasized. There are two devices available to firms through a corporate environmental strategy which will enable them to exercise greater power in the market: influencing environmental legislation in their favour, and building supply chain linkages.

Influencing legislation

Firms are also able to build resources if they influence or pre-empt legislation. By influencing legislation, firms may be able to deflect unfavourable environmental legislation. For example, British firms have been effective in avoiding a carbon tax in large part because of heavy lobbying from oil companies (Bansal, 1995). The Contaminated Lands Register was delayed in 1993 in part because of heavy lobbying from financial institutions who were concerned that major tracts of financed land would be devalued. Also, firms which voluntarily demonstrate concern for the environment may be provided special privileges by the government. For example, Princess Cruises was able to secure long-term access to the Grand Cayman Island because they had volunteered to anchor offshore to avoid further congestion. Other cruise ships must reapply every two years to gain access to Grand Cayman Island.

Supply chain management

Firms can also foster resources by building linkages with suppliers through effective supplier management policies. A supplier management policy means that a firm requires that its suppliers meet specific environmental management standards. By doing so, firms establish stronger and tighter links with their suppliers. With these tighter alliances, the firm can build greater security of supply and because the supplier is managing its environmental risk, it is less likely that there will be disruptions of supply, because the resources are sustainable.

Avoiding a strategic disadvantage

The environment offers not only numerous opportunities for firms but, if not managed properly, poses a threat to a firm's success. It does so in two ways. First, if firms do not respond to environmental opportunities, and their competitors do, they risk placing themselves at a competitive disadvantage. Firms must, therefore, respond quickly to the changing desires of customers so that they do not lose market share. Secondly, by not responding to constituent demands, firms also risk the possibility of losing stakeholder support and, therefore, losing legitimacy among stakeholders. Such a loss of legitimacy could eventually threaten the firm's operations if the firm's licence to operate is withdrawn.

Whereas the discussion of opportunities relies heavily on our study of competitive advantage, the discussion of threats relies more heavily on our notion of organizational legitimacy (Meyer and Rowan, 1991; Suchman, 1995). Although legitimacy is widely understood, its precise definition has remained obscured by its multiple interpretations. In this section, the notion of organizational legitimacy is defined within the context of environmental management and, then, the ways in which it is maintained are outlined.

Organizational legitimacy is defined as 'cultural support for an organization' (Meyer and Scott, 1983: 201). A firm's constituents, or stakeholders, judge a firm's legitimacy. If the firm is illegitimate in the opinion of the stakeholder, the stakeholder will withdraw support for the organization: customers will stop purchasing product, employees will withhold best efforts, shareholders will sell shares, government officials will withdraw the firm's licence to operate. Significant withdrawal of stakeholder support will destabilize the corporation and could threaten its survival.

By aligning themselves with the views of constituents, firms can ensure that they remain legitimate. The firm is legitimate when congruence is achieved. This relationship is illustrated in Figure 8.3.

There are no degrees of legitimacy; there are only degrees of illegitimacy. Because legitimacy is the summation of the incongruities across all constituents and across all business functions, even the most honourable firm will be considered illegitimate by some constituents. The greater the degree of illegitimacy the greater the likelihood that stakeholders will withdraw support. When a sufficient number of improprieties are affecting a sufficient number of people, a critical mass will be reached making the firm's performance volatile.

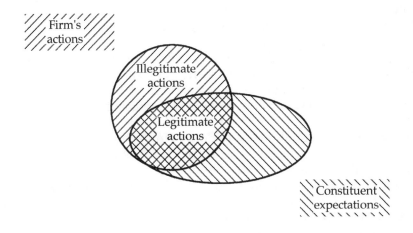

Figure 8.3 Legitimate actions

The relationship between constituent expectations and firm's actions is dynamic. Firm's actions will change over time as its competitive strategies are adjusted, but more importantly, stakeholder values will change over time as more information about the environment is gained and fashions change. Hence, the firm must engage in continuous monitoring of stakeholder values.

Whereas firms earn strategic advantage by being different from other firms, firms avoid a strategic disadvantage by being similar to other firms. Firms are able to retain congruence by making substantive changes to their activities, by making symbolic changes so that constituents believe that the organizational activities are congruent with their expectations, or the firm can attempt to enact change by influencing the expectations of constituents. Each of these three changes will be reviewed in the following sections.

Substantive change

Reducing environmental impacts

A substantive change requires that the firm change its practices so that it more closely aligns itself with constituent expectations. In the case of environmental management, it requires that the firm reduce its environmental impacts. As each constituent has different expectations of the firm, it is often difficult for the firm to know which set of expectations it should meet. The clearest expression of expectations is articulated in law and regulations.

Obeying the law suggests that the firm is meeting the minimal conditions for legitimacy. Non-compliance with legal requirements is often judged as a clear defiance by the organization to a minimum standard. The imposition of fines and penalties for breaking the law is a clear signal to stakeholders that the firm has stepped outside a social norm.

Often legal standards do not go far enough in meeting the demands and desires of stakeholders. For example, there is no UK law which requires that car manufacturers regulate the emission of paint dust. However, when there is a significant amount of paint dust in the air, it will collect on the cars, houses and gardens of the nearby community. Whereas the car manufacturer is not compelled to minimize these emissions, it is good practice to do so in order to avoid conflicts with the local community.

Another example is provided by the noxious fumes associated with the reformulated petrol sold in California. Because of the recent development of reformulated petrol, there was no legislation to protect consumers against its noxious fumes. Consequently consumers were becoming sick from exposure to this fuel. At first, firms were defiant, not willing to recognize the distress being caused to individuals. Later, to retain legitimacy, they withdrew the reformulated petrol recognizing that the sales of other products were being jeopardized because of it. The firm must, therefore, assess whether the law goes far enough in controlling environmental impacts so that the concerns of stakeholders are met.

As constituents set expectations and judge a firm's legitimacy, the firm must be cognizant of these expectations if it wants to remain legitimate. Because these expectations change, and because the power of individual constituents can also shift, the firm must negotiate relative demands. Constituents, which may initially appear to have little power, can mobilize sufficient support to influence organizational health. Such was the case with Shell in 1995 when it had requested to sink the Brent Spar in the North Sea. Greenpeace was able to significantly raise the exposure to the issue so that the firm faced consumer boycotts throughout Europe. Shell caved in and later decided to ferry the oil platform to land and dismantle it. Ironically, there still remained considerable debate as to the most environmentally responsible action.

Adjusting organizational structure

An organization is designed so as to buffer the pressures within its environment. Firms will organize themselves so that they are better able to meet competitive pressures and normative pressures from powerful constituents. It is often argued that a firm's organizational structure must fit its strategy. Similarly, organizations can be designed so as to accommodate technical or social considerations. Positions are created to provide technical information such as a legal analyst and government liaison officer. Also, formal decision-making structures can be adjusted in order to alter the patterns of coalition and domination and absorb greater information flows. In the area of environmental management, this could involve the striking of an environmental committee, the creation of an environmental department, or the appointment of an environmental manager.

Adjusting the organizational structure assists in buffering environmental pressures. When the firm encounters an environmental issue, the environmental director, who is informed in such matters, can ensure that the organization is receptive to responding the issue. Without designating formal decision-making the organization takes the risk of ignoring the issue whose importance could escalate tremendously over time. Managers could effectively influence corporate culture so that internal constituents are apprised of the environmental responses of the firm. For the purposes of environmental management this could mean staff training or awareness programmes, internal memoranda and newsletters dealing with environmental issues, awareness-raising campaigns such as those aimed at paper recycling and waste reduction, highly visible environmentally responsible activities and a corporate environmental policy.

Managing environmental risk

Finally, firms suffer greater losses in legitimacy with a major crisis. A firm's illegitimacy gap increases at an increasing rate with each infraction. Therefore, it is important for the firm to minimize major disasters by investing wisely and ensuring that equipment is operating correctly. Environmental audits and environmental impact assessments will help to ensure that this is the case. Also, by spending more time understanding the future direction of legislation and potential environmental impacts of a new or existing process, changes can be made in order to minimize disaster.

Union Carbide's gas leak in Bhopal, India, in 1984, the nuclear meltdown in Chernobyl in 1986 and the oil spill off the coast of Alaska by the *Exxon Valdez* in 1989 are all reflections of poor risk management. The results were catastrophic, environmentally and financially, and they were magnified unnecessarily by the response of the organization after the environmental incursion.

Firms can manage risks in three ways. First, by issues management they can develop a process which ensures that they scan the environment for important social and political issues. Issues management serves two purposes. First, it minimizes surprises to the organization because it acts as an early warning system. Second, issues management provides a rapid systems response so that surprises are more effectively absorbed through greater coordination and integration within the organization. Exxon, through its Oil Spill Response System, monitors carefully oil spills and has outlined the steps which must be taken to mitigate both the damage of the spill and the damage to the firm's legitimacy. This system was developed after the *Exxon Valdez* incident in 1989.

Second, the organization may also attempt to alter the mix of constituents and the degree of its dependence on them (Pfeffer and Salancik, 1978). Altering resource dependencies permits greater latitude in the firm's actions. By developing long-term contracts, alternative suppliers and slack resources, the organization can develop greater degrees of freedom in behaviour. Therefore, if a firm is suffering a legitimacy crisis from one set of stakeholders, it can shift resource dependencies to alleviate some discontent. For example, a firm which uses tropical hardwoods may have difficulty in procuring supply and may suffer the wrath of some constituents.

By securing the supply of hardwoods from sustainable sources, the firm can retain legitimacy and gain better security of supply.

Finally, in cases in which a firm has an unmanageable amount of risk, the firm can reduce that risk by outsourcing activities. The firm essentially shifts the risk to the supplier of these activities. The firm would engage in only those activities for which there is low environmental risk and regulate their suppliers for adequate environmental policies. For example, large oil companies will often outsource the storage and transportation of crude oil. In the unfortunate event of a spill, the firm is able to dampen the associated negative publicity by insisting that another firm was responsible for the accident. Although this response does not eliminate responsibility, it does help to mitigate some of the negative effects.

Symbolic change

Accreditation

By aligning itself with a set of symbols, a firm earns greater credibility and legitimacy. If concerns are raised by stakeholders of the firm's legitimacy, the firm can point to past exemplary performance demonstrated by the symbols with which it is aligned. Firms can align themselves with people or with intangible symbols to help buffer the impact. By using socially acceptable procedures to carry out controversial activities, organizations can maintain an appearance of legitimacy even when such activities clash with social norms (Epstein and Votaw, 1978).

An increasing number of firms are seeking BS 7750 accreditation as well as applying for environmental awards. In environmental management, there are numerous awards for which firms may apply including the Chartered Association of Certified Accountants award for Environmental Reporting and the RSA's Award in Environmental Management. Aligning the firm with high profile environmental spokespeople, or endorsing some of the activities of green advocacy groups such as Greenpeace or Friends of the Earth may also help secure the firm's legitimacy. The Co-operative Retail Society (CRS), for example, was associated with David Bellamy who is a popular environmental advocate. Gateway has employed the services of Bryn Jones who was at one point closely aligned to the Green Party.

Changes in language

Changing organizational structure often implicitly involves changing vocabulary. Language will adapt to accommodate constituent views so as to offer legitimate accounts. Organizations may espouse socially acceptable goals while actually pursuing less acceptable ones. Organizations are able to forestall enquiry or divert attention through the use of language. Many organizations, in fact, formulate and publicize environmental policies but do not establish procedures for monitoring compliance or meeting goals. Given the ambiguity pertaining to environmental compliance and measurement, management can change how constituents perceive organizational actions. Several organizations in the 1980s were accused of making environmentally friendly claims for products which did not meet the stated standards. Part of the difficulty lay in the ambiguity of the terms used.

The organization may also attempt to colour its actions with a hue of responsibility. Legitimating is largely a retrospective process inasmuch as an organization interprets its past actions in light of current social values. The gas leak at Bhopal provides a good example of the use of language and personal accounts to gain legitimacy. After the leak, company officials deflected blame pointed at the company for negligence by blaming a saboteur (Shrivastava, 1992). Although sabotage was not supported by any accounts, the firm was able to shift some of the negative public opinion.

Changes initiated through language can be fraudulent and benevolent simultaneously. Even if changes in language are not accompanied by substantive changes, language serves as an instrument of generating support from constituents. Internal constituents, especially, may become more committed to the task at hand. The institutionalization of the language creates its own reality so that people support the activity which, in turn, effects substantive changes. A company can create a new set of shared meanings which become integral aspects of not only reflecting change but also instigating change.

Enveloping myths with rationality assists, as well, in selling social issues as technical ones, and hence gives them greater legitimacy (Elsbach, 1994). For example, firms will often use scientific arguments to rationalize their approach to environmental management, or they will point out the lack of scientific consensus to justify their position. Science blurs our understanding of the situation. For example, the debate about the environmental effects of diesel versus that of unleaded petrol rages on. Even in cases where the science is more certain, as in the negative effect of CFCs on the ozone layer, the ways in which to resolve the problem are unclear. Until a good alternative to CFCs is developed, firms will be slow to change, looking to scientific experts to provide reasons to rationalize their inaction.

Offering apologies, denial and concealment

The organization can manage any loss in legitimacy by offering apologies for, or denying past infractions. By acknowledging openly its responsibility for environmental infractions, the firm could potentially save face in the long run with constituents. Johnson and Johnson in 1980 was able to retain, arguably build, legitimacy through its rapid, effective and apologetic response when its Tylenol bottles were found laced with cyanide.

In some cases, a firm is able to buffer threats to its legitimacy by denying and concealing illegitimate trespasses. By concealing its activities, the firm cloaks its operations in secrecy. Hence, it effectively decouples illegitimate parts of the organization from others, highlighting the socially acceptable practices in which the firm engages while simultaneously avoiding discussion of less acceptable practices. Firms will avoid evaluation and inspection from outside agencies in this case because these audits would signal to stakeholders that the firm is not acting competently. Firms seeking to deny environmental incursions often dramatize their ritual commitment to the environmental policy by adapting basic structural elements to concur with constituent expectations. For example, such an organization would not permit access to the contents of its internal audits, but merely hold them up as an act of good faith hoping to pacify constituents.

Enacted change

Education and information

Firms not only have to rely on changing their operations, they can also choose to change the expectations of constituents. The firm has several tools available which can shape constituent values. For example, firms can correct constituent perceptions through education and information, they can reframe the issue so that it is understood differently, and change constituent expectations to be more closely aligned to the firm's activities.

The organization may seek to influence socially institutionalized practices, laws and traditions to meet their own ends. Firms can reduce their illegitimacy in business–government relationships by either attempting to change legislation through lobbying the establishment or by complying with government mandates relating to ethical issues. For example, Miles (1982) shows how the tobacco industry was able to form various coalitions of tobacco interests and influence social values so that the health risks of smoking were never fully understood.

Building networks

Networks of people and organizational members generally increase the coherence in a social system, while at the same time building stability for the participant firms (Zucker, 1988). This process increases the institutionalization of corporate activities permitting the firm greater latitude in its actions. For example, TransAlta Utilities established a panel of local citizens and company staff in 1989. Thirteen Albertans were asked to join TransAlta Utilities to discuss the firm's environmental mission and policy statements. The panel also provided a useful mechanism for TransAlta to hear community concerns, and for community representatives to hear directly from company officials about the company's plans and initiatives. Through this network, TransAlta has secured greater trust within the local community, and the two-way access to information and opinions has given the firm a better understanding of community concerns while simultaneously granting them the opportunity to shape some of those views.

Conclusion

The focus of this chapter was on defining a corporate environmental strategy and the threats and opportunities that the natural environment poses to firms. Many firms will argue that an environment strategy is costly, time-consuming, or attention-distracting, or they will suggest that the uncertainty and complexity pervading environmental science, consumer demand and stakeholder concerns make it difficult to assess whether an environmental strategy is profitable. However, there still exist compelling reasons for an environmental strategy.

In this chapter, I argued that there were three reasons why firms should adopt an environmental strategy: to gain a strategic advantage (leveraging opportunities), to avoid a strategic disadvantage (mitigating threats) and to act responsibly (feeling good). The first two of these motivations were discussed in this chapter. The last, which is rooted in a discussion of corporate social responsibility and ethics, is left to Nigel Roome in Chapter 2.

The natural environment offers a strategic opportunity by exposing new ways in which to earn a strategic advantage over other firms. First-movers may be able to earn a sustainable competitive advantage if they are able to gain experience early and build stakeholder trust and loyalty. Competitive advantage can be earned by exploiting changes in resource conditions and, hence, reduce costs and by differentiating their product in line with customer desires. The natural environment also poses the opportunity to leverage new core competencies, build links with government officials to shape legislation in their favour, and to develop networks with suppliers which offer favourable conditions. By leveraging these opportunities, firms can secure above normal profits.

The natural environment also poses a strategic threat if firms do not comply with the expectations of constituents. These include the rules and expectations dictated by government legislators, customers, shareholders, the local community and other key constituents. The failure to respond will threaten the firm's legitimacy. A substantial increase in the organization's illegitimacy can threaten the firm's survival as governments impose fines and penalties, customers withdraw purchases, employees withhold best efforts and the local community denies its licence to operate. Firms can respond to constituent expectations by making substantial changes to their operations, by making symbolic changes to their operations so that constituents believe that the firm is complying to their expectations, or by changing the expectations of constituents. By accommodating the expectations of constituents firms introduce greater stability in their environment by building trust with stakeholders and consequently, they are better able to secure their long-term survival.

This chapter does not advocate the adoption of a corporate environmental strategy but it suggests that environmental strategies are becoming increasingly relevant to organizational effectiveness. The failure of organizations to analyse the opportunities and threats exposed by the changes in science and constituent expectations to the natural environment could seriously jeopardize their competitive position.

References

Bansal, P. (1995). Why do firms go green? The case for rational legitimacy, PhD thesis, University of Oxford.

Economist Intelligence Unit (EIU) (1993). *Best Practices: Environment.* Report number I-769, EIU.

Elsbach, K. D. (1994). Managing organizational legitimacy in the California cattle industry: the construction and effectiveness of verbal accounts. *Administrative Science Quarterly*, **39**(1), 57–88.

Epstein, E. M. and Votaw, D. (eds) (1978). *Rationality, Legitimacy, Responsibility: Search for New Directions in Business and Society.* Goodyear Publishing.

Global Environmental Management Initiative (GEMI) (1991). Proceedings of the First Conference of the *Global Environmental Management Initiative: Corporate Quality Environmental Management.* GEMI.

Hart, S. (1995). A natural-resource-based view of the firm. *Academy of Management Review,* **20**(4), 986–1014.

Hill, J., Marshall, I. and Priddy, C. (1994). *Benefiting Business and the Environment.* Institute of Business Ethics.

Meyer, J. W. and Rowan, B. (1991). Institutional organizations: Formal structure as myth and ceremony. In *The New Institutionalism in Organizational Analysis* (W. W. Powell and P. J. DiMaggio, eds) pp. 41–62, University of Chicago Press.

Meyer, J. W. and Scott, W. R. (1983). *Organizational Environments: Ritual and Rationality.* Sage.

Miles, R. H. (1982). *Coffin Nails and Corporate Strategies.* Prentice Hall.

National Round Table on the Environment and Economy (NTEE) (1992). *Prosperity and Sustainable Development for Canada.* Advice to the Prime Minister.

Newall, J. E. (1990). Managing environmental responsibility. *Business Quarterly.* Autumn, 90–4.

Pfeffer, J. and Salancik G. R. (1978). *The External Control of Organizations: A Resource Dependence Perspective.* Harper and Row.

Porter, M. E. and van der Linde, C. (1995). Green and competitive: ending the stalemate. *Harvard Business Review,* September–October, 120–34.

Prahalad, C. K. and Hamel, G. (1991). The core competence of the corporation, In *Strategy: Seeking and Securing Competitive Advantage* (C. A. Montgomery and M. E. Porter, eds) pp. 277–99, Harvard Business School Publishing.

Schmidheiny, S. (1992). *Changing Course: A Global Business Perspective on Development and the Environment.* MIT Press.

Shrivastava, P. (1992). *Bhopal: Anatomy of a Crisis.* Paul Chapman.

Shrivastava, P. (1995). Environmental technologies and competitive advantage. *Strategic Management Journal,* **16**, 183–200.

Stern, A. (1994). *Managing the Environment Challenge in Europe.* The Economist Intelligence Unit.

Suchman, M. (1995). Managing legitimacy: strategic and institutional approaches. *Academy of Management Review,* **20**(3), 571–610.

Tully, S. (1989). What the greens mean for business. *Fortune,* 23 October, 46–52.

Zucker, L. G. (1988). Where do institutional patterns come from? Organizations as actors in social systems. In *Institutional Patterns and Organizations, Culture and Environment* (Lynne G. Zucker, ed.) pp. 23–49, Ballinger Publishing.

9 Environmental marketing

Ken Peattie

Introduction

To many people the concept of environmental, or green, marketing appears to be an anachronism. As a key driver behind the expansion in consumption and production since the late 1950s, marketing has contributed strongly to a level of economic growth which is not environmentally sustainable (or in the terminology of Johnson, 1991, is 'grey' rather than 'green'). Over-consumption, and the marketing which stimulates it, has also been strongly implicated in putting many elements of the global ecosystem under severe pressure (Durning 1992). The word 'marketing' tends to conjure up images of 'hard sell' advertising using changes in fashion or technology to leverage consumers into buying yet another generation of products that they do not need, to replace those they have not yet made full use of. It is perhaps not surprising that in marketing agency Gerstman and Meyer's third annual survey of attitudes to the environment among US consumers, marketers were identified as the profession 'least concerned about the environment' by 91 per cent of respondents.

Despite such negative associations, marketers and marketing have often been at the forefront of the commercial response to the environmental agenda and the challenge of moving towards sustainability. For some companies this has been a reactive measure, with marketers being drafted in to conduct damage limitation exercises and rebuild stakeholder confidence in the wake of some form of environmental public relations disaster. For more proactive companies environmental marketing is simply an extension of their desire to respond to customer needs, or it may develop in response to perceived opportunities for competitive advantage through improved ecoperformance. Whatever the motives behind an individual company's decision to adopt the principles and practice of environmental marketing, it is a very different form of marketing and requires a wide range of new approaches.

The uses of the word 'marketing' are many and varied; it can refer to:

1 activities that producers engage in to get their market offerings to their customers;
2 a business function responsible for activities such as market research, advertising and customer service;
3 a philosophy or concept that guides the actions of the company;
4 an academic discipline.

An important distinction to draw is between 'selling' and 'marketing'. Although selling is an important marketing activity, a selling orientation involves a company creating a product and then trying to persuade consumers to buy it, regardless of the degree to which that product meets the needs of the customer. A marketing-orientated company begins with the customer's needs, and seeks to generate profit by integrating all its efforts and resources behind the drive to meet those needs. An important point to note is that much of the activity which has reflected badly on both 'marketing' and 'environmental marketing' are actually a result of companies adopting a selling orientation, particularly when faced with the threats and opportunities which the environmental challenge presents.

The evolution of environmental marketing

Marketing is one of many areas to have experienced profound changes resulting from the emergence of the loosely-knit web of socioenvironmental concerns encompassed in the term 'green movement'. The wave of environmentalism during the early 1970s spawned the 'ecological marketing' concept (Henion and Kinnear, 1976), which complemented the more established 'societal marketing' concept. These remained relatively separate but parallel themes until the mid-1980s when the emerging concept of sustainable development highlighted the indivisible nature of the social and environmental agendas. This background often causes contemporary environmental marketing to be treated with a sense of *deja vu* by marketing academics and practitioners. However, there are some important differences between the environmentalism which confronted marketers in the 1970s and the green movement of the 1990s, and these are summarized in Table 9.1.

Table 9.1 The evolution of environment concern

Factor	1970s environmentalism	1990s green
Emphasis	On 'environmental' problems	On the underlying problems with our social, economic or legal systems
Geographic focus	On local problems (e.g. pollution)	On global issues (e.g. global warming)
Identity	Closely linked to other anti-establishment causes	A separate movement embraced by many elements of 'the establishment'
Source of support	An intellectual élite, and those at the fringes of society	A broad base
Basis of campaigns	Used forecasts of exponential growth to predict future environmental problems (e.g. Limits to Growth)	Uses evidence of current environmental degradation (e.g. the hole in the ozone layer)
Attitude to businesses	Business is the problem, generally adversarial	Businesses seen as part of the solution More partnerships formed
Attitude to growth	Desire for zero growth	Desire for sustainable growth
View of environment/ business interation	Focused on negative effects of business activity on the environment	Focuses on the dynamic inter-relationship between business, society and the environment

Source: Peattie and Charter (1994).

Environmental marketing: definition and fundamentals

Environmental marketing can be defined as: 'The holistic management process responsible for identifying, anticipating and satisfying the needs of customers and society, in a profitable and sustainable way.' (Peattie and Charter, 1994). Three important factors distinguish it from conventional marketing, each of which requires a new perspective on marketing principles and practice (Peattie, 1996). The first is the emphasis on environmental *sustainability*. This extends the time horizon of marketing to become much more open-ended, because the marketer must look beyond a product's economic life cycle to consider the environmental impacts of its long-term use and ultimate disposal or reuse. The pursuit of sustainability will force companies to judge the success of their marketing not just in terms of products' technical and economic performance in the marketplace, but also in terms of the socio-environmental impacts of the company and its products. It should be stressed that sustainability is an ultimate goal, rather like total quality or absolute customer satisfaction. Some companies' environmental marketing has attracted media criticism (including environmentally excellent companies such as Body Shop) because a failure to reach sustainability has been confused with a failure to strive towards it.

The second key element of environmental marketing is the emphasis on *holism*. The marketing concept demands an integrated effort to satisfy meet customers' needs, but conventional marketing tends to define customer needs and satisfaction rather narrowly. In the past, customer satisfaction has been judged in terms of the performance of the product at the moment (or during the period) of consumption. A green consumer, by contrast, may reject a product because they become aware of the socio-environmental harm that a product causes prior to consumption during the production process, or after consumption in terms of product disposal. They may also avoid a product because of activities of the producer, its suppliers or investors but which are not directly related to the product itself. The boycotting of Nescafé relating to Nestlé's activities in the marketing of infant formula milk is a well-known example.

The final key element is the emphasis on balancing the needs of customers with *societal welfare*. Although some commentators have dismissed environmental marketing as societal marketing in a new wrapper, environmental marketing is significantly different in its emphasis on the physical sustainability of the marketing process (as well as its social acceptability); the more holistic and interdependent view of the relationship between the economy, society and the environment; the open-ended rather than just long-term time frame; the treatment of the environment as something with intrinsic value over and above its usefulness to society; and the focus on global concerns, rather than those of particular societies.

Both economics and marketing place a great deal of emphasis on the individual benefits of consumption, while the collective consequences of consumption are assumed to be taken care of by Adam Smith's concept of the 'invisible hand'. This is so strongly ingrained in western culture that moves to curb consumption on the basis of environmental protection are often attacked as being contrary to cherished principles such as freedom and democracy. It was World Bank economist Herman Daly who asserted that individualism represented 'the invisible foot that kicks the heck out of the common good' (Stead and Stead, 1992: 79). Every traffic jam illustrates the problems caused by the collective consequences of individual consumption decisions, and underlines the fact that we cannot assume that trying to maximize satisfaction for individual consumers will maximize the overall benefits of a strategy in terms of customer satisfaction and societal welfare.

Figure 9.1 shows how a concept of eco-performance can be

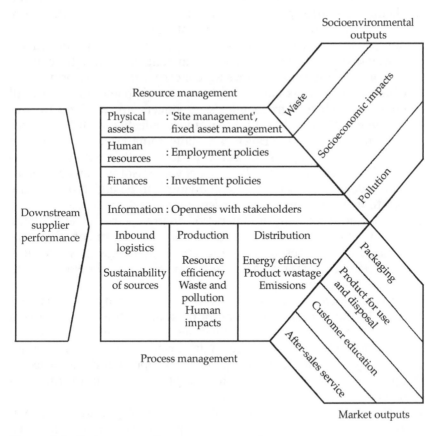

Figure 9.1 Components of corporate eco-performance
(*Source*: Peattie and Charter, 1994).

developed to complement existing notions of economic and technical performance, which embodies the principles of holism, societal welfare and the pursuit of sustainability. This notion of ecoperformance can become central to the marketing of products, brands and entire companies who find themselves on the ever-expanding environmental 'front line'.

Green products

At its most basic, marketing is the process of appropriately marrying up product offerings and customers. Environmental marketing requires new perspectives on both customers and products. There are many ways in which product offerings are changing in response to the green challenge, including:

1 *Product redefinition*: a suntan lotion in the 1990s is less the glamour-enhancing browning agent that it was in the early 1980s, and is much more a skin protector.
2 *New product features*: economy cycles for washing machines, power-save mode on electrical equipment and catalytic converters on cars all reflect increasing concern with ecoperformance.
3 *Changes to product use*: in the case of potentially harmful products such as agrochemicals, producers are working to help customers to use less of them more effectively. ICI's award-winning electrodyn sprayer can allow some crops to be treated effectively with up to 98 per cent less pesticide than conventional application methods and Ecover washing powder comes with a separate bleach sachet allowing it to be added only to the 'white' washes where it is needed.
4 *Product redesign*: car designers for many years have designed cars to hang together regardless of the treatment they are subjected to. In response to the green challenge they are now being asked to design cars which can be easily disassembled to aid recycling initiatives.
5 *Increased product durability*: the actual durability of consumer durables has become an important issue on the environmental marketing agenda with a trend away from disposability and towards 'lifetime' purchasing. Agfa Gevaert switched to a design brief based on durability for their photocopiers and succeeded in upgrading the lifespan of their copier drums from under 3 million copies to over 100 million.
6 *Packaging changes*: with 50 million tonnes of packaging thrown away annually in the EU, packaging has become a major area for response to environmental concern, particularly since for marketers it provides opportunities to make significant improve-

ments in ecoperformance without the costs and risks involved in changing the core product. The challenge is to decrease the amount of packaging used, and its environmental impact, while still promoting and protecting the product. Packaging is also being redesigned by companies in response to legislation such as the EU Directive on Packaging and Waste, which is based on the concept enshrined in the German packaging ordinances, that producers should take responsibility for the eventual fate of their packaging materials.

At a more fundamental level, the emphasis on holism that environmental marketing brings is causing the product concept itself to be re-evaluated. If green consumer satisfaction depends upon the production process and on all the activities of the producer, we are approaching the situation where the company itself is becoming the product consumed. Drucker's famous concept that 'Marketing is the whole business seen from its final result, that is from the customers' point of view' (Drucker, 1973: 74), seems set to become an enforced reality for many businesses, because the green movement means that customers (or those who influence them) are now actively looking at all aspects of their company. As Bernstein (1992) points out, companies are becoming increasingly unable to hide anonymously behind their brands.

The question of what represents a 'green' product is a difficult question. There are absolute green products which actually contribute to environmental improvement about which there will be no debate. For other products it is a question of the degree as to whether they are relatively green (sustainable) or grey (unsustainable), and this can change significantly according to the weightings that are attached to different forms of environmental impact. While companies like BMW and Volvo argue over who produces the greenest car, many environmentalists are trying to interrupt the debate to point out that there is no such thing. There are several elements that can influence the perception of a product's greenness including its constituents, its purpose, the consequences of product use and misuse, product durability and product disposal.

We can define a product or service as 'green' when its environmental and societal performance, in production, use and disposal, is significantly improved and improving in comparison to conventional or competitive product offerings (Peattie, 1996). This definition has the following important characteristics:

1 A dual focus on environmental and societal performance. Only performing well on one dimension is unlikely to create a credible green strategy.

2   A continuous improvement orientation. Since what constitutes 'green' is constantly changing, it requires improvement to be a continuous process rather than a single event.
3   A use of both competitor offerings and past products as a yardstick for comparison. Therefore a company could still become greener while lagging behind competitors in terms of ecoperformance, providing it could demonstrate significant and continuous ecoimprovement.
4   An emphasis on significant change in response to customer and other stakeholder needs.

Such a broad definition, can be criticized as being vulnerable to abuse by unscrupulous marketers, but to go to the other extreme and only allow sustainable products to be marketed from an environmental platform would simply remove any incentives for improvement among the companies that need it most.

Green customers

The word 'consumer' epitomizes a view of customers, not as people, but as a means of consumption. Marketing theory tends to deal with individual customer wants or needs, but in reality people have many wants, some of which will conflict, such as a desire to own and drive a car, and a desire to live in an unpolluted environment. Just as products can be more accurately analysed as a 'bundle of benefits', a customer should be considered as possessing a 'bundle of wants and needs'. In the face of conflicting desires to consume and conserve, customers may increasingly seek satisfaction through non-purchase decisions (such as repairs). By contributing to reduced environmental degradation, green consumer behaviour addresses an inherent human need for a viable environment, which may sometimes be at the expense of more explicit material wants.

Customer needs drive the marketing process, and the efforts of marketers are dedicated to meeting those needs, and sometimes to persuading consumers that their needs can be met. If businesses are to become more sustainable, then green consumer demand will have an important part to play, alongside legislation, green investment and the influence of other key stakeholders. In the past consumers have often used their influence, and sometimes have refused to patronize particular companies and products, in response to socioenvironmental concerns. Following the concern created by Limits to Growth, concepts such as 'responsible consumption' (Fisk, 1973), 'responsible simplification' (Mead, 1970) and 'socially conscious consumption' (Anderson and Cunningham, 1972) emerged. Despite the development of such concepts, environmentally motivated consumer behaviour was seen as a marginal marketing issue until the late 1980s. However, Kardash as early as 1974, suggested that virtually everyone can be classified as an 'ecologically concerned consumer'. This is because, providing that other factors such as price are relatively equal, most people would discriminate in favour of an environmentally superior product.

It was the worldwide boycott of CFC-driven aerosols, orchestrated by environmental groups in response to growing concern about ozone layer depletion, that drew companies' attention to consumers' ability to express their environmental concerns in a way that could affect businesses suddenly, profoundly and on a global scale. Since then in the EU, environmental concern has continued to rise in virtually all member states (Leeflang and Raaij, 1995), as it has in the majority of the world's societies.

Ten years after the arrival of 'green consumer' companies are still trying to work out exactly who they are, what they want and how to market to them. Ottman (1992 a) points out that the term 'green consumer' is something of an oxymoron, since consumption and the resultant creation of waste is the antithesis of a truly green philosophy. Although 'green customer' and 'green purchasing' might be more accurate terms, with the publication of *The Green Consumer Guide* (Elkington and Hailes, 1988) and its translation into a wide range of languages, the term 'green consumer' has developed into something of a global standard, despite its inherent contradictions.

The guide defined the green consumer as one who would avoid products which:

1 endanger the health of consumers or others;
2 significantly damage the environment in production, use or disposal;
3 consume disproportionately large amounts of resources during production, use or disposal;
4 cause unnecessary waste through overpackaging, excess product features or an unduly short lifespan;
5 use materials derived from endangered species or environments;
6 involve cruelty to, or needless exploitation of, animals;
7 adversely affect other countries, particularly developing countries.

Such a definition is rather narrow because it does not encompass consumers discriminating in favour of environmentally improved products, and it excludes non-purchase consumption behaviour. Environmental concern can be expressed through recycling products and packaging; through different forms of purchase (for example leasing instead of buying); through frugal product use and in the maintenance and reuse of consumer durables. Marketers are seeking ways to respond appropriately to the greening of consumers, and Ottman (1992b) suggests four E principles:

1   *Easy*: make it easy for your customers to be green;
2   *Empower customers*: by providing them with solutions and information;
3   *Enlist support*: from customers;
4   *Establish credibility*: with all the businesses' stakeholders to guard against any form of backlash.

One difficulty for the environmental marketer is that the conventional view that 'the customer is king' and a marketing process based around serving explicit customer needs is that it assumes that consumers actually know and understand their needs. However, on socioenvironmental issues consumers are often interested, but very confused or poorly informed. A survey of 1500 US *Consumer Reports* members found that even among these very well-informed consumers, the majority got at least ten out of sixteen straightforward questions about the environment wrong. In such a situation, marketers need to take a more responsible attitude towards consumers, and instead of treating them as a monarch to be obeyed, treat them as someone they have a responsibility to inform and educate as well as serve. Although such a concept may appear overly paternalistic to some, it actually reflects the style of marketing already well established in professional service markets and replaces the simple notion of customer satisfaction with the concept of 'consumer welfare' (Mulhern, 1992).

Segmenting green markets

A key question for marketers is how to identify green consumers, and whether there is some basis on which they can be separated out into distinct green market segments in order to be targeted. There have been many attempts to define green consumers in terms of age, gender, socioeconomic status, education level, location, environmental knowledge and lifestyle. Most of these studies have created inconsistent, and sometimes contradictory, results (Peattie, 1996). The only reliable conclusion that can be drawn is that there is no such thing as a typical green consumer. There is an ultra-green segment with a lifestyle highly orientated towards the environment, who offer a potential target to companies who can produce a highly credible green offering. Otherwise environmental concern appears to cut across other conventional segmentation bases. Table 9.2 demonstrates a 1989

Table 9.2 A green segmentation of the UK market

Group	Level of knowledge and concern	Comparison with 1988	Main environmental concerns	Comments
Girls 15	Low – main focus on self	Same	Animals – cosmetic testing; whale and seal hunting	Could grow into green consumers later on
Men 16–22	Moderate concern, but limited personal involvement	Increased knowledge	Whatever the current media focus is on	Cynical about government and manufacturers' motives
Women 18–30	Moderate	Increasing knowledge, trial of green products	General	Will try green products, but can revert if functional performance is poor
Women under 30 with 1 child	High	Growing activity – definitely becoming greener	Those affecting children's health – food production, pesticides, leaded petrol	The most obvious green consumers
Women 35–45 with children 13–18	High	Growing knowledge and activity	All major issues that will affect their children's future	Children acting as educators
Retired men and women	High	Increased knowledge and activity	Deterioration in quality of life	'Have to regard the fight for the environment like the Blitz – all do your bit'
Men and women 25–45 'embarrassed capitalists'	High	Growing sense of individual responsibility. Greater knowledge	General – depends on media focus	Environmental concern becoming normalized
Men and women 'empty nesters' (no children at home)	High	Growing concern	Environmental issues have become the greatest threat of the twentieth century (replacing communism)	'Every little bit helps'

Sources: Brand New and Diagnostics Market Research.

green segmentation of the UK market conducted by Brand New and Diagnostics Market Research. It demonstrates the variety of influences on consumers, including the media, values and beliefs, environmental knowledge and family relationships, each of which have the ability to motivate someone in any one of the segments towards green consumer behaviour. Consumers cannot be classified as 'green' in the same, relatively enduring and consistent way that they could be classified as female, French, left-handed, professional or teenage. Different consumers will respond to different issues on the overall green agenda; they will connect these issues to some products but not others, and they will vary in the way that this concern impacts their behaviour.

Consumerism and consumer boycotts

A powerful and direct influence that consumers can have on a company is through the action of a consumer boycott. Boycotts vary between a relatively passive refusal to purchase and consume, to more active, organized and direct protests against companies. Consumer boycotts can be related to a social issue, such as the campaign against Nestlé over its marketing of infant formula milk in developing countries, or an environmental issue such as the those organized against oil companies such as Shell. Rehak (1993) notes that in the USA an annual publication entitled *National Boycott News* put forward a conservative estimate of at least 125 active boycotts in force across America by the end of 1992. He also suggests that such formalized boycotts are only the 'tip of the iceberg' since the 71 per cent of American consumers who had switched brands over environmental issues were each involved in their own private boycotts.

Environmental marketing strategies

The need for a holistic approach to environmental marketing makes it very difficult to draw distinctions between corporate and marketing strategies. One subsidiary within a corporation cannot hope to succeed in an environmental marketing campaign if the activities of other greyer parts of the company will be viewed as discrediting it. Conventional marketing tends to view strategy-making as an intensely competitive process. Although many companies are trying to compete on the basis of ecoperformance, a significant trend within many green markets is an unprecedented level of collaboration between rivals in the development of new technologies to solve common environmentally related problems.

For those companies that are serious about developing an environmental marketing strategy, the success factors can be summarized as the seven Cs:

1 *Customer-orientated*: in addressing environmental issues that concern customers and creating product offerings that balance improved ecoperformance with customer needs for functionality, value and convenience.
2 *Commercially viable*: in ensuring that any technical and economic barriers can be overcome to produce a product offering that will both meet customer needs and make a profit.
3 *Credible*: to customers, senior managers and other stakeholders.
4 *Consistent*: with corporate objectives, strategies and capabilities.
5 *Clear*: it should not be shrouded in environmental or technical jargon. The use of mysterious claims for green detergents such as 'Contains no NTAs' has been heavily criticized by the Consumers' Association.
6 *Co-ordinated*: with the operational strategies and plans of the other business functions.
7 *Communicated*: effectively internally and externally. Internal marketing does just not mean launching environmental policies to staff; it also means keeping the momentum going as the environment becomes just another key business issue.

Implementing environmental marketing: the extended marketing agenda

The green marketing process (Peattie, 1992), as illustrated by Figure 9.2 calls for a broadening of the agenda for marketers in terms of the external forces they must respond to, the internal marketing mix elements that they must manage, and the criteria for success which they must meet. Figure 9.2 attempts to summarize this challenge, and since marketers seem to be comfortable dealing with groups of Ps, the model presents an agenda of 'green Ps', each representing an area which the prospective green marketer needs to understand and respond to.

The marketing environment consists of 'the external actors and forces that affect the company's ability to develop and maintain successful transactions and relationships with its target customers' (Kotler, 1994: 134). For the environmental marketer, key external factors which need to be monitored and understood include the following.

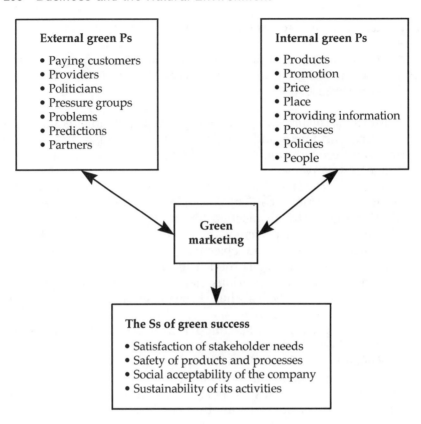

Figure 9.2 The green marketing process
(*Source*: Peattie, 1992).

Paying customers

Market research shows environmental concern and a demand for greener products from greener companies (and unfortunately cynicism about current market offerings and the motives behind them) to be increasing all around the world. The demand for green products (and a willingness to pay a premium for them) has been expressed in traditionally concerned markets like Germany by up to 80 per cent of people, and by 50 per cent even in previously unenthusiastic markets like France (Hassan and Vandermerwe, 1994). In contemplating the responses of their customers, companies will need to know: How deep are their green concerns? How well informed about environmental issues are they? Which issues concern them? Do they want greener products, and if so, what sort? What environmentally related information do they require?

Providers

The ecoperformance of a company will be strongly affected by the ecoperformance of companies who provide them with everything including raw materials, energy, office supplies and services such as waste disposal. Marketing a company and its products on the basis of superior ecoperformance requires complete confidence that environmental damage has not just been passed back down the supply chain. For this reasons companies are becoming actively involved in lifecycle analysis and supplier eco-audits. In addition to green consumers, the inclusion of environmental criteria in the buying behaviour of large companies and public sector organizations is having a significant effect in many industries. Large corporations seeking to improve their ecoperformance such as IBM are using their purchasing power to insist that suppliers undertake environmental audits and meet tough new environmental criteria. British Telecom for example dropped the 'dirtiest' 10 per cent of its supplier base. In this way the adoption of environmental marketing by a relatively small number of big companies can set up a disproportionately powerful supply-chain reaction. The power of public sector green purchasing is demonstrated by the following anecdote from Kiernan (1992: 133): 'One of the world's largest paper companies commits a minor technical environmental violation in the state of Maine. As a result, in May of 1992, the US federal government imposes a three-year ban on government paper purchases from the company. Cost to the company in lost revenues? Over $100 million.'

Politicians

Although marketing theory stresses the primacy of the consumer, so far in driving forward corporate environmental response, consumer pressure has come second to legislation in importance. Partly this is a continuation of the conventional compliance-based response to environmental concerns, but also now awareness is growing that new tough legislation is sparking a wave of technical innovations which in turn present significant marketing opportunities. The green political agenda will continue to be an important one for marketing strategists to monitor. A major change to legislation or taxation, for example through the introduction of a carbon tax, could have a monumental impact on the costs and structure of a range of industries.

Pressure groups

Another important external force are environmental pressure groups. Some groups, like Friends of the Earth, embrace the entire green agenda, while others such as the Whale and Dolphin Conservation Society who administer the 'dolphin friendly' tuna labelling scheme, are concerned with specific issues. The approach of groups varies in terms of whether they favour lobbying and information dissemination or direct action, and whether their attitude to business is adversarial or based around partnership approaches.

Problems

The degree to which companies are associated with specific environmental problems will strongly influence the degree to which they embrace environmental marketing. McDonalds' environmental strategy was strongly influenced by the company being linked to particular environmental problems. The contribution of their disposable packaging to the landfill crisis in the USA, combined with the link between blown foam hamburger 'clamshells' and CFC releases led to the adoption of new quilted burger wraps (even though the 'clamshells' were no longer produced with CFCs). McDonalds were also wrongly linked to the production of beef on cleared South American rain forest land, and embarked on a major customer education campaign as a result. Marketing strategists need to be vigilant for any issues emerging where a part of the company, their suppliers, or any of its competitors are linked with environmental and social problems.

Predictions

Many of the environmental problems which emerge are predicted long before they are proven. The complex nature of environmental systems make it difficult conclusively to prove cause-and-effect relationships between commercial activities and environmental damage. Proactive companies will respond to environmental prediction and change their products and production processes as a precautionary step, instead of defending potentially harmful products until environmental science can uncover a 'smoking gun'. Johnson Wax abandoned the use of CFCs in aerosols as long ago as 1976, in response to scientific predictions which took a further nine years to be accepted as true.

Partners

There are many opportunities for companies to demonstrate their commitment to socioenvironmental progress by becoming involved in partnerships to achieve change. Companies are increasingly moving away from an adversarial relationship with green groups and are working with them instead. Finnish company Nokia, for example combined with the World Wide Fund for Nature to launch its recycled paper products in a campaign which outsold its nearest rival two-to-one despite a 50 per cent smaller advertising budget. Companies may also enter into partnerships with one another, with educational institutions or with local communities in order to solve problems in line with the philosophy of business becoming 'part of the solution instead of part of the problem'.

The internal green Ps in Figure 9.2 represent an expanded marketing mix which needs to be audited, managed and hopefully improved to support a green strategy.

Products

Since the mid-1980s there has been rapid growth in the number of products being launched and marketed under a green banner, and Vandermerwe and Oliff's (1990) survey of multinationals found some 92 per cent claiming to have made changes to their products on environmental grounds. In some cases existing products have been repositioned to take advantage of their ecoperformance advantages over rivals. In the late 1980s Audi changed their marketing from an emphasis on the technological excellence of their cars to emphasize their relative ecoefficiency.

Promotion

Promotion was initially the most popular response to the green challenge, as producers competed with each other to position their existing product offerings as green on the basis of particular attributes. This accounted for much of the 'bandwagon-riding' of the late 1980s which led the UK Advertising Standards Association to comment that 'some advertisers seem to be paying more attention to making sure that their wares are perceived as sitting on the right side of the green fence than to checking the factual accuracy of their claims' (Bernstein, 1992). The early 1990s witnessed fewer explicitly green advertising campaigns, with ecoperformance being integrated into more conventional campaigns. One of the difficulties in developing green promotional campaigns is that environmental issues are complex, and do not easily lend themselves to the superficial images and soundbites of conventional advertising, or to encapsulation on a packaging label or a public relations handout. Some campaigns have managed to combine credibility with commercial effectiveness. Volvo ran a highly successful campaign in Japan with a headline in a full-page daily paper advertisement reading 'Our products create pollution, waste and noise' this frank admission about the societal costs of cars was followed by an explanation of Volvo's efforts to improve the ecoperformance of its products. The forthright approach was viewed as so remarkable that part of the campaign's success was due to the media coverage it provoked.

Price

The issue of the pricing of green products has been an important one on the environmental marketing agenda. Many companies are now finding that the economics of their industry are changing with costs relating to regulatory compliance, waste disposal, insurance and raw material source changes. In many cases changes involve increased costs which must be passed on to customers. Conventional 'grey' products are sold at prices which do not reflect the socioenvironmental costs of their production and use. These products are therefore often less expensive than greener products which attempt to integrate such costs and are usually produced at lower volume. Market research from many countries suggests that consumers are willing to pay about 5 per cent more for *credible* green products. By framing questions in terms of the acceptability of 'green premiums', such surveys simply reinforce a view of environmental protection as unrealistically expensive. Increasingly, however, companies such as 3M, who fully embrace the environmental principles of simplification, pollution avoidance and waste minimization, are finding that ecoefficient products and processes can create savings.

Place

The distribution of physical products, particularly within increasingly international markets, accounts for a great deal of businesses' environmental impact. Some products pose a specific environmental risk when in transit, as the *Braer* or *Sea Empress* oil spills, vividly demonstrated. For most the consumption of fossil fuels and the resulting emissions account for the environmental costs of distribution, and since conventional marketing treats these costs as 'externalities' this means that distribution costs are artificially low, resulting in some very ecoinefficient patterns of distribution. Issues relating to the location and management of distribution facilities can have a significant bearing on product ecoperformance, and many of them are encapsulated in Figure 9.3.

Another important 'place' issue is that of distribution channels, and in consumer goods markets retailers have had a powerful influence on the greening of marketing. It was supermarkets that first felt the brunt of consumer concern about CFC-driven aerosols, and supermarket stocking policies are often instrumental in the adoption of new green products and the demise of unacceptably grey products. German retailer Hertie withdrew, changed or introduced around 2000 products on environmental grounds during 1989 alone. There has been a gradual emergence of retailers based around an explicitly environmental philosophy, such as Terra Nova in the USA or Body Shop in the UK; and also the adoption of environmental strategies in response to customer demand and as a form of competitive differentiation among established retailers, such as Migros in Switzerland, Tenglemann in Germany or Tesco in the UK.

Providing information

The marketing concept is founded on an assumption that companies are interested in consumer needs and will provide useful information to allow consumers to match products to need. There are a number of ways in which companies can provide information to help customers understand the environmental dimensions of their consumption decisions and behaviour. In marketing at the company level, corporate environmental reports such as the highly successful 'Miljorapport' produced by Norway's Norsk Hydro, have become an important communication medium. At a product level, labelling, informative advertising and customer information services have all been used effectively. A number of proactive companies have set out to contribute to environmental education in schools and elsewhere. Although some such initiatives are somewhat cynically promotional, others have been welcomed as valuable and constructive.

Processes

An important difference between environmental and conventional marketing is the degree to which the way a product is made becomes important. Free-range eggs, rod-and-line caught tuna, cruelty-free cosmetics, sustainably managed timber or unbleached paper are all products marketed on the basis of the production processes used. Chapter 5 explores some of the issues relating to processes further.

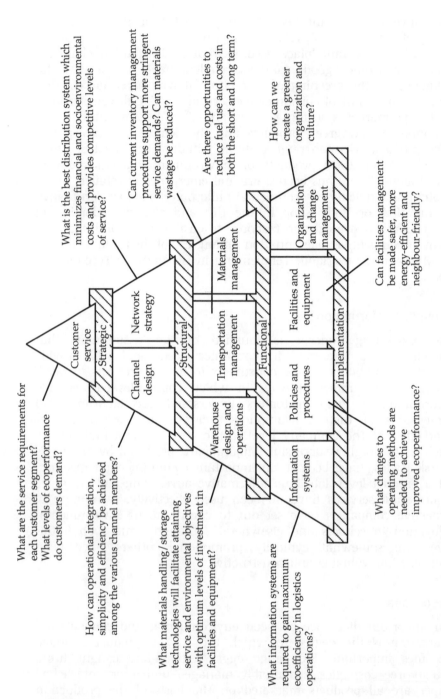

Figure 9.3 Key issues – logistics strategy
(Source: Peattie 1996: 251).

Policies

The policies of a company relating to purchasing, corporate invest-ment, openness with information, company cars, environmental training or disaster response can all provide evidence of environ-mental commitment and strengthen the basis of credibility from which environmental products are marketed. Without 'soft' management policies to motivate, monitor, evaluate and control ecoperformance improvements, investments in 'hard' environmental technologies, products and systems are unlikely to produce signifi-cant benefits.

People

The marketing philosophy demands that marketing activity and commitment to meeting customer needs is spread throughout the company, and not confined to a department with a sign that says 'Marketing' hanging on the door. Environmental marketing needs a similar commitment to the environment to permeate the entire company and its culture. This requires a great deal of attention in terms of training and recruitment (see Chapters 10 and 11).

In terms of criteria for success, conventional marketing theory implies that if the four Ps of product, price, place and promotion are right, then success will follow in the form of a fifth P, 'Profits'. Environmental marketing success involves ensuring that the marketing mix and the company meet four S criteria (Peattie, 1990):

1 *Satisfaction* of customer needs; in terms of technical performance of products, economic value and ecoperformance.
2 *Safety* of products and production for consumers, workers, society and the environment.
3 *Social acceptability* of the products, their production and the other activities of the company.
4 *Sustainability* of the products, their production and the other activities of the company.

Environmental marketing management

The green challenge has had a considerable impact on the nature of marketing as a role in many companies and industries. The concept of companies taking greater responsibility for their customers and products has been reflected in the idea of 'brand managers' being replaced by 'brand stewards'. In agrochemicals markets where difficulties with correct product use often occur in countries with low literacy rates among farmers, some companies are using the concept of brand stewardship to ensure that products are used correctly. Dow Corning, for example, demands that its sales staff:

1 inform customers about known hazards relating to the products;
2 advise customers to use products in accordance with label recommendations;
3 insist that distributors pass on handling, use and disposal information to their customers;
4 report and respond vigorously against cases of misuse;
5 co-ordinate visits by company staff to customer sites, to ensure safe use and disposal of products.

The contribution of marketing management to corporate environmental strategy

Marketing has an important leadership role to play within companies in relation to the environment. Coddington (1993) recommends that companies engaged in a greening process should set up an environmental task force in which marketers play a leading role. He identifies two sets of strengths that marketers can contribute to the greening process, the marketing perspective and the marketing skill set. The greening challenge requires creativity, the ability to work effectively across internal organizational boundaries and excellent communication skills. Coddington identifies marketing managers as being often 'superbly qualified' for the task because:

1 Marketers are able to identify and analyse the marketing implications of corporate environmental exposures and initiatives.
2 Marketers can help to identify new business product and service opportunities that arise out of those same environmental exposures and initiatives (for example using hazardous waste clean-up obligations as a springboard for entry into the hazardous waste remediation business).
3 Marketers can work to ensure that when corporate environmental policies are developed, the marketing implications are given due consideration.
4 As a matter of course, marketers must co-ordinate their activities across multiple departments (R&D, manufacturing, packaging, sales, public relations).

5 Marketers are professional communicators. This skill is enormously useful in virtually every aspect of environmental management – on the task force itself, and in such areas as environmental management training, emergency response training, community relations and other domains which put a premium on communications.

An important but often neglected element of the marketing process, and one which requires all of the marketer's skills, is the need to market any particular strategy internally to gain the support of stakeholders within the company. Unless a strategy has the clear support of top management, and unless it is understood and accepted by those who will ultimately be responsible for its implementation, the chances of success are relatively slim. A switch to an environmental marketing approach usually represents a radical change for a company and its culture, and there can be a great deal of resistance to the changes that are involved. The decision of Mercedes to produce a smaller and more environmentally responsible car in partnership with SMH (the maker of Swatch) produced board-room power struggles which nearly split the company in two.

The environmental marketing challenge

Environmental concern represents an unparalleled challenge to the practice and philosophy of marketing. At a conceptual level marketing theory is hampered by its reliance on conventional neo-classical rational economics to explain exchanges between companies and customers, and on concepts borrowed from military science to explain the interaction between companies. Given that both conventional economics and military science and activity are notoriously environmentally hostile, this is something of a handicap. A more practical difficulty that many environmental marketers face is in persuading customers to accept compromises in technical performance or price increases in exchange for improvements in ecoperformance. In an ideal world all greener products would be able to match conventional products in technical performance and price. However, an economic system which fail to make the polluters pay, and grey products which frequently fail to address in any way customers' genuine concerns about the environment and product ecoperformance make the task of creating products which are credible in both environmental and competitive terms very difficult.

Another challenge relates to the fact that what constitutes a green product also varies over time. It is perhaps a sobering thought that CFCs were originally marketed as being exceptionally environmentally inert. As our understanding of the environmental challenge evolves, so do the issues of concern that may be translated into changed purchasing behaviour. Sudden interventions by the media, or by newsworthy celebrities can also rearrange the priorities on the green agenda. Technology changes or competitor actions can also render a particular green product obsolete. For the marketer there is a very strong temptation to step onto the sidelines of the environmental debate and declare that they are not getting involved until things are clearer in terms of scientific evidence, political directions and customer wants and understanding. The environmental agenda will unfold at different rates for different companies in different industries and countries, and concern among consumers, politicians and marketers is bound to fluctuate over time. However, barring relatively miraculous technological innovations or environmental interventions, the environmental marketing agenda will evolve in three stages (Peattie and Charter, 1994):

1 *Substitution.* Characterized by green consumers differentiating between products on the basis of perceived ecoperformance, much confusion over concepts and terminology, and with a great deal of sales and public relations activity dressed up as green marketing. There has also been a great deal of 'spot-lighting', the singling out of particular industries, companies and products for praise or condemnation, sometimes with little relation to the actualities of ecoperformance. Environmental improvements are often limited to end-of-pipe changes to production systems, the substitution of damaging ingredients such as CFCs and the elimination of excess packaging.

2 *Systemization.* The establishment of BS 7750 for Environmental Management Systems, ISO 14000 and the EC Ecolabel Scheme should move the entire 'game' on to a new plane of recognized (if flawed) performance criteria and evaluation. Businesses will move towards the redesign of products and production systems, and the implementation of environmental reporting and management systems. Better information for consumers will allow more informed and consistent green purchasing. Provision of environmental information and provision for the recycling of products will become standard practice, and governed by increasingly stringent legislation.

3 *Societal change.* The deepening environmental crisis will eventually lead to a more radical shift in consumer behaviour challenging the very basis of demand and consumption. This will be part of a wider social, political and economic upheaval to develop a more sustainable society. Consumers will increasingly

become conservers and will seek opportunities to recycle or recondition products, and to achieve satisfaction through non-purchasing based activities.

If marketers fail to keep up with these developments, and indeed fail to contribute to driving them forward, they will have neglected the fundamental marketing concept of responding to customer needs. The environmental challenge represents a turning point for marketing as a management philosophy, discipline and function. Despite corporate rhetoric about social responsibility and responding to customer needs, a widespread perception about marketing is that it is used to leverage people into patterns of consumption that are not socially or environmentally sustainable. The marketing concept which most companies fervently embrace, brings with it a commitment to create long-term shareholder value by co-ordinating the whole business behind the effort to meet customer needs. To achieve this in the new millennium, companies will need to radically change their products, production systems, business relationships and communications efforts to work towards a more sustainable economy. This is a daunting task for all of those who practise or preach the doctrine of marketing, but without a concerted effort to market sustainability to managers, customers and investors, the shadow of environmental disaster will be cast over the long-term future of every company's customers and investors.

References

Anderson W. T. and Cunningham W. H. (1972). The socially conscious consumer, *Journal of Marketing*, **36**, July, 23–31.

Bernstein, D. (1992). *In the Company of Green: Corporate Communication for the New Environment*. ISBA.

Coddington, W. (1993). *Environmental Marketing*. McGraw-Hill.

Drucker, P. F. (1973). *Top Management*. Heinemann.

Durning, A. T. (1992). *How Much is Enough?* Earthscan.

Elkington, J. and Hailes, J. (1988). *The Green Consumer Guide*. Victor Gollanz.

Fisk, G. (1973). Criteria for a theory of responsible consumption. *Journal of Marketing*, **37**(2), 24–31.

Hassan, S. S. and Vandermerwe, S. (1994). A global view of 'green' marketing. In *Global Marketing: Perspectives and Cases* (S. Hassan, and R. D. Blackwell, eds) Dryden Press.

Henion, K. E. and Kinnear, T. C. (eds) (1976). *Ecological Marketing*. American Marketing Association.

Johnson, C. (1991). *The Green Dictionary*. McDonald Optima.

Kardash, W. J. (1974). Corporate responsibility and the quality of life: developing the ecologically concerned consumer. In *Ecological Marketing* (K. E. Henion and T. C. Kinnear, eds), American Marketing Association.

Kiernan, M. J. (1992). The eco-industrial revolution. *Business in the Contemporary World.* 4(4), 133–43.

Kotler, P. (1994), *Marketing Management: Analysis, Planning, Implementation and Control.* (7th edn), Prentice-Hall.

Leeflang, P. S. H. and Raaij, W. F. (1995). The changing consumer in the European Union: a meta analysis. *International Journal of Research in Marketing,* 12, 373–87.

Mead, M. (1970). Responsible simplification of consumption patterns. *Ekistics,* 30, October, 324–26.

Mulhern, F. J. (1992). Consumer wants and consumer welfare. In *Marketing Theory and Applications* (T. C. Allen et al. eds), Proceedings of the 1992 AMA Winter Educators' Conference, pp. 407–12, American Marketing Association.

Ottman, J. (1992a). *Green Marketing: Challenges and Opportunities for the New Marketing Age.* NTC Business Books.

Ottman, J. (1992b). The four E's make going green your competitive edge. *Marketing News,* 26(3), 7.

Peattie, K. J. (1990). Painting marketing education green: or how to recycle old ideas. *Journal of Marketing Management,* 6(2), 105–27.

Peattie, K. J. (1992). *Green Marketing,* Pitman.

Peattie, K. (1996). *Environmental Marketing Management: Meeting the Green Challenge,* Pitman.

Peattie, K. and Charter, M. (1994). Green marketing. In *The Marketing Book* (M. J. Baker, ed.), Butterworth-Heinemann.

Rehak, R. (1993). *Greener Marketing and Advertising.* Environmental Marketing and Advertising Council, Rodale Press.

Stead, W. E. and Stead, J. G. (1992). *Management for a Small Planet.* Sage.

Vandermerwe, S. and Oliff, M. (1990). Customers drive corporations green. *Long Range Planning,* 23(6), 10–16.

10 Putting systems into practice

Allerd Stikker

Ideally, business decision-makers should understand ecological principles, and should be able to relate these principles to the effect their specific business has on the natural environment and turn this understanding into environmentally sound business practice. In order to achieve this aim the decision-makers will have to integrate environmental considerations into existing and new management systems. These systems include total quality management, environmental care, responsible care, environmental auditing, life cycle analysis, and integrated chain management. Putting all this into practice is however still very much more complicated than it would seem. The reason is that decision-makers in business are engaged in combat for market share, cost control, profit improvement and financial resources. A business unit is sometimes described as a combat unit, constantly on the alert for threats and opportunities and usually working with time-scales of six months to three years. This condition does not allow for much time to consider conceptual theories such as on sustainable development in the twenty-first century or on global biodiversity. As previous chapters have shown however, the relationship between ecology, economy and business will require changes in management attitudes for the business to survive in an ecologically competitive setting, where environmental liabilities and opportunities are very real. In Figure 10.1 a survey is presented showing the various drivers that may cause changes in management attitudes, leading to a sustainable enterprise.

Awareness

Most business managers will become actively interested in the technicalities of environmentally sound management when they are exposed to the issue of sustainable development in a way and in a language that is accessible to their frame of mind and measurable

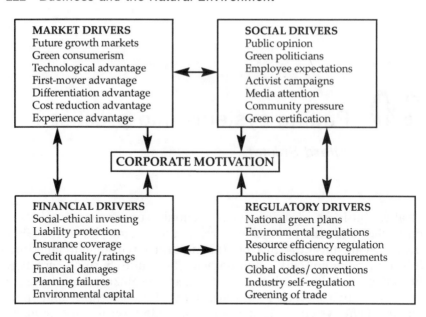

Figure 10.1 Drivers for sustainable enterprise
(*Source*: Thomas N. Gladwin, 1992).

by familiar parameters. This will obviously include translating ecologically sound management in economic terms. Although it seems obvious that depleting non-renewable resources or using renewable resources faster than they renew will make these resources more expensive in a relatively short time, these facts must be shown in monetary terms. Also the fact that causing pollution and handling pollution become every year more expensive at a faster rate than inflation must be made visible in profit and loss projections. Only then, in most cases, will an awareness emerge that will lead to a broadening of management practice to include environmental factors.

In order to illustrate this, three examples will be given where global sustainable development is translated into business targets. These examples are particularly useful in helping to precipitate change related to environmental issues in business. The first is related to the need not to further increase the 'environmental burden' of the planet. By environmental burden we mean the combined effect of pollution and depletion as they affect the earth's resources and quality of life. If we set a target to at least keep this burden constant at present levels, and take the year 2030 as a reference point we can estimate the consequences for pollution and depletion control. Let us assume, not unrealistically, that the world population will have doubled by that time and that the standard of living per capita in developing and newly industrialized countries will have, again not unrealistically, increased by 5 per cent per year, which means, over the period of thirty-five years about five times. This would mean that the burden would increase by $2 \times 5 = 10$ or ten times the present level. Only if depletion of resources and pollution of the habitat were reduced to one-tenth of the present practice per unit of production, would the burden remain constant. For business this would mean developing within a relatively short time the technologies and the management systems to reduce resource depletion and pollution by 90 per cent.

When managers become convinced that this target is politically necessary, technologically possible and economically feasible, the creative and innovative mind of industrial entrepeneurship will start working on it. In fact this has begun to happen in a great number of cases in the world, as extensively illustrated in publications by the Business Council for Sustainable Development (Schmidheiny, 1992), the World Resources Institute (Smart, 1992) and the International Chamber of Commerce (ICC, 1992).

A second example, related to the technological aspect of the previous illustration of sustainability is the concept of back-casting. Assuming that the challenge of a reduction of pollution by 90 per cent is accepted, Figure 10.2 shows, for illustrative purposes only and not referring to a specific technical example, what might be achieved with successive steps of improvement in emission levels of a certain substance.

An end-of-pipe solution will reduce the level of a specific emission, say acid drops in exhaust air, but the acid drops are collected and end up in waste water, so the problem has in fact been solved by shifting from one pollution to another. In environmental care systems, usually a further reduction can be achieved by doing better than present practice, in other words improving existing processes.

A further step is reducing emissions by adapting the technical processes and the resource base. But these subsequent steps may well not achieve the 90 per cent reduction target. The conclusion is that new technologies, sustainable technologies, will be required. As the development of new technologies to maturity takes, judging by experience in many industries, up to twenty-five years, R&D (research and development) departments should start working on them now. A third example of how to let the goal of sustainability enter the mind and the agenda of industrial business management, is the environmental learning curve, as illustrated in Figure 10.3.

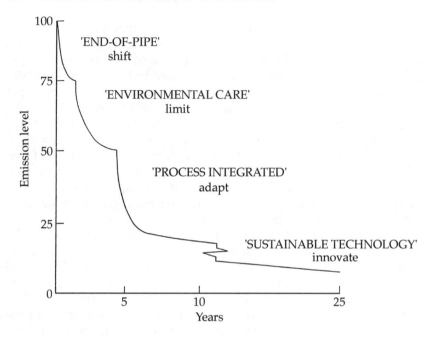

Figure 10.2 Emission reduction with technology
(*Source*: VROM, 1992).

In this curve the successive levels of sophistication of environmentally responsible management are set against a relative time factor. The scales measure where a specific business unit is situated on the curve today and how much time will be needed to reach a level of sustainable business.

Sustainable business means a maximum use of renewable resources, allowing for the time needed to renew, and a maximum reduction of pollution so as not to irreparably damage the environment, including human health. The curve in Figure 10.3 can be used to help to understand the process of moving toward sustainability. It shows that the road to improvement goes in stages and demonstrates that the present level of effort contributes to the learning process of how, where and when to improve further. In other words sustainability cannot and will not be implemented at short notice, but it represents a goal that should gradually, but consciously, be achieved. The positioning on the learning curve is not an absolute fact, but an indication of managerial attitude. It also indicates commitment to management systems and is a measure of progress.

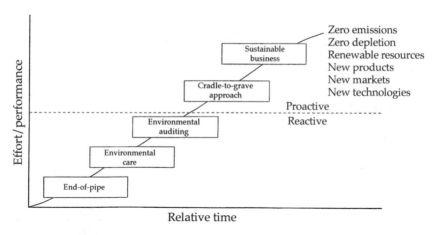

Figure 10.3 Environmental learning curve

The three examples are useful instruments to create an awareness that has to be aroused before a convincing and consistent policy can be formulated and put into practice.

Deciding on sustainability goals

Assuming that management of a certain business unit or company has gone through the process of raising awareness of the environmental element in decision-making and that consensus is reached within the management team on the position of their specific business on the environmental learning curve, an analysis is required of the options offered by sustainability goals. First, an analysis is needed of whether the business is involved in activities that in general are negative, mixed or positive with regard to perceived contributions to environmental sustainability.

Figure 10.4 illustrates a guiding classification, based on an opinion poll. The classification will give an indication of the actual need and urgency to decide on change. Then, as a result of the analysis on the positioning on the learning curve, as discussed in the previous section and on the basis of the ultimate goal of being sustainable business, certain guidelines can be formulated to adapt the present three or five-year plan of the business unit. These guidelines refer to the introduction of new environmental care systems but they also refer to organizational changes, contractor/ supplier specifications, sustainable technology programmes and specific emission reduction targets. A practical example of setting

NEGATIVE	MIXED	POSITIVE
COAL/OIL	BIOTECHNOLOGY	SOLAR/WIND ENERGY
BEEF	TIMBER	ENERGY EFFICIENCY
PESTICIDES	METALS	MASS TRANSIT
MOTOR VEHICLES	PACKAGING	POLLUTION CONTROL
WEAPONS	TOURISM	LOW-INPUT AGRICULTURE
TOBACCO	PULP/PAPER	RECYCLING
ADVERTISING	CHEMICALS	ELECTRONIC OFFICE
LIMOUSINES	AIRLINES	TELECOMMUNICATIONS
MINING	HYDROPOWER	CONTRACEPTIVES
DISPOSABLES	HAZARDOUS WASTE	MICRO-LENDING
CFCs	PRINT MEDIA	WATER/SANITATION
OFF-ROAD VEHICLES	BANKING	HEALTH CARE
SPEED BOATS	PLASTICS	EDUCATION
SUPERSONIC TRAVEL	NUCLEAR ENERGY	SMART MATERIALS
SPACE EXPLORATION	DELIVERY SERVICES	EXTRACTIVE RESERVES

Figure 10.4 Perceived contribution to environmental sustainability (*Source*: Thomas N. Gladwin, 1992).

these targets provides the Du Pont Company with a statement in their corporate environmental plan (Figure 10.5).

When the business management team accepts the guidelines toward sustainability, a priority list can be selected that will contain the elements where concentration of effort should be focused. This will then lead to action plans for purchasing, R&D, production, marketing and sales. Obviously the new plans need to be evaluated for their ecological and economic effects. On one hand the effect must at a minimum be in line with governmental and legal regulations and on the other hand the effect must be of an order of magnitude for which it is worth making the effort. The economic effect must be such that either in the short term it contributes to profit improvement (which it does more often than many managers

---

| **Corporate Environmental Plan Purpose** |

The Corporate Environment Plan (CEP) is a global planning tool and management system used to integrate environmental and business thinking at sites, in businesses, and at the corporate level. The intent of the CEP is to improve awareness of, alignment with, and implementation of the SHE Commitment to meet stakeholder needs. The CEP provides a framework that will:

• Predict resources needed to:
  – implement SHE Commitment, environmental policy and standards
  – meet or exceed environmental goals and targets
  – ensure compliance with addditional regulatory requirements

• Measure and predict progress toward environmental targets/goals

• Indentify opportunities for synergy and leveraging

• Facilitate improved initiative prioritization

• Facilitiate identification of strategies to achieve the SHE Commitment goal of zero waste and emissions

---

Figure 10.5 Corporate environmental plan purpose
(*Source*: Wika, 1996).

expect), or it must lead to a competitive advantage that will eventually lead to a better market position, resulting in better profits in the longer term. In this economic analysis it will be essential for the decision to be taken that the business also makes an evaluation of what full environmental cost-pricing would mean for the company at the resource level, at the production process stage and in the final product destination.

Performance measurement

When awareness has been created, sustainable business goals have been formulated and priorities have been identified, the next step is to decide on a method for monitoring the progress towards the targets to be reached, using performance indicators and bench-marking techniques, taking into account competitors' performance. The monitoring methods can be divided into two categories. One focuses on the degree of commitment and implementation with respect to policies, systems, education and response to the various external relationships and requirements. The other focuses on specific quantified goals that can be measured by technical and accounting methods, and expressed in volumes, toxicity, efficiency, effectiveness, costs and benefits etc. The first category is the more qualitative and second the more quantitative. Both methods can result in performance indicators showing the percentage of the extent to which the goals has been achieved.

Qualitative monitoring

This category is a useful tool for corporate and general management. The Global Environmental Management Initiative in the United States has devised a useful methodology, the Environmental Self-Assessment Program or ESAP (GEMI, 1992). The methodology was developed in 1992 by twenty-one major US companies in co-operation with Deloitte and Touche, and has now been tested and further refined. Related to the ICC *Business Charter for Sustainable Development* (ICC, 1991), containing sixteen principles, the ESAP method provides for regular rating of the performance level of a company or business unit regarding these principles. Each principle is divided into a set of elements and each element contains four successively comprehensive performance level descriptions. The four levels are: compliance systems, development and implementation, integration into general business functions, and total quality approach. A fifth level indicates whether a particular element is not relevant to a company's operations, due to the nature of the company's industry profile. The rating by participants in the performance evaluation is done by scoring their business practice against each element and subsequently by assigning an 'importance weighting' to each element. The weighting is based on the relative importance that the implementation of the principle currently receives in the company or business unit. This enables a weighted average principle score to be calculated.

Figure 10.6 summarizes the sixteen ICC principles and the elements developed by GEMI and tested in practice by industries participating in the programme. An example of the scoring method according to this schedule is shown in Figure 10.7 and Figure 10.8. Figure 10.7 shows a format for principle 8, as an example. Since 1993 a substantial number of multinational corporations have started to apply the ESAP system of performance indicators.

Quantitative monitoring

With regard to the quantitative approach, the methodology is based on traditional scientific and technical engineering skills and can often be linked to health and safety statistics as well to total quality management techniques. The main areas for quantitative measurements are effluents to water, emissions to air, and waste to soil in the various stages of the life cycle, energy use, noise generation and resource depletion. The purpose of these quantifiable measurements is usually to understand impacts, to improve performance, to define quantitative objectives or for public reporting or a combination of the four. The specific systems and skills to set objectives and to measure performance are dealt with in other chapters and are extensively covered in a publication by Business in the Environment (BiE, 1992), with actual recent cases of fourteen companies of different natures. With respect to implementation, according to the BiE publication, the following key factors need to be observed by any company committed to install environmental measurement systems.

Test case

Before committing resources to a full-scale implementation project, much effort can be saved by first carrying out a pilot project in one part of the organization, or in the whole organization in a focused test of performance. The basis tasks in any pilot will involve:

1 planning;
2 data collection and analysis;
3 review and reporting;
4 implementation.

Descriptions of these tasks follows.

Planning

It is essential to assign adequate time to planning the project if it is to be effective. This may involve wide consultation and communications within the company to help provide 'ownership' of the problem and solution. The three key tasks in planning are: bringing the right people together; defining the scope and objectives of the project; and preparing a plan, including tasks and timescales.

1 *Bring the right people together.* How a company chooses to run the project will depend on its size and management style. The following elements should be included:

ICC principles	*Elements*	
1. Corporate priority	1.1	Scope of corporate policy
	1.2	Management involvement
	1.3	Resources
	1.4	Communications
	1.5	Implementation
	1.6	Accountability
2. Integrated management	2.1	Planning
	2.2	Reporting
	2.3	Information flows
	2.4	Control
3. Process of improvement	3.1	Technical developments, scientific understanding and external expectations
	3.2	Improvement of policies
	3.3	Improvement of programmes and products
	3.4	Improvement of performance
	3.5	Process for change
4. Employee education	4.1	Awareness programmes
	4.2	General skills and training
	4.3	EHS professionals training
	4.4	Management development
	4.5	Motivation
5. Prior assessment	5.1	Property plus business acquisition or divestiture, and joint facility or venture planning
	5.2	Site closure planning
	5.3	New business activity or project planning
6. Products and services	6.1	Environment impact
	6.2	Product and service safety and integrity
	6.3	Energy consumption
	6.4	Use of natural resources and raw materials
	6.5	Stewardship of natural resources
	6.6	Waste minimization and management
7. Customer advice	7.1	Advice to customers and distributors
	7.2	Advice to transporters
	7.3	Advice to consumers
	7.4	Advice to the public and environmental groups
8. Facilities and operations	8.1	Internal operations standards and practices
	8.2	Solid and hazardous waste reduction and treatment
	8.3	Waste residue management and disposal
	8.4	Energy minimization programmes

	8.5	Natural resources extraction and raw materials usage
	8.6	Habitat protection
	8.7	Pollution control and reduction
	8.8	Employee health and safety
	8.9	Risk evaluation and reduction
9. Research	9.1	Research on raw material procurement and use
	9.2	Research on products
	9.3	Research on processes
	9.4	Research on waste minimization and emissions
10. Precautionary approach	10.1	Process changes
	10.2	Marketing changes
	10.3	Changes in products and services
	10.4	Changes in conduct of activities
11. Contractors and suppliers	11.1	Contractor priority suppliers
	11.2	Contractor performance
	11.3	Supplier priority and performance
12. Emergency preparedness	12.1	Hazard and incident assessments
	12.2	Emergency response plans
	12.3	Product and service safety
	12.4	Employee training
13. Transfer of technology	13.1	Technology information
	13.2	Management methods
	13.3	Transfer to industrial sector
	13.4	Transfer to public sector
14. Contributing to the common effort	14.1	Public policy common effort
	14.2	Contribution to environmental protection programmes
	14.3	Environmental education initiatives
15. Openness to concerns	15.1	Employee workplace concerns
	15.2	Customers' and consumers' concerns
	15.3	Community concerns
16. Compliance and reporting	16.1	Environmental audits
	16.2	Progress measurement
	16.3	Internal performance reporting
	16.4	External performance reporting

Figure 10.6 ICC principles and elements
(*Source*: GEMI, 1992).

ENVIRONMENTAL SELF-ASSESSMENT PROGRAM

– Principle 8: Facilities and Operations –

"To develop, design and operate facilities and conduct activities taking into consideration the efficient use of energy and materials, the sustainable use of renewable resources, the minimization of adverse environmental impact and waste generation, and the safe and responsible disposal of residual waste."

Mark an "X" on the continuum which best estimates the overall performance level of your company. On the line next to the word "Score" write the number that corresponds to the "X" on the continuum. If an element is not applicable, put an "X" on the line next to "NA".

PERFORMANCE LEVEL →	NOT APPLICABLE	1	2	3	4	ELEMENT IMPORTANCE Please Assign an Importance Weighting to Each Element A = Greatest Importance B = Medium Importance C = Less Importance	NOTES
8.7 POLLUTION CONTROL AND REDUCTION	Corporation responds to laws requiring pollution control.	Formal systems exist to *identify potential spill* risks and prioritize emissions sources and implement leading cost-effective solutions to *reduce or prevent* spills and emissions. Spill and emissions prevention, control, monitoring and warning systems *exceed legal* requirements.	Pollution prevention and reduction systems are *integrated* with facility and process engineering and activity planning functions. *Direct and indirect impacts* of facilities, operations and activities are addressed. A system exists to *measure progress* toward spill and emission reduction goals.	Pollution prevention and reduction systems are continuously *evaluated* through total quality improvement opportunities. System exists to *solicit, accept and respond* to input and feedback from employees and appropriate external sources (e.g. regulators, community leaders, technical experts and industry leaders).	A B C	
	NA ___ 0	1	2	3	4	Score: ___	
8.8 EMPLOYEE HEALTH AND SAFETY	Corporation responds to employee health and safety laws.	System in place to *identify and prioritize* health and safety risks and implement cost effective risk reduction technologies and practices that *exceed legal* requirements.	Employee health and safety considerations are *integrated* with the planning and management systems of business functions. *Direct and indirect impacts* of facilities, operations and activities on employee health and safety are addressed. Systems exist to *measure progress* toward corporate health and safety goals.	*Systems are continuously evaluated* through total quality management techniques to identify and implement opportunities for improvement. Systems exist to solicit, accept and *respond to input* and feedback from employees and appropriate external experts (e.g. medical community, industry leaders, health and safety professionals).		
	NA ___ 0	1	2	3	4	Score: ___	

Figure 10.7 Environmental Self-Assessment Program
(*Source:* GEMI, 1992).

– Principle 8: Facilities and Operations –

"To develop, design and operate facilities and conduct activities taking into consideration the efficient use of energy and materials, the sustainable use of renewable resources, the minimization of adverse environmental impact and waste generation, and the safe and responsible disposal of residual waste."

Mark an "X" on the continuum which best estimates the overall performance level of your company. On the line next to the word "Score" write the number that corresponds to the "X" on the continuum. If an element is not applicable, put an "X" on the line next to "NA".

Please indicate your perception of your company's overall performance against this Principle. For best results, calculate your overall score using the weights you assigned to each element above.

Overall Rating

PRINCIPLE 8 $\longrightarrow$

```
|----+----+----+----| Score:____
0    1    2    3    4
```

Basis for Assessment Please note for your company's records the documentation or other evidence you would use to verify the score you assigned for each element:

Element 8.1 Internal Operating Standards/Practices

Element 8.3 Waste Residue Management and Disposal

Element 8.2 Solid and Hazardous Waste Reduction and Treatment

Element 8.4 Energy Minimization Program

Figure 10.8 Example of ESAP assessment (*Source:* GEMI, 1992).

(a) A management team responsible for running the project, responsible for setting project objectives (consistent with company policy and objectives) and for reporting.

(b) Top management commitment to implementing an environmental policy throughout the organization.

2 *Definition of scope and objective.* The scope of the pilot project will need to be defined in relation to those areas addressed in steps 1 to 4, namely:

(a) the environmental performance area and specific objectives to be addressed (e.g. waste reduction by 40 per cent in volume by the year 2000);

(b) the types of performance measure that will be considered including impact, contributor, risk and external relations measures;

(c) whether or not qualitative measures will be included, as well as quantitative measures;

(d) whether or not measuring requiring new data can be accepted.

3 *Preparation of plan.* All tasks should be defined with resource requirements and timescales.

Data collection and analysis

The definition of information requirements during the planning stage should define the nature of the information that is needed to measure performance. Information may already be available, such as energy consumption. The main task will then be to analyse and present this information in a format useful for monitoring and control. For supplier performance measures, information will be required from the suppliers themselves, normally through an appropriate questionnaire or through meetings. For contributor measures, particularly in measuring the effectiveness of management systems, some form of appraisal rating or testing method may be needed.

Review and reporting

The ultimate test of any performance measure lies in whether it is effective in informing the appropriate target groups, and/or in achieving intended performance improvements through motivation. The extent to which the pilot can be assessed in these terms will depend on its timescale. A project of less than six months' duration may not yield results that can be interpreted effectively, especially in performance areas such as energy where seasonal and other variations need to be examined.

A longer pilot is not always possible or desirable, however, and companies will need to rely on a different process to decide whether given performance measures should be integrated with existing management systems. A review by the project team should suffice, provided that the team has been set up to include representatives of those people/units who will be the 'recipients' of the performance measures. In the case studies, those companies which involved managers and staff at different levels derived the greatest benefits. The results of the project should therefore be reviewed against:

1 specific project objectives;
2 the effectiveness of performance measures in providing information;
3 the effectiveness of performance measures in motivating managers/staff to meet environmental objectives;
4 compatibility with environmental policy;
5 practicality of implementation and integration with management systems;
6 other benefits, such as encouraging different people to work together, within different business functions and/or at different levels.

Benchmarking

An effective way to stimulate the setting of environmental sustainable goals and their improvement, is benchmarking. Benchmarking is the comparison of environmental performance of a company or business unit with other companies or business units, both internally and externally. Practice has shown in recent years that companies are quite willing to exchange facts and figures on subjects related to safety, health and environment. For instance in 1992 AT&T in the US carried out a benchmarking project with Xerox, DuPont, 3M, HB Fuller and Dow Chemical in order to identify areas for improvement (Mallette and Tomlinson, 1992). For the method to be successful it is essential that the benchmark is not the average but 'the best in class'.

The method implies extensive and well-prepared interviewing of other firms. It is obviously helpful if implementation and monitoring methodologies are comparable. This is another good reason for co-operation among industrial companies on the development of methodologies. On the other hand, within corporations a corporate methodology will make it possible to compare performances of divisions or business units within the corporation and introduce a competitive element. This will also facilitate the use of environmental performance as a measure for remuneration, and is increasingly being introduced in corporate remuneration programmes.

Environmental cost-accounting

In recent years systems of environmental costing have entered the accounting profession. These provide insight into the actual environmental costs a company is incurring and thereby enable it to identify savings or changes in product or process design or to minimize these costs. This method, called total or full environmental cost-accounting, will become important as a business management tool.

Environmental costs include (CACA, 1996):

1   *Usual costs.* These include direct and indirect costs usually associated with the project of both a capital and revenue nature.
2   *Hidden costs.* There are additional costs which are usually found in overheads/general accounts. These would include regulatory, environmental management system, monitoring and safety costs – both capital and revenue in nature.
3   *Liability costs.* These are 'contingent liability costs' which are not presently incurred in a conventional accounting sense. These may emerge depending on circumstances (for example, if the law changes) and their likelihood can be estimated. Such costs include fines, future clean-up costs and regulatory costs associated with a project.
4   *Less tangible costs.* Costs and benefits are likely to arise from improved environmental management which may be able to be assessed in financial terms. These costs and benefits could include the loss/gain of goodwill arising from a project; changing attitudes of suppliers, customers, and employees; and advertising/image issues arising from environmental performance of projects.
5   *Environment focused costs.* Estimation of the costs that would be incurred if an environment focused approach was taken to a project. Costs to ensure that a project had zero net environmental effect could be estimated. It is unlikely that such costs would become real costs in the absence of a radical change in the regulatory and operating environment.

Full environmental cost pricing including category 5 is not yet accepted and implemented in present governmental and industrial practice, but pressures are mounting that this should be applied to achieve global sustainable development. It is to be expected that full environmental cost pricing will be achieved by a mixture of economic measures (such as ecotax on energy), regulations and business initiatives. Ecologically responsible management should take these elements into account today when making business plans.

Communication

For successful implementation and monitoring of both qualitative and quantative goals towards an environmentally sustainable enterprise, the company or business unit involved will have to set up a continuous and consistent communication programme for both internal and external customers. This is becoming more important now that the financial community, banks, insurers and investors are becoming increasingly critical of the environmental performance of their clients in view of future liabilities and legislative constraints. The risks also pose opportunities, and communicating how these are dealt with and their effects on corporate image need to be addressed.

Summary

Putting systems into practice requires an awareness programme, a goal-setting exercise, an implementation and monitoring methodology, and a communication programme. The awareness programme is essential for any effective environmental management system. If employees do not understand and accept the need for and benefits of environmental management, the system will not work. Of essence in the awareness programme is the emphasis on the link between environmental performance and financial performance and the continuity of the business.

As resources, technologies and markets vary considerably, putting systems into practice is business-specific and is a part of the responsibility of the management team. In order to gain experience and prevent pitfalls, implementation should be introduced on a test case basis.

References

Business in the Environment (BiE) (1992). *A Measure of Commitment.* BiE. London.
Chartered Association of Certified Accountants (CACA) (1996). *Business Conceptions of Sustainability and the Implications for Accountancy.* Research Report No. 48, Certified Accountants Educational Trust.

Gladwin, T. N. and Leonard, N. (1992) Envisioning the Sustainable Corporation. Internal Document. Stern School of Business, New York University.

Global Environmental Management Initiative (GEMI) (1992). *Environmental Self-Assessment Program (ESAP)*. GEMI.

International Chamber of Commerce (ICC) (1991). *Business Charter for Sustainable Development*. ICC.

International Chamber of Commerce (ICC) (1992). *From Ideas to Action*. ICC.

Mallette, K. and Tomlinson, J. (1992). *AT&T Benchmarking: Focus on World-Class Practices*. AT&T Customer Information Center.

Schmidheiny, S. (1992). *Changing Course: A Global Business Perspective on Development and the Environment*. Massachusetts Institute of Technology.

Smart, B. (1992). *Beyond Compliance: A New Industry View of the Environment*. World Resources Institute, Washington.

VROM (1992) Sustainable Technological Development. Internal document, Ministry of Housing, Physical Planning and Environmental Affairs, The Netherlands.

Wika, W. G. (1996). Dupont's corporate environmental plan: deriving maximum business benefit from environmental progress. GEMI Conference, 20 March.

This chapter © A. Stikker, 1997.

11 Management systems: environment and economic management

Mike Monaghan

Introduction

Twenty-five years ago it was rare within industrial circles to even hear mention of the phrase 'environmental management'. If the subject did arise at all it was probably confined to the obvious larger 'polluting' industries, such as chemical companies and power generators who, by and large, confined their environmental management systems to ensuring that they met the, generally somewhat lax, legislation applying to emissions. The situation in the 1990s presents a strikingly different picture and one which continues to evolve rapidly. It is perhaps instructive to trace the growth of awareness within industry and the determining factors in this growth.

Elkington and Knight (1991) highlighted the external events which created the impetus among a widening range of business sectors about environmental matters. These included discovery of the hole in the ozone layer and people's reaction to it, concern about marine oil spills, damage to forests from acid rain and growing worries about global warming. Business was seen as the prime culprit and a growing body of opinion, soon backed up by legislation, forced industry to look harder at how to clean up its act. No company can now consider itself to be outside the environmental firing line.

The 1992 United Nations Conference on Environment and Development (UNCED) in Rio was widely acknowledged in industrial circles as having confirmed that environment was firmly on the agenda for all businesses. Reports prepared for the Rio conference by, for example, the Business Council for Sustainable Development (Schmidheiny, 1992), now the World Business Council for Sustainable Development (WBCSD), and the earlier International Chamber of Commerce Charter *Business for Sustainable Development* (ICC, 1991a) were further pointers to the acceptance by industry that environmental management was no longer the province of the few or a subject to be confined to a specialist department.

Environmental management in the 1990s can be categorized as having three key features. First, it is as much part of the agenda within service industries as it is in the traditional 'smokestack' industries. This is typified by the widespread acceptance within, for example, the tourist industry, often described as the world's largest industry, that their activities can have far-reaching environmental impacts. The work of the World Travel and Tourism Environmental Research Council based in Oxford (WTTC, 1992) and the International Hotel Environmental Initiative (IHEI, 1994) have highlighted these. Similar patterns of activity are emerging among other non-manufacturing sections of industry.

The second feature is that environmental management can no longer be confined simply to regulating emissions to comply with the law. As our understanding of the complex interaction between the environment and human activity generally, and industrial activity in particular, has grown so too has the scope of what constitutes environmental management. Industry finds that it is no longer adequate to be solely concerned with what 'comes out of the end of the pipe' but needs to manage issues as wide-ranging as where it locates its facilities, what materials it purchases, what resources it consumes, etc. Environmental management also extends to issues such as how employees travel to work and what role the company can play in local community environmental improvement programmes. This has been described as moving from a focus on 'Compliance' through 'Good Housekeeping' to 'Beyond Compliance' (O'Riordan, 1996, unpublished data, University of East Anglia).

The third feature is that environmental management can no longer be seen as the province of a specialized department. It now has to be seen as being similar to any other major management discipline within the company, such as health and safety, personnel or even marketing. The environmental implications of all decisions taken by a company need to be addressed, whether these are a major capital investment, relocation of a plant, change in packaging or revision of the company car policy.

This is particularly true in medium-sized companies where specialist departments, if they exist at all, will be small and normally responsible for issues in addition to environment, such as Health and Safety. If environmental management is to be carried out systematically and effectively, a formal system is essential. This requires a culture change for most companies. An informed commitment from the very top of the company is required if such a change in corporate culture has any chance of being achieved. Once such a commitment is in place, there are five basic stages to be activated for a successful implementation. These are broadly

similar to the processes to be undergone in any effective management discipline. For environmental management the stages are.

1 Carrying out a review of the environmental impacts/effects of
   the activity and the relevant legislation.
2 Preparing an environmental policy geared to the business of the
   company and its environmental impacts.
3 Establishing a management structure to implement the policy,
   including training of those responsible.
4 Setting environmental objectives and improvement targets.
5 Introducing an auditing and review process.

External systems such as the European Community, Eco-auditing
and Management System (EMAS) (EC, 1993), the British Standards
Institution Environmental Management System (BS 5750) (BSI,
1994) and the International Organization for Standardization
Environmental Management Systems (ISO 14001) (ISO, 1995), will
become of increasing importance for companies wishing to gain
external verification and accreditation of their procedures. However,
many companies are finding in the initial stages especially that
adopting the above systems in their entirety is not essential, particularly whilst issues of compatibility between them are being sorted
out. Nevertheless, the methodology and structures of the systems
provide valuable insights and a basis for preparing an in-house
system, without the inevitably onerous and costly documentation
and verification procedures.

It is increasingly clear that companies can no longer rely entirely
on internal procedures and programmes to meet the concerns of
customers, suppliers and the public. The public's 'right to know' is
as firmly attached to environmental issues as it is to any others.
This manifests itself in various ways. The most obvious is the
demand for corporate environmental disclosure, but is also evident
in the calls for independent verification of the 'green' claims of
suppliers of equipment and services.

The elements of an effective environmental management system
are therefore beginning to emerge more clearly. These may be
summed up as follows. It must have commitment from the top, be
seen as part of the mainstream management of the business;
address itself to all activities of the company; be formalized through
structures and programmes; be capable of being externally verifi-
able; and be publicized.

This may sound like a daunting task to any management but
there is now a body of information to draw on and experience
suggests that once the task is embarked on, progress can be
surprisingly quick and employee commitment readily achievable.

Managers are often surprised to find that much of what constitutes sound management practices and 'good housekeeping' forms the bulk of their environmental management programme.

The concept accepted?

Previous chapters in the book explained the external pressures which led to the environment being firmly on the agenda of businesses. For companies which are generally considered as major polluters, for example, the chemical industry, the steel industry and power-generation plants, environmental controls have been a feature of their activities for many years. They have been concerned in the past principally with the level of pollutants arising from their processes, but now increasingly take into account the environmental impact of the products they manufacture, including their eventual disposal, and also their overall environmental interactions. Life cycle analysis is now becoming the norm.

Even companies with apparently well-established environmental control systems had a rude awakening during the 1970s and 1980s when their environmental performance was challenged by well-informed pressure groups representing widespread public concern which, in turn, was translated into ever tougher legislation, and demands for disclosure of emissions and other environmental information. This has led such companies to rethink the nature and purpose of their environmental control systems, and to accept the need to be far more open about environmental issues and the steps being taken to reduce the overall environmental impact of their activities.

Whilst large companies from the traditional polluting industries have been the primary target for environmental pressure groups and legislators, there has been a growing awareness among small and medium-sized companies, (SMEs), which constitute the bulk of businesses worldwide, that their activities have a substantial environmental impact. This growing awareness within smaller companies, particularly those in the burgeoning service sector has coincided with larger companies realizing that a substantial part of their own environmental impacts may well arise from those parts of their business contracted to just such SMEs.

To date the larger environmental pressure groups have normally targeted larger companies, but it is also worth noting that local communities' concerns about their environment have led to a substantial growth in the number of local, single issue, environmental groups whose principal concern may well be the activities of the small, local companies. The first time an SME may realize that environmental management is important to them, is when an enforcement officer calls following a complaint from the local community or they encounter a demonstration by local residents outside their plant.

Whilst the need for action is now widely accepted, putting it into practice has proved quite a tall order. To start with, there is seldom anyone in such companies with the relevant technical background in environmental matters. Although the reality is that in-depth scientific knowledge is not essential for setting up an effective environmental management programme, managers faced with such a potentially huge concept as 'the environment' and how to tackle it are not surprisingly somewhat daunted by the prospect.

It also has to be said that environmental 'activists' have sometimes been counter-productive in their campaigns by demanding absolutist solutions, e.g. 'stop producing this nasty product now', 'cut out all emissions immediately', 'get all goods off trucks on to trains', etc. which are seen to be so impractical that managers are in danger of being pushed into concluding that as they can never meet such demands economically, trying to manage environmental issues is just too difficult. The most they will accept is that they will 'keep the law', but going beyond that will bring little or no benefit to the company and is likely to cost too much and so reduce profits. Doing the minimum to stay within the law and hopefully keep environmental pressure groups 'off your back' is sadly an only too common position among many SMEs.

However, this is by no means the universal response to the pressures. Whilst it is generally the case that legislative pressure has been the major impetus for companies to accept the environment as one of their priorities, and that initially the issue tended to be treated as a technical matter, allocated for example to the Health and Safety executives, as awareness of the importance and scope of the environment has grown, allocation of environmental responsibilities to a board member has become increasingly common and the positive benefits of well-sustained environmental management have been more apparent.

Accepting that environmental concerns could no longer be treated as a matter for a specialist, or as a passing phase, was perhaps the easy part for many companies. Difficulties arose in translating a general feeling that 'something needs to be done' into a co-ordinated, economic and sustained action programme. It is in translating concerns into an action programme that the importance of a well planned, environmental management system (EMS) becomes of paramount importance.

The implementation dilemma

The perception that many people, including many employees, have of business managers, is that environmental concerns rank quite low with them. The facts, however, would appear to be rather different.

A survey was carried out with groups of managers from a wide spread of European-based non-manufacturing businesses over a period of two and a half years. The managers, who were mainly in the age range 35–45, were asked to indicate which of the five indicative environmental scenarios shown below they most identified with personally i.e. which best described their view of the state of the environment.

1 The state of the environment is deteriorating to such a extent that a 'sustainable revolution' is required within fifty years, otherwise the well-being or even the very existence of human life is threatened.
2 The environmental problems facing the world are very serious. Whilst technology is capable of solving them, it will require a significant shift in priorities in the developed world to bring about the necessary improvements.
3 There are serious environmental issues facing the world, but technology can solve the problems and, with some increase in effort by governments, industry and individuals and continued international co-operation, matters will be resolved.
4 The seriousness of environmental problems has tended to be exaggerated by the 'greens'. There are environmental issues which will have to be tackled, but other issues are perhaps of greater importance to the world, and require greater attention.
5 'Green concerns' are largely a fashionable issue. We are over-reacting and probably wasting money solving largely non-existent problems.

It was significant that, during the two and a half year period which stretched from approximately mid-1991 to 1994, the proportion of managers who considered that scenario 2 best described the 'state of the world' steadily increased to a point where some two-thirds opted for this. Managers were clearly concerned to an increasing extent, about the state of the environment, and were probably more 'green' than the population at large.

Understandably the same group of managers experienced considerable difficulty in translating these concerns into changes in their working practices which would be commensurate with their perceived seriousness of the problem.

A comment on how people outside the business world, many of whom are customers or potential customers, perceive business's attitude to the environment was provided by surveys of non-business groups carried out by the author. They were asked which scenario from the list they thought business managers were most likely to opt for; the majority considered they would choose 4. Clearly, business has a long way to go to convince the 'outside world' of the seriousness of its commitment to environmental improvement.

Although this exercise is somewhat limited, it serves to illustrate an important point which is perhaps not always faced squarely, namely that many thoughtful managers recognize the tension between their business activities (where pressure to maximize profits is often seen as being at variance with environmental improvement initiatives) and their personal concerns for the environment as it affects themselves, their children and society. A major benefit, therefore, of a management system is that it provides a process which helps overcome the danger of managers feeling overwhelmed by the size of the problem set against what they feel they can achieve in their own companies. Agreeing on clear and achievable targets for the company and individual managers within the context of an overall policy and strategy at least partly overcomes this dilemma.

There are, however, many barriers to effective action, and they need facing squarely. Some have already been described above and a number of others are outlined below.

1 Fear that embarking on an environmental improvement programme could be costly and have a negative impact on profits.
2 Not convinced of company's seriousness about the issue, is it just public relations?
3 Uncertainty about what are the genuinely important environmental issues.
4 Difficulty in relating the company's activities to global environmental concerns.
5 Uncertainty about whether certain actions will genuinely benefit the environment, given the sometimes conflicting information in the media, etc.
6 Fear of getting caught up in a 'green knee-jerk reaction'.
7 Feeling that anything they do will have little effect.
8 Conflicting demands on time and resources.
9 Impossibility of meeting the demands of pressure groups.
10 Shareholders/investors do not support the extra costs of greening the company.

11 Anticipated indifference of employees/trade unions to environmental issues.
12 Unconvinced that many customers are bothered about the company's environmental standards.
13 Not sure if suggested cost savings, e.g. on energy and waste disposal costs, will be achieved.

These views were again obtained by the author from discussions with a range of managers. They raise a number of important points.

The 'business case' for the environment is yet to be accepted by all managers. Too many still see it as a cost rather than as a positive contribution to business well-being and added value.

The need for sound and balanced information to overcome uncertainty and confusion highlights the crucial importance for staff, including top management, to receive background environmental education. Once some of the negative myths are cleared away and the mystique surrounding the topic is eliminated, many inhibitions to action can be overcome. Simple guides to action can be helpful in this (see for example BiE, 1991; and Earthworks Group, 1993).

Perhaps the strongest message which emerges is the fundamental requirement of staff to be convinced of a commitment 'from the top' and for this to be translated into the provision of adequate resources and allocation of priorities.

Making a start

Whilst the introduction of the structured environmental management system described below will help overcome many of the inhibiting factors outlined in the list of barriers, there are two essential prerequisites for this to be effective.

First, the chief executive of the company must be fully committed to the concept of environmental improvement, and must communicate this to the company. This requires the chief executive to be adequately informed of the major environmental issues and why businesses need to be concerned about them. This is not an easy task for a busy manager, especially one whose managerial experience has normally been in the 'pre-environment' era. Getting a board member or a very senior executive with the necessary skills and background to provide the necessary leadership is most often the route which ensures an appropriate level of informed leadership; not always an easy task for a smaller company.

The second prerequisite is the need for an effective education programme. It is particularly important in the early stages for management at the most senior level in the company to receive some general environmental awareness training. The programme should include a summary of the main global and local environmental issues and their relevance to business, the pressures on business and the benefits to it of good environmental practices, the legislative background and the elements of the proposed environmental management system including auditing.

Specialists within the company, who will be responsible for implementing the programme, may well require additional training, but it is desirable that those with general management responsibilities receive sufficient training for them to be aware of the key issues and to be able to offer appropriate support.

Education can take many forms. In larger organizations internal courses using some external expertise tend to be most effective. In smaller companies attendance at external courses and use of 'do it yourself' manuals may be more effective and economic. Provision of simple task-oriented guidelines may well assist individuals and groups charged with the responsibility for policy implementation.

The five basic stages

The stages outlined below and shown in Figure 11.1 are a simplified version of those contained in, for example, the ISO 14001 environmental management system. They comprise a practical programme for most companies and if subsequently the company wishes to proceed to the full accreditation, the stages outlined will form a valuable basis on which to proceed.

Carrying out an environmental review: the planning stage

Faced with the questions of how companies stand in relation to the environment and what they should be doing about environmental matters, many are unsure of how to proceed.

One effective approach is to appoint a small group led by a senior manager to carry out a preparatory environmental review. This should result in a report which highlights the significant impacts that the activity has on the environment (including the products or services it produces), and indicate the main areas for action to control and reduce these. This is not a simple exercise and a number of guides, including checklists of items to be examined exist (see, for example, BiE, 1991). The review should identify what environmental legislation applies to an organization and whether there are any known breaches of this which have occurred in the past or are likely to occur in the future.

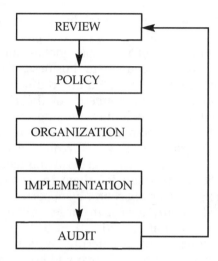

Figure 11.1 Simplified environmental management system

Almost every activity of an organization has some impact on the environment. When preparing a list of environmental effects/ impacts it is therefore important to try to limit them to those of significance. The major impacts can be categorized in many ways; the following may prove helpful:

1   Emissions to air.
2   Emissions to water.
3   Contamination of land.
4   Production of waste materials, some of which may be hazardous.
5   Use of land and visual impact of developments.
6   Use of resources including energy and water.
7   Emissions of noise, odours, dust and vibration.

These broad categories can be further broken down in various ways. For example each department or section of a company can be asked to assess to what extent they contribute to the issue.

The environmental implications of office activity should not be forgotten. In many companies the total consumption of energy and resources in an office may be the main direct impact of the company on the environment. Companies often employ a significant proportion of the workforce in their offices, and it is important that the staff have the opportunity to be involved with the environmental programme.

An alternative approach is to take the major global and local environmental issues and relate each sector of the company to them. For example, ask how a department or process or activity impacts on, say, global warming, acid rain, ozone depletion, marine pollution, low level air pollution, and secondly what steps might be possible to reduce this.

The review will inevitably highlight gaps in knowledge about the impacts and their significance and what are feasible steps to bring about improvements. These can be highlighted in the review and earmarked for future investigation and analysis. The review may well raise as many questions as it answers.

At this initial stage it is not important that the review is not comprehensive and does not cover all the areas of impact. Indeed, it would be unlikely that any company carrying out a review for the first time would cover all the significant areas.

Other matters to be covered during the review may include:

1 Whether to set targets beyond regulatory requirements.
2 Expected changes to legislation.
3 Quality of environmental records held within the company, e.g. on emissions.
4 Communication on environmental matters.
5 Environmental aspects of any products or services provided.
6 Waste minimization options.
7 Recycling opportunities, purchase of recycled materials.
8 Transport policies.
9 Noise, odours, and usual impact of activities.
10 Suppliers and contractors.
11 Education programme.

Simple user-friendly reporting of the results of such a review is important.

An example of the outcome of an environmental review, for a shipping company, incorporating policy objectives and practical targets, is shown in Figure 11.2 in respect of one of the specific effects identified. This relates to one topic – Halon. The other topics treated similarly included garbage, sewage, CFCs, VOCs, anti-fouling paints etc.

Having completed the review/impact assessment it is helpful to prioritize the issues in order of importance. This will inevitably be somewhat subjective as the precise impact cannot be known at this stage and is indeed a difficult issue to settle definitively. Provided the major issues have been identified and an action programme to begin dealing with them is launched, there is no need to expend excessive effort on attempts to determine precise rankings of all the issues identified.

ITEM	HALONS
Environmental Issues:	Release of halons to atmosphere is a significant cause of upper atmosphere ozone depletion.
Current Practice – Environmental Impact:	Halon firefighting systems are fitted on board four ships. Office computer room also fitted with halon system. Use of or leakage from these systems would add to ozone depletion.
Alternative Practice –Environmental Impact:	Replace halon system with alternative. Currently CO_2 is the practical alternative – this has minor environmental impact in that release would add to global warming. Other alternatives under development – overall effect and safety not yet known.
Advantages/ Disadvantages of Alternative:	CO_2 – avoids ozone depletion. Less safe for individuals in that risk of suffocation exists if released before area cleared. Greater storage space required for additional CO_2. Cost of replacement programme.
ACTION PLAN – Policy Objective:	Minimize the emission of halons from ships' firefighting systems by specific attention to plant integrity and leak detection arrangements. Consider the early replacement of existing halon systems – review and report on alternatives.

Specific Tasks:	*Action By/Date*
1. Introduce system for monitoring.	
a. Halon use	CT 31/3/93
b. Plant integrity and leakage	
2. Ensure plant can be maintained in working order without testing by release of halon.	CT 31/3/93
3. Investigate and report on removal of office computer room system, with safe recovery of halons by qualified contractor; and replacement with suitable substitute system.	AB 31/6/93
4. Investigate and report on alternative systems for ships with aim of replacing existing systems when practical alternative available.	CT 31/6/93
5. Use of alternative systems for new ships and premises.	MD Ongoing

Figure 11.2 Sample environmental review and action plan

Among the criteria for choosing what to include in the initial programme could be that the initiative is likely to have short-term, easily identifiable benefits preferably with cost savings. Nothing succeeds like success, especially if hard-pressed managers can see financial savings.

The outcome of reviews and audits can be very revealing and often surprising to management who often wrongly assume they are controlling environmental issues well even if they have not previously analysed activities under that heading.

Two examples will illustrate this. A large company with a substantial refrigeration plant were confident of their refrigerant leak controls. It was only when an audit forced them to list and analyse the refrigeration plants consumption that the magnitude of the problem became apparent. The information was available but had never been collated and reviewed. The findings triggered an overhaul of the system which brought about a 30–40 per cent reduction in leakage and many thousands of dollars in saving.

A small facility in the UK was prodded into assessing how it could save water as a result of an environmental review. Within weeks, simple new water-saving devices were installed. Savings of up to 80 per cent were achieved with a payback of around six months on the investment.

Not all checks lead to cost savings. A query during a review at a remote facility about the effectiveness of the garbage separation revealed that potentially hazardous materials were being mixed with routine waste and being tipped together in a non-registered site. Segregating the hazardous waste and disposing of it in a registered site resulted in higher disposal charges. However, in addition to contributing to environmental enhancement, the change prevented a potentially costly fine for illegal dumping, with the attendant adverse publicity.

Experience shows that well-conducted reviews identify many areas where environmental improvements are possible, many of which will save money; all will help protect the corporate reputation.

Developing an environmental policy

As we have already seen, different companies will have different reasons for wanting to address environmental issues. Whatever the reasons, an environmental policy document is of crucial importance. The environmental policy is generally a company's first form of environmental communication and needs to send a clear message both internally and externally about the company's position in respect of the environment. It should be signed by the chief executive of the company.

There is no right way or wrong way to draft an environmental policy and there will be as many policies as there are companies. What is important is that the policy addresses the specific needs of the company. The needs of the company and its understanding of environmental issues and their importance will evolve over time.

At the initial stage the priorities are likely to include:

1 Ensuring as far as practicable the demands of the regulator, the local community and relevant pressure groups are met.
2 Ensuring that they comply with all legislation.
3 Keeping to a minimum, or avoiding, any adverse environmental impacts within reason.
4 Developing their business or particular products by being greener than competitors.
5 Making a positive contribution to global/local environmental problems.

All of the above reasons for addressing environmental issues are perfectly valid. ISO 14001 suggests a number of criteria to be met by environmental policies. Ideally the policy should:

1 Be relatively brief, i.e. not more than two pages and preferably one.
2 Be communicated to, and be easy to understand by, all levels within the company.
3 Be available to the public.
4 Include an acceptance by the company of their areas of impact and a commitment to progressively reducing them.
5 Where practicable, be industry specific, i.e. refer *inter alia* to the key environmental impacts of the business in question.
6 Include a commitment to meet all current environmental legislation.
7 Go beyond legal compliance and enshrine a statement about setting environmental standards.
8 Indicate that individuals will be assigned direct responsibility for environmental matters.
9 Indicate that an auditing programme will be set up to measure the implementation of the policy.
10 Have a commitment to review the policy after, say, two years.
11 Be consistent with Health and Safety and quality policies of the company.

It will be advantageous, although not essential, for the review to be carried out before the policy is prepared. This will help focus the policy and ensure it is seen as part of a process rather than as a stand alone document. As reviews may take some time to complete, it is often necessary to introduce a policy in advance. The initial policy may well need modifying in the light of the review findings, by listing some of the key areas identified from the review as ones of particular relevance and importance to the company.

Examples of two policies are given in Figures 11.3 and 11.4. The first illustrates how the policy of the group with a wide range of activities worldwide has set broad objectives and requires the individual operating companies to formulate their own policies to be consistent with the group policy but directed to their own specific business areas. The second example is from a subsidiary company of P&O – Bovis Construction Limited. The policy, after acknowledging the company's wider impacts and responsibilities, focuses specifically on Bovis's major environmental impacts relating to its activities on construction sites.

Establishing a management organization for environment

Simply having an environmental policy is clearly inadequate to ensure that the necessary actions follow. Whilst the strategic aim may be to integrate fully environmental management with traditional management functions, experience shows that those organizations which have had most success in introducing effective environmental management programmes, in a relatively short timescale, have appointed a manager or managers whose responsibilities have been to 'champion' the initiative.

Whether companies choose to fully integrate environmental management or to initially adopt a champion, by taking on board environmental protection they will find themselves potentially facing a series of new tasks. Clearly, if the new organization is to work, then it is necessary to define these tasks, establish who will be responsible for carrying them out and provide the necessary education and training.

If, for example, a company decides that its initial key objective in adopting environmental management is compliance with all legislation, then understanding of the legislative issues will form the key element of any training. (This explains why many companies chose to add environmental responsibilities to managers who were dealing with Health and Safety and who were already concerned with issues of legal compliance.) However, companies who adopt a longer-term strategic approach to environmental management, find that legislative compliance is only a part of effective environmental management and training and education will need to reflect the wider concerns. The personnel/training department will have a particular role to play in encouraging employee motivation and providing education on environmental matters. However, the necessary expertise may well not be available within the company and certainly in the initial stages may need to be resourced from outside.

P&O GROUP POLICY STATEMENT

ENVIRONMENT

1 It is the policy of The Peninsular and Oriental Steam Navigation Company to recognise its responsibility to protect the environment and minimise, as far as is safe, practicable and economically sound any adverse environmental impact of its activities.

2 Each operating subsidiary of the Company is similarly responsible for managing its own activities to minimise environmental impact.

3 The Main Board of Directors of the Company considers that environmental matters are management responsibilities that rank equally with health and safety; finance; marketing and personnel.

4 A Main Board Director of the Company has a special responsibility to maintain an overview of environmental matters throughout the P&O Group.

5 The Company will assist and support its operating subsidiaries in establishing and implementing their environmental policies by means of advice and training, and by periodic auditing of their activities.

6 It is the policy of the Company to require each operating subsidiary to:

6.1 appoint a Director to be responsible for environmental matters

6.2 comply fully with all legal requirements at every location where it operates

6.3 ensures where legislation does not exist, that it sets its own standards enshrining best industry practice in comparable activities

6.4 carry out and document a review of the environmental impact of its activities and establish policies and procedures and set targets to minimise such impacts; this review to be updated periodically

6.5 produce and keep up to date its own environmental policy

6.6 establish a regular internal environmental auditing programme

6.7 provide training to management and staff in environmental matters

6.8 set targets to reduce progressively the consumption of energy and materials and the production of waste

6.9 ensure that the environmental implications of all investment decisions are considered

6.10 encourage full participation and commitment of all employees in carrying out the policy

6.11 contribute appropriate resources to developing standards and solution to environmental problems

6.12 co-operate as appropriate with external bodies and with local communities who may be affected by its activities

6.13 investigate all environmental incidents, keep records of these and ensure that they are reviewed by its Board of Directors

6.14 report any serious incidents to the Main Board Director responsible for Environment and to the Director for Environment

6.15 submit an annual report on environmental matters relevant to its activities to the Main Board Director responsible.

February 1994

Sir Bruce MacPhail
Managing Director

Figure 11.3 P&O Group policy statement

Bovis Construction Limited

ENVIRONMENTAL POLICY STATEMENT 1996

Bovis Construction Limited recognises that its activities have wide ranging environmental implications. These can potentially be either damaging or beneficial.

It is therefore the policy of the Company to:

1. comply with legislation and establish and continuously improve best environmental practice in the industry;
2. assess and consider the environmental impact of its activities and take action as appropriate;
3. promote personal responsibility and effort on the part of employees to prevent environmental damage and to act as good neighbours to those affected by construction activities;
4. provide such assistance, training and information as may be necessary to personnel at all levels.
5. audit environmental performance;
6. provide and display this policy and review it annually;

For the execution of this policy the following organisation and arrangements apply:

The senior Manager/Supervisor on site, or at a place of work will be responsible for the implementation of the Environmental Policy and will ensure, so far as is reasonably practicable, that;

(a) work is carried out in accordance all relevant legislation and company Environmental Policy
(b) waste is removed by registered carriers to licensed tips;
(c) measures are taken to prevent ground, river and coastal water pollution;
(d) measures are taken to minimise noise pollution;
(e) a good neighbour policy is implemented;
(f) ozone depleting gases such as CFCs and Halons are not discharged to the atmosphere;
(g) wild life, habitats, flora and fauna, trees, archaeological and heritage remains are protected as appropriate;
(h) materials wastage is minimised, recycling options promoted and water, paper and energy conserved;
(i) vehicle exhaust pollutants are minimised.
(j) environmental incidents are investigated, reported and preventative action taken against repetition.

The Company provides environmental assistance and auditing through its safety and enviromental managers, who will be responsible for bringing to the notice of management any deficiency observed, and for providing guidance, information and training.

Within the organisation, arrangements will be made to submit environmental reports and discuss environmental matters at Board Meetings and safety and environmental consultative and management meetings.

Mr. K. W. Evans is the Director responsible for the implementation of this policy, together with each Director whithin his own sphere of responsibility viz:

Head Office	- Mr. D. Kingston
	- Mr. D. Bate
	- Mr. L. Chatfield
Operations & Regional Offices	- Mr. J.E. Spanswick
	- Mr. J. Lelliott
Bovis Lelliott	- Mr. J. McCloy
Bovis Lehrer McGovern	- Mr. G.A. Taylor
Bovis Program Management	- Mr. S. Blagdon
Yeomans & Partners	- Mr. J. Crowe
Ashby & Horner	- Mr. K. W. Evans
Bovis Engineering Limited	

Project Manager

J.H.F. Anderson,
Managing Director
January 1996

Figure 11.4 Bovis Construction Limited's environmental policy statement 1996

Adequate resources are essential if introduction of what are often quite substantial changes to an organization's culture and procedures, are to be effective and sustained. However it is seldom necessary or even appropriate for a separate environmental department to be established, other than in the largest companies with high levels of environmental impact. The danger of such a department is that it will tend to take away from line managers their sense of responsibility for introducing and managing environmental improvement within their own sphere of activity.

The key issue here is to integrate the environmental activities into the normal management processes of the company. The role of the environmental specialist(s) is primarily one of enabling, guidance, education and subsequently auditing. The process of introducing an 'environment' culture is similar in many ways to that undergone in the 1970s and 1980s when safety was given a much higher profile in many companies.

The environmental 'specialist' in addition to providing guidance on day-to-day implementation should also monitor legislation and bring relevant changes to the attention of the company.

Senior management are primarily responsible for developing the policy and ensuring adequate resources are provided to introduce the policy and monitor its effectiveness. The finance department should, as required, provide systems for assessing the costs or quantifiable benefits arising from environmental activities. Department managers should have clear delegation of responsibility for the environment within their own areas of control, i.e. purchasing, transport, operations, design, marketing, personnel, etc.

The key to the introduction and long-term success of an environmental management organization is the integration of environmental activities into the normal management process of the company. Line managers must 'own' the policy and the programme.

Establishing objectives and an implementation programme

The major policy objectives follow from the environmental review and may require assessment and strategic decisions by the board. However, many of the objectives will be capable of being broken down into achievable tasks for individual departments within the company. A wide range of specific environmental objectives can be set.

For example, to a manager in one department, objectives could be to 'measure and then reduce the quantity of waste generated by 5 per cent' or 'segregate the waste into specified categories'. An office manager might well be charged with 'reducing the consumption of paper by 10 per cent' or 'reducing the consumption of water by 20 per cent by introduction of saver systems'.

The purchasing department could be asked to report on an investigation into environmentally friendly alternatives to some of the current products they buy, e.g. solvent-free paints, goods made from recycled materials. The engineering department might target on measuring reduction of the CFC consumption within the refrigeration plant etc. The personnel department could take on planning education and awareness raising for all employees.

The accounts department might have a project on how to record and measure the costings of environmentally related items such as energy and water consumption with a view to tracking progress, or how they could reduce the consumption of paper within their own department. The transport department could be tasked to reduce total mileage per delivery, or propose improvements to the fuel efficiency of the company car fleet. Many opportunities exist for recycling. Marketing could focus on how to exploit the company's environmental performance with key clients, and possibly how to involve clients in the process.

All sections of the company can and should be involved. Where performance appraisals are in existence, environment should be included within the performance criteria. It is important that the various departmental objectives are understood as being part of an overall whole, that targets are widely publicized and are all directed to the major environmental objectives of the company (this being one of the key tasks of the company environmental specialist), whilst at the same time being sufficiently discrete and specific to be attainable for the individual managers concerned. The twin dangers to guard against are being too ambitious in the first instance or being too vague and non-specific when setting the targets.

The question may also be raised – should the agenda for the action programme be set by what are the perceived priorities of environmental pressure groups? If, for example, Greenpeace are targeting on transport, Friends of the Earth on the ozone layer and innumerable local groups setting their own agendas, how is a company to respond?

There is no simple answer. As a starting point companies should seek to ascertain their major environmental impacts and to set their own agendas in such a way as to genuinely understand, control and progressively reduce these major impacts. External pressures may, however, mean that on occasions effort and attention has to be devoted to more high profile issues which may be of less genuine significance. However, if a company is to be successful in preserving the integrity of its response to 'helping to safeguard the environment', it cannot constantly be deflected from its determined priorities.

It would, of course, be naïve to ignore potentially sensitive issues, e.g. use of tropical hardwood, even though they may represent an insignificant proportion of a company's business. Prudent steps can head off adverse publicity which might undermine the overall programme, but companies need to be on guard against knee-jerk reactions to each new 'green wave'. Be aware, but be proactive not reactive would seem to be the watchwords.

Environmental auditing

There is a danger of rushing into setting up an environmental auditing programme at a very early stage, on the assumption that this provides the necessary evidence that a company is managing the environment effectively. This is a mistake. An effective auditing programme needs careful preparation and can take place more effectively after the above steps have been completed, rather than in advance of them.

The environmental review/effects assessment will in many ways fulfil the requirements of an initial audit. However, in essence an audit is geared to assessing the performance of an organization against a number of clearly established policies, targets and priorities. Two definitions of environmental auditing are useful:

A management tool comprising systematic documented periodic and objective evaluation of how well environmental organization management and equipment are performing with the aim of helping to safeguard the environment by:

1. Facilitating management control of environmental practice.
2. Assessing compliance with company policies which would include regulatory requirements.
(ICC, 1991b: 2)

An Environmental Audit is the systematic examination of the interactions between any business operation and its surroundings. This includes all emissions to air, land and water; legal constraints; the effects on the neighbouring community, landscape and ecology; and the public's perception of the operating company in the local area.
(CBI, 1990: 3)

The definitions merit attention. Both stress the need for audits to be systematic and periodic, i.e. not one-offs, and based on clearly defined protocols listing the issues to be examined. Documenting the findings is also essential.

The CBI definition is interesting in that it calls for an examination of the 'public's perception of the operating company'. This suggests that it is not enough to be doing the right thing, it is important to be seen to be doing so and to convince one's neighbours of this. This implies that assessing external corporate reporting in various forms as well as good neighbour policies should form part of audits.

An audit typically will seek to review the activities of a company or a site by a combination of discussions, completion of questionnaires, review of documentation, covering policy, legislative compliance, systems and procedures and existing practices, followed by evaluation of the actual implementation 'on the ground'.

There are generally no absolute standards against which auditors will be working other than those involving legislative compliance. The key questions auditors will be asking will be: does the performance of the company conform to its environmental policy, and are the activities and procedures achieving the targets and objectives set by the company?

A number of useful guides to auditing have been prepared, CBI (1990), ICC (1991b) and Spedding, Jones and Deering (1993). A section of a typical in-company guide for auditors is shown at Figure 11.5. This points to the main areas to be covered. In addition, more specific protocols may be found helpful.

It has been found that a practical approach to auditing is to have a relatively simple procedure developed for the initial audit and for this to be progressively enlarged during subsequent audits. Many companies have well-established Health and Safety audits and it is generally helpful to combine the environmental auditing with a Health and Safety audit, as many areas common to both are covered. It is, however, important that a distinct environmental audit protocol is established in advance and understood by those to be audited.

Environmental auditing is a specialized and skilled activity and many companies find it helpful either to send the individuals who are going to be responsible for auditing to receive specialized training which is quite widely available, or alternatively for a limited period only to use the services of environmental auditing specialists to assist in the initial audits.

Both approaches have proved helpful but it is important that the main auditing is ultimately carried out by members of the organization rather than purely relying on external auditors as the latter approach will tend to devalue the commitment by the organization to the whole programme, and probably be less effective. Periodic spot checks by independent auditors of the process and the quality of the audits may prove to be of value however.

AUDITOR GUIDE – ENVIRONMENTAL MANAGEMENT	
1. Environmental Review/ Impact Assessment	
To check whether a documented Review has been carried out and if it is satisfactory.	Is review document available? (Obtain copy) Who prepared it/was involved? Does it cover key environmental impacts? Does it summarize Policies to deal with them? Does it set out an action programme? If a formal document is not in existence, is there an equivalent process in place?
2. Air Emissions	
To ensure major sources are identified and steps in place to reduce impact.	Are major sources of air pollution identified? Are they documented? Have they been quantified? Do any require permits/licences? Are any incinerators used? What are current policies to control emissions? What steps are in place to measure and reduce? Comment on vulnerability of adjacent properties to air pollution from facilities/operations
3. Waste Management	
To ascertain that wastes generated are properly controlled and plans to reduce are being considered.	Are amounts quantified by type? Segregation arrangements? Any hazardous wastes? Are hazardous wastes properly identified and segregated? Are Duty of Care or equivalent procedures in place? What wastes are generated?
4. Recycling	
To check if opportunities for recycling are being taken.	What wastes are potentially recyclable? What proportion are currently recycled? What steps are being considered to extend this?
5. Energy Management	
To assess if systems are in place to progressively reduce energy consumption.	Is the energy consumption by category known and logged? What are the trends in energy consumption? Have the areas for potential energy saving been identified? What steps have been taken to date to reduce energy consumption? What are future plans and have specific energy reduction targets been set? Is there anybody assigned to manage the energy reduction programme? Would the use of outside consultants be helpful?
6. Material Consumption	
To assess the steps taken to reduce the quality and environmental impact of materials purchased.	What are the major material purchases (excluding fuel)? Have the environmental implications of these purchases been considered? Have any steps been taken to reduce consumption, e.g. by materials substitution, recycling, etc. Have any alternative materials been considered which have lower environmental impacts? Is information readily available on the quantity of materials purchased and waste generated from them? Any steps taken to reduce packaging?

Figure 11.5 Auditor guide: environmental management

Benchmarking

After a period of formalized environmental activities, companies rightly wish to ascertain how their performance compares with industry norms or accepted 'best practice'. For multidivision or diverse groups criteria for judging how different divisions are performing is also likely to be helpful. There are no universally accepted norms against which performance can be judged although meeting BS 7750 and ISO 14001 requirements may ultimately provide some measures to use for benchmarking.

In the USA, environmental benchmarking is relatively well developed albeit against relatively restricted criteria, e.g. on the EPA emissions data on toxic chemicals, or pollution prevention programmes. Arthur D. Little has assisted companies to measure their performance against worldwide 'state of the art' performance. Such exercises can help companies decide if they need to devote greater attention to, for example, water minimization or energy conservation. Another example is the Global Environmental Management Initiative's (GEMI) Environment Self-Assessment Program, which is very comprehensive and was described in Chapter 10.

Business in the Environment and the CBI have launched benchmarking exercises comparing the performance of different companies. The BiE survey took the top 100 UK companies and prepared an 'Index of Corporate Environmental Engagement' which is published, and which it is intended will be revised annually to gauge the extent to which companies are improving their management of environmental issues. It is also hoped to raise awareness and encourage competition. This index covers a limited number of key management areas including environmental management systems, ecoaudits, policies and board-level responsibility, but at this stage does not include quantified data which is more appropriate when companies within a restricted industry group are being compared.

Eco-labelling

One of the frequent complaints of anyone wishing to purchase more environmentally friendly products is that sorting out competing 'green claims' of suppliers is very difficult. It also makes it difficult for manufacturers who genuinely believe their production processes and products to have significant environmental enhancement to have their position recognized.

The net effect of such confusion has unfortunately been such that many have given up the attempt to 'green' their purchasing and some manufacturers have questioned the benefit of pursuing improved environmental standards. However, help is at hand.

A number of organizations have carried out so-called 'life cycle analyses' of products and ranked them according to their cradle-to-grave environmental impacts. Even with such scientific and seemingly objective studies, results can be disputed and there has been a suspicion that the outcome of studies is not always unrelated to the organization commissioning the study.

Schemes such as Germany's 'Blue Angel' eco-labelling have been successful against initial scepticism from manufacturers in raising the credibility of eco-labelling to a point where over 80 per cent of consumers are aware of it and influenced in their buying decisions by it. The scheme has also had a marked effect on manufacturers. Once the criteria are published, e.g. on oil heaters or paint, manufacturers rush to bring out products to meet them. Low solvent paints are a case in point. When the criteria was set only 1 per cent of paints sold met the standard – within a few years, over half the paints sold via do-it-yourself outlets met the criteria – leading to a reduction of thousands of tons of solvent emissions. Other ecolabels include the Nordic Council Label, the Canadian Environmental choice and the Japanese Eco-mark.

The EC has developed an eco-labelling system, the label being shown in Figure 11.6. This was the first regional, as opposed to national scheme. Progress has inevitably been slow. Problems on agreeing the criteria have proved difficult due to the complexity of the issues and the differing weight put on them by different countries. However the first EC eco-labelled products were on sale

Figure 11.6 EC ecolabel

early in 1994 and it is expected that it will become an increasingly common and much desired symbol in the years to come. By 1996 ecolabels had been awarded to paint, washing machines and kitchen towels/toilet paper and the criteria agreed for many more products including detergents, light bulbs, T-shirts and copying paper.

The scheme is voluntary, and will exclude food, drink and pharmaceuticals. For many businesses it could be important to target achieving an ecolabel for their products, and it will hopefully be a benchmark to be used by buyers in specifying environmentally acceptable products.

Communicating the message

Communicating the environmental message both internally and externally is vital. The way in which this is carried out clearly depends on the systems used within the company for communication on other policy matters.

What is it that people want to know and who are the most important audiences? It is suggested that the key audiences for a company are its staff, its immediate neighbours, its customers, its shareholders, its suppliers, relevant enforcement authorities, trade associations, insurers and, finally, environmental pressure groups. Relative importance is also probably in this order although circumstances may change this from time to time, e.g. communicating a 'green' message to customers will be particularly important if the company is marketing a 'green product'.

As far as staff are concerned, a sudden rush of environmental announcements and items, reaching them through company channels, followed by a long period of silence is disastrous, creating the impression that it is a 'seven-day wonder' or a 'flavour of the month', and that the company will then settle down to its previous passive attitude to the environment. It is, therefore, crucial to set up a system to ensure that information on environmental matters is provided on an ongoing basis, and in particular that updates on progress are disseminated widely within the organization. Staff need to be aware of the company policy and in broad terms the objectives and targets arising from it. Information on who is responsible for the programme at corporate and departmental level is also vital.

The in-company communication programme should cover everything from company annual reports and messages from the chairman through to company newspapers, briefings, notice-boards, environmental competitions and posters. Experience suggests that this is one of the most difficult and yet most important areas in helping to transform an organization's attitude to the environment. The environmental message should permeate the normal flow of information and not be confined to special environmental publications.

External communication is rather more problematic. A recent international survey of 690 companies (KPMG, 1995) revealed that even among the major companies, external corporate environmental reporting was in its infancy; among small and medium-sized companies it has probably not yet been born.

Less than 15 per cent of companies surveyed produced a separate report although some two-thirds referred to environmental issues somewhere in their annual report. The authors of the report note that whilst the trend in environmental reporting is growing, it is doing so more slowly than expected and they suggest this is so partly because of the higher standards now being demanded, 'green glossies' no longer suffice, if they ever did, and to produce a comprehensive, detailed report is seen by many companies to be too demanding.

Whatever the difficulties, external environmental reporting seems set to grow.

Conclusion

Managing the environment is as important as but no different from, managing any other aspect of a company's business. Managers should not be overawed or inhibited by the apparent scale of global environmental problems and the complexity of solving them. As has been remarked, the world got into an environmental mess by lots of small steps and that is the way it is going to get out of it; this is as true for companies as it is for individuals.

Sound management systems will allow rapid progress to be made, and by using the wealth of experience already available companies can avoid misdirecting their energies. Most of the solutions are already available to be used; it is largely a matter of identifying and applying them.

Meeting legislative standards, and embarking on the road to pollution prevention and minimizing the use of resources follow naturally from the review of the environmental impacts and the formulation of a programme to minimize the impacts.

A steady, sustained approach initiated from the top and 'owned' by the line managers and all staff is the ideal model, rather than an imposed, 'big bang' approach. There is a fund of goodwill and an unexploited willingness to 'green' the company among staff, especially when commercial benefits can be demonstrated. One of the benefits of a sound environmental programme can be a real improvement in staff morale.

The factors inhibiting adoption of effective environmental programmes are real but can be overcome as is proved by the experience of companies both large and small worldwide. Management should be in no doubt that progressive companies which are successful over the long term are characterized, among other things, by enlightened environmental programmes.

References

British Standards Institution (BSI) (1994). *Environmental Management Systems*. BSI.

Business in the Environment (BiE) (1991). *Your Business and the Environment*. BiE.

Confederation of British Industry (CBI) (1990). *Environmental Auditing Guidelines for Business*. CBI.

Earthworks Group (1993). *50 Simple Things Your Business Can Do to Save the Planet*. Greenleaf Publishing.

Elkington, J. and Knight, P. (1991). *The Green Business Guide*. Victor Gollancz.

European Community (EC) (1993). *Eco Audit and Management Scheme (EMAS)*. EC.

International Chamber of Commerce (ICC) (1991a). *Business Charter for Sustainable Development*. ICC.

International Chamber of Commerce (ICC) (1991b). *Effective Environmental Auditing*. ICC.

International Hotel Environmental Initiative (IHEI) (1994). *Green Innovations*. IHEI.

International Organization for Standardization (ISO) (1995). *Environmental Management Systems*. ISO.

KPMG (1995). *Survey of Environmental Reporting*. KPMG.

Schmidheiny, S. (1992). *Changing Course*. MIT Press.

Spedding, L., Jones, D. and Deering, C. (1993). *Eco Management and Eco Auditing*. Chancery.

World Travel and Tourism Environmental Research Council (WTTC) (1992). *Environmental Guidelines*. WTTC.

Conclusion

Pratima Bansal and Elizabeth Howard

The chapters in this book have been ordered to move from the more theoretical to the more applied. The earlier theoretical chapters address different questions pertaining to the business–environment relationship from those asked in later chapters. Table 12.1 outlines what we as editors see as the main question being asked in each chapter and the main conclusions derived. In this final concluding note, we outline how the chapters contribute to understanding some of the dilemmas in studying the business–environment relationship, and some of the common themes that can be extracted from them.

Our overall question has been about how we should think about business and the environment, as a matter of philosophy, economics, systems management and so on. Three more detailed questions have been addressed:

1 How should we understand the science of environmental management; how can we know the effect of changing our environmental impacts and therefore what we should do?
2 What are the values by which we should make decisions to change; whose values are they?
3 How could or should environmental concerns be incorporated into the economic decision-making of competitive businesses?

Each chapter takes a position on at least one of these questions which leaves us with several perspectives on them and provides us with multiple insights. Let us summarize some of the differences in perspective and approach to each of these questions.

Several chapters discussed the question of how we should understand the science of environmental management, and how we know the effect of changing environmental impacts. There seemed to be three distinct approaches to answering this question. The first is that it is assumed that the science is a given (e.g. Bansal, Cameron and Mackenzie, Monaghan, Stikker, Peattie, and

Williams). That is not to say that the science is not contentious, but that there are areas in which businesses have sufficient scientific evidence to suggest that there is an issue confronting them. In this approach, the firm assumes that there are solutions in addressing these issues. In the second approach, the authors assume that scientific views are contentious and that values play a significant role in choosing which science prevails (Gladwin and Kennelly, and Roome). There are several alternatives, such as technocentrism, ecocentrism and sustaincentrism, and the individual must choose from these. As a result, it is the individual's personal values which direct firms towards uncovering science. The third approach attacks the very basis of what we assume is good science, arguing that the science can be constructed or be a structural attribute (Grint) or that it is a consequence of cultural diversity where it fits the environment in which we operate (Milton). In other words, there is no absolute sense of 'good science': it is a product of our society, it is beyond our ability to judge absolutely because we are instrumental/ integral in defining science and what is good. There is no point in arguing which process businesses should adopt because we will construct what is most appropriate given that we define the criteria for what is 'appropriate'.

Secondly, the issue of values has been addressed. What values should guide our decisions and whose values are they? Here, we see two tacks. In the first, the author assumes that responsible corporate environmental management is a good thing (Monaghan, Pearce, Peattie, and Stikker). The chapters written by Cameron and Mackenzie and by Williams suggest to us that those values are assigned by society via governing agencies. Stikker discusses the processes of changing organizations in response to changing values and Monaghan the systems for managing the business operation. Some of the other chapters explain from where values are generated (Grint, Milton, and Roome). These authors do not take sides on the debates, explicitly acknowledging the plurality in values and providing us with some thoughts as to the source of these values, and in some cases providing us with insights into how we can choose.

Most of the authors in the later chapters address a third dilemma, the method or methods by which environmental concerns should be incorporated into the decision-making of competitive businesses (Bansal, Cameron and Mackenzie, Monaghan, Pearce, Peattie, Stikker, and Williams). All of the authors in some way attempt to examine this question through their own disciplinary lens. Whereas some offer a specific 'how to' manual (Monaghan, and Stikker), others attempt to broaden the scope of management issues and ways in which to address them (Gladwin and Kennelly, and

Table C.1 Chapter summaries

Chapter	Disciplinary root	Main questions	Main conclusions
1	Sustainable development	How do we wish to live and what is the role of organizations in such living?	The objective of sustainable development is a reasonable one, but the conventional paradigm of technocentrism and the ecocentrism do not push us in that direction. The paradigm of sustaincentrism embodies the principles of sustainable development which aims at assuring ecosystem and sociosystem health and integrity.
2	Corporate social responsibility and applied ethics	How does sustainable development guide managerial decision-making?	Strategic decision-making must be guided by values and ethical systems. The existing utilitarian ethic will not direct us to sustainable development. If sustainable development is to be valued, we must incorporate a wider scope of ethics and values into decision-making.
3	Anthropology	From where do our attitudes and discourse of environment stem?	Our knowledge of environment is cultural; it is generated by the ways in which we engage with the physical world and with each other. Environmental discourse is an interaction between diverse cultural perspectives.
4	Sociology	Does society shape the environmental agenda?	Sociology offers three theoretical insights in answering this question: external structures which determine action, the interpretative actions of individuals; or social constructions where problems are what society defines them to be.
5	Economics	Why is it in the best interest of firms to invest in environmental assets? How can the costs of environmental assets be minimized?	Firms will invest in environmental assets when the benefits exceed the costs. Corporate accounting can be revised to reflect environmental investments.
6	Government policy	What are the government structures and principles which influence government environmental policy?	For successful management, managers must understand the logic of the legal and regulatory context, the people with whom they must negotiate and regulations which they must interpret.
7	Law	What systems of environmental law influence good business management?	The interlocking legal systems set limits and impose conditions on actions of which managers must be aware, and this system also sets limits and imposes conditions on action which will provide scope and incentive for new types of activity, marketing and innovation.

Table C.1 continued

Chapter	Disciplinary root	Main questions	Main conclusions
8	Strategic management	Should the natural environment influence a company's strategy and, if so, how?	Environmental strategy can be perceived as an opportunity or threat. When treated as an opportunity, it can enhance the firm's competitive position. When treated as a threat, it can assist in the firm's survival.
9	Marketing	Should a firm engage in green marketing and, if so, how?	Green marketing assists in building stakeholder support. It requires, however, a radical change in the organization's structure, processes and culture.
10	Organization	How does a firm employ organizational practices which encourage sustainable development?	Stikker offers a six-step plan to ensure cultural and organizational change.
11	Systems analysis	How does a firm successfully apply an environmental management system?	Five elements are necessary for constructing an environmental management system. There are some prerequisites for successful implementation.

Milton). In fact, the chapters move from the general issues of 'why do we have an environmental issue' and 'how do we define it' to 'what can we do about it'.

In the previous paragraphs we have noted some areas in which the authors have taken different approaches to answering similar questions. To conclude, we identify three areas in which we believe all the chapters agree: that the environment is *relevant* to business, that organizations will have to *change* to respond to the environment, and that the definitions of environmental management and sustainable development are *ambiguous*.

The relevance of environment to business is underlined by the implicit assumption throughout this book that organizations *must* respond to environmental issues. In none of the chapters did the author question whether the natural environment warrants consideration. Rather the issue has some urgency as a result of the way in which society is acting, because of the legal implications, because of ethical concerns, or because of profit-related financial considerations.

Firms cannot continue with the status quo if we are to respond to environmental concerns. Although there seems little consensus about the degree of required organizational change, the message is that some change is required. Cameron and Williams suggest that firms should respect 'the polluter pays' principle and the precautionary principle. Pearce suggests that it should be ensured that the marginal costs of not acting equal the marginal benefit of acting responsibly. Gladwin and Kennelly and Roome suggest that we will need a paradigm shift to achieve a sustainable solution.

Finally we must recognize the amorphous nature of the concept of 'environment'. In these pages it has been frequently challenged, explicitly or implicitly. Its definition is likely to change over time. It is also likely to reflect the context in which it is provided, and the individual providing the definition. Deterministic or possibilist, ecocentric or humanistic, our concepts of environment tell us how we see our world.

The natural world can be a prison, with limits to growth, constraining what business can or should do. It can be a paradise, with intrinsic value, where humans should tread lightly. It can be a treasure trove awaiting our exploitation and the development of the technological ability to supply more of our needs and wants. It is what we construct.

This book has brought together a wide selection of approaches to the environment–business relationship. The variety makes clear the reasons for the dilemmas and conflicts and the lack of action in many areas of business. Different disciplines have different approaches; competing paradigms exist; value systems conflict. Understandably, then, the answers and practical prescriptions which business derives may vary too.

Index